Monetary Policy

Monetary Policy

John Fender
University of Birmingham

John Wiley & Sons Ltd

This edition first published 2012

Copyright © 2012 John Wiley & Sons, Ltd

Registered office

John Wiley & Sons Ltd, The Atrium, Southern Gate, Chichester, West Sussex, PO19 8SQ, United Kingdom

For details of our global editorial offices, for customer services and for information about how to apply for permission to reuse the copyright material in this book please see our website at www.wiley.com.

Library of Congress Cataloging-in-Publication Data
Fender, John.
  Monetary policy / John Fender.
      p. cm.
  Includes bibliographical references and index.
  ISBN 978-0-470-01909-2 (pbk.)
1.   Monetary policy.   I. Title.
  HG230.3.F428 2012
  339.5'3—dc23
                          2011041450

A catalogue record for this book is available from the British Library.

Set in 9/13pt Kuenst480 BT Roman by Thomson Digital, India

Printed in Great Britain by TJ International, Padstow, Cornwall

Contents

Acknowledgements

I would particularly like to thank Colin Ellis, David Miles, Peter Watt, John Whittaker and one anonymous reader who read the first draft of the book and made many helpful comments and suggestions. I have also had helpful suggestions from Rebecca Driver, Michael Henry, Neil Rankin and Peter Sinclair. Tom Allen was very helpful in gathering some of the data used and Steve Hardman at Wiley has shown considerable patience as well as encouragement throughout the project. Therese Gleitman was very helpful in checking the proofs.

Introduction

The aim of this book is to present an up-to-date analysis of monetary policy. It has been written primarily with advanced undergraduate courses in monetary policy in mind, but hopefully it will also be of interest to many who are not taking such courses. It may be useful for several other undergraduate courses as well as introductory graduate macroeconomic courses. Although there is some focus on the UK, other countries' experiences, particularly those of the USA and eurozone, will be discussed as well. The approach adopted is to explore the various aspects of monetary policy through the exposition of a series of models that illuminate some facet of the question at issue. So the overall approach might be described as basically theoretical, but the theory is not advanced. We do not discuss dynamic stochastic general equilibrium (DSGE) models, which dominate the contemporary research agenda in macroeconomics, at any great length, nor do we discuss the intricacies of the various econometric tests employed in testing relationships. Important as these topics are, there is not enough space for such a discussion in this book, nor is such a discussion too relevant given the intended level and audience of the book. Those who do wish to pursue these issues at greater length will have to look elsewhere. Instead, the author will apply what he considers to be his comparative advantage, namely that of expounding a number of simple models and using them to shed light on current monetary policy. Doing this provides ample material for a book of this size.

The idea of writing this book occurred to the author some time ago, when teaching third year undergraduate courses in Monetary Policy at the University of Birmingham there did not seem to be a suitable textbook. The idea of writing one himself seemed to be an obvious solution, and this is the result. Perhaps the book which is most similar, in topics covered, overall approach and level is Goodhart (1989). But there have been enormous changes in both macroeconomic theory and monetary policy since 1989. Another excellent book is Walsh (2010); but this is an advanced graduate textbook, intended for second-year postgraduate courses; it is far too difficult even for advanced undergraduates. Woodford's monumental treatise (Woodford, 2003a) should be mentioned as well, but this is even more demanding than Walsh.

The book may be of interest to many who are not students, but who have some knowledge of basic economics and who wish to acquire an understanding of monetary policy. We consider questions of how policy actually works in practice, and what it should do. We now know a great deal about monetary policy and how it operates, although there is much we are still ignorant about. One of the aims of the book is to impart this knowledge in an intelligible way to those who have a reasonable grasp of basic economics.

There is a great deal of literature on virtually all the topics covered by this book, and we can cover only a tiny fraction of it here. We hope that readers will wish to find out more about many of these topics, and, where appropriate, we have tried to include some appropriate references for those who do wish to investigate these issues further.

The basic structure of the book is as follows: Chapter 1 explores some basic issues concerning the foundations of a monetary economy, and Chapter 2 presents a very brief history of macroeconomics, in particular emphasising Keynes's contribution and the IS-LM frame-work. Chapters 3 and 4 discuss two of the main components of aggregate demand, consumption and investment, whereas Chapter 5 considers what used to be absolutely fundamental topics for a course in monetary policy, the demand for, and supply of, money. The move towards the use of a short-term interest rate as the instrument of monetary policy means that these topics are much less important than they once were but they are still, we argue, not to be ignored. Chapter 6 analyses the fundamental issue of nominal price and wage rigidities, a crucial ingredient of the approach to macroeconomics we take in this book. Chapter 7 explores the vital question of the relationship between inflation and unemployment, and Chapter 8 considers the theoretical underpinnings of the institutional reforms which have taken place in monetary policy in the last quarter of a century or so. The fact that inflation is socially costly is a crucial reason for having inflation targets, and we explore reasons why and how inflation is socially costly in Chapter 9. Much of macro-economics and monetary economics ignores the existence of financial intermediaries, particularly banks. This is not so in this book, however, which considers their relevance for monetary policy in Chapter 10. Chapter 11 studies a topic that is also somewhat neglected in monetary policy texts, the significance of the open economy for monetary policy and Chapter 12 is devoted to another important yet often neglected topic, that of the term structure of interest rates. One of the main ways in which monetary policy works is, we argue in this book, through affecting asset prices so Chapters 13 and 14 focus on two of the main assets through which monetary policy has an impact, namely the stock market and the housing market. Although the book is about monetary policy and not fiscal policy, there are relationships between the two, and therefore we feel justified in devoting Chapter 15 to fiscal policy. Chapter 16 considers the evidence for the effectiveness of monetary policy, and Chapter 17 focuses on the targets and instruments of monetary policy. In Chapter 18 we summarise much of the discussion in the previous chapters and put together a picture of the transmission mechanism of monetary policy. Chapter 19 discusses monetary policy in practice in the UK, the US and the eurozone. Chapter 20 considers the significance of the extraordinary events that unfolded in 2007 and 2008 and Chapter 21 discusses what is perhaps the main innovation in monetary policy recently, that of 'quantitative easing'. Chapter 22 presents some concluding thoughts about current and future policy.

Once upon a time, monetary policy was analysed using a framework where it was assumed that the money supply was the instrument of monetary policy, something the monetary authorities chose and implemented. Those days are long gone, and there seems to be a widespread consensus that monetary policy is implemented (mainly) through the central bank choosing a short-term interest rate. While we agree that this is the appropriate way to characterise monetary policy, it does not mean that we can dispense with all discussion of the supply and demand for money, for a number of reasons. Firstly, sometimes the analysis using the money supply as the instrument is the same as that using the interest rate as the instrument, as in the simple IS-LM framework. Secondly, some issues are easier to handle in a framework where the money supply is the policy instrument; that of exchange rate overshooting is an obvious example. It is not clear that overshooting has any meaning in an interest-targeting framework, and considerable insights can be derived from distinguishing and analysing both the shorter run and longer run implications of a money supply increase. Thirdly, the demand for money is particularly relevant for the costs of inflation. Fourthly, much of the literature, both theoretical and empirical, especially the older literature (some of which is still worth reading), considers a framework where the money supply is the instrument of monetary policy. Fifthly, much of undergraduate macroeconomics is taught using the assumption that the money supply is the policy instrument and it might be too abrupt a transition to move to considering monetary policy being conducted exclusively in terms of an interest rate rule. Sixthly, changes in the money supply may contain useful information about the state of the economy, so it should be, at least, something policy makers should pay attention to. For example, M4 (the main measure of the money supply in the UK) was increasing at an annual rate of about 15% in the years before the financial crisis whereas in the last two years or so its growth has effectively been zero. Had policy makers paid more attention to what now seems to be excessive monetary growth in the pre-crisis era, it might have set off warning bells and perhaps the worst of the crisis could have been averted. Seventhly, and finally, monetary aggregates still play a role in some central banks' policy-making frameworks, most notably the 'twin pillars' approach of the ECB.

So, while we agree with those who emphasise that the main instrument of monetary policy is the short-term interest rate, there are a whole host of reasons why this book will not dispense entirely with discussion of the money supply and monetary aggregates.

There may be a certain amount of overlap between chapters. This is not necessarily unintended; it may not be inappropriate to discuss, for example, measures designed to stabilise house prices both in the chapter on the housing market and in a more general discussion of monetary policy later in the book. The author is aware that readers are under no obligation to read the entire book. Some readers who are particularly interested in the housing market, for example, may wish to read just Chapter 12. Those who are interested mainly in monetary policy in practice might concentrate on the last five or six chapters. Nevertheless, the book is intended to be structured in a fairly logical way and there should be no problems if a reader starts at the beginning and reads it straight through. The topics are ordered in the sequence the author would cover them in a course on monetary policy, and hopes that such a sequence is not too eccentric.

There may be some slight discrepancies in notation between chapters. One reason for this is that when we are expounding a particular model, we may well use the notation customarily used for that model, or used in the original exposition, and sometimes notation differs between such models. We hope such differences are not too confusing to readers; we try to define notation where appropriate, and to avoid inconsistencies within chapters.

Finally, readers should be aware that this edition of the book was completed in late July 2011, so when the 'current situation' is discussed, it is the situation as of that date that is meant.

CHAPTER 1

Foundations of a Monetary Economy

There is a problem faced by economists who wish to study money. Typically, economists make a number of basic assumptions about the economy; they assume that consumers derive utility from consuming various goods and disutility from supplying labour, that firms seek to maximise profits by producing goods using factors of production such as labour and capital in accordance with a production technology, and so forth. But it seems that this approach does not contain any role for money.[1] One would guess that the existence of money has something to do with avoiding the 'double coincidence of wants' problem that occurs under barter – in the absence of money, if agents have to find a trading partner who wants to consume what they produce and vice versa, then carrying out such transactions can be a long, arduous and costly process. It is easy to see how money can help to reduce these costs: agents can accept money (a generally accepted medium of exchange) in exchange for the good they wish to sell and then take the money and exchange it for the good they wish to acquire. However, although it may be easy to see what the problem is, solving it is by no means straightforward. The reason is that for the 'double coincidence of wants' to be a problem, there must be certain frictions in the economy. If there were perfect information and no transactions costs, there would be no problem in finding a suitable trading partner and trading (so no need for money). It seems, then, that the existence of money requires there to be various frictions in the economy, but modelling these frictions

---

[1] Hahn states the problem thus: 'The most serious challenge that the existence of money poses to the theorist is this: the best developed model of the economy cannot find room for it.' (Hahn, 1982, p. 1.)

and explaining how they give rise to the existence of money is no trivial task. Going beyond this and deriving a satisfactory theory of monetary policy from such foundations is a major challenge and something economists are far from achieving. In this chapter we shall discuss some of the approaches that have been taken in the literature to solving this problem and modelling the existence of money rigorously. Inevitably, we shall have to be highly selective; the models we discuss will be just a very small subset of those that have been produced. But hopefully our account can give some idea of how economists have sought to explain the existence and role of money, discuss some of the conclusions that have emerged and suggest directions for future research.

1.1 The Emergence of a Medium of Exchange in a Primitive Economy

To fix ideas, we might start by thinking of a primitive economy where agents produce goods which, by and large, they do not consume. In order to obtain the goods they do wish to consume they need to find someone who is willing to exchange what they have produced for their product. Such a search may be long and arduous – a hairdresser who wants a pair of shoes will have to find a shoemaker who wants a haircut. In such an environment, not much trading may take place; agents may instead produce what they consume and hence do not obtain the benefits of specialisation and trade according to comparative advantage. Considerable benefits may be derived by establishing a 'market place' with a stall for each possible pair wise exchange of goods and this might be a way of reducing the search costs (that of finding a 'double coincidence of wants') of barter. So the hairdresser who wanted a pair of shoes would go to the stall where haircuts were exchanged for shoes. However, it is easy to see that if there are a large number of goods in the economy, then to allow for every possible pair wise exchange, there would have to be a large number of stalls. A simple calculation establishes this – if there are n goods in the economy, then there would be $(n-1) + (n-2)+(n-3)+ \ldots +2+1=n(n-1)/2$ stalls. (There would need to be stalls for the first good to be traded against each of the other $n-1$ goods, and stalls for the second good to be traded against each of the remaining $n-2$ goods, and so forth.) Even with a small number of goods, this means a large number of stalls: with 100 goods there are 4950 stalls. It follows that:

1. If there are costs in establishing and running a stall, this arrangement could be very costly.
2. Some markets might be very thin. One might have to wait a long time at a particular stall until a suitable trading partner arrived; alternatively, some stalls might hold inventories, but this too would be costly, and of course some goods are not storable, so this solution would not be available for them.
3. It is easy to see that most stalls are redundant. It is sufficient that there be stalls which enable one particular good to be exchanged against every other good. If this good is good i, then an exchange of good j for good k can be achieved by first of all exchanging good j against good i and then exchanging good i for good k. So no more than $n-1$ stalls are required. This argument is not, however, sufficient to establish that one commodity will

emerge which acts as a medium of exchange. Can one rule out, for example, one good being generally acceptable in exchange against some goods, with another good acting as a medium of exchange for all other goods, and the two goods exchanging for each other? It is difficult to say more without modelling the forces that might lead to the emergence of a medium of exchange more explicitly.

We might ask whether there are any characteristics which the commodity that comes to be used as a medium of exchange might have. We would surmise that portability, divisibility, homogeneity and durability would be important characteristics. It is easy to see why. For example, if a good is not homogenous – if some units of the good are, for example, in some way better than others – one might expect the poorer units of the good would be passed on in exchange and the better units retained: the expression 'bad money drives out good' comes to mind. However, it is difficult to say much more at this level of generality. The issue really needs to be considered in the framework of a formal model, and to a consideration of some formal models we now turn.

1.2 Money and Overlapping Generations

Samuelson (1958) discussed the possibility of introducing money into an overlapping generations (OLG) model. OLG models are employed frequently in economics and are useful for analysing a number of issues. They assume the economy is made up of finitely lived agents who are born at different times, but although individuals have finite lives, the economy may go on forever. Samuelson considered an OLG model without production where each agent lives for two periods (youth and old age) and is endowed with one unit of a perishable commodity in the first period of their lives. Population grows at a rate n, so the number of young is $(1+n)$ times the number of old. Since the good is perishable, agents cannot consume it in the second period of their lives. How do they consume, then, in their old age? They would be willing to trade some of their endowment in the first period in exchange for the promise of delivery of the consumption good when they are old. However, this is not something the only possible trading partners the young have when young (the old generation) can deliver. There is hence no trade and the market equilibrium involves each generation consuming their entire endowment when young and nothing when old. This is clearly inefficient and a rather stark example of dynamic inefficiency.[2] (It would clearly be preferable, and feasible given the economy's resource constraint, for each generation to transfer a portion of the endowment received when young to the old generation. The real interest rate is effectively -1, which is always less than the population growth rate, so the criterion for dynamic inefficiency – that the interest rate is less than the population growth rate – is met.)

---

[2]Dynamic inefficiency is where a central planner can make every generation better off by transferring goods between agents. It can occur even when all the usual conditions for Pareto Efficiency are satisfied.

Money may solve the problem. Suppose the government gives to the currently old H completely divisible pieces of paper (called money) and individuals believe they will be able to exchange money for goods, at price P_t in period t. It is straightforward to show (e.g. Blanchard and Fischer, 1989, pp. 158–60) that Pareto efficiency is restored – in fact, what happens is that prices fall at a rate n, keeping real per capita money balances constant. The (gross) return on saving is now $1 + n$, and hence the private and social rates of transformation are equated.

However, if the money stock is increased at a steady rate, the welfare properties of the resultant equilibrium depend on how money is introduced. If additions to the money supply are paid as interest on the existing money stock, then there is no real effect – the nominal rate of return on money and the rate of inflation increase by the same amount, hence leaving the real return on money unaltered. However, if it is paid as, say, transfers to the older generation, then in equilibrium, the real rate of return on money falls and the allocation of resources is altered in an unfavourable direction.

One question that might be asked about this result is how the beliefs necessary to sustain an equilibrium in which money is held are generated? (No-one will hold money unless he believes it will be possible to exchange money for goods when old.) The result is that if these beliefs exist then money can lead to a Pareto improvement, but these beliefs need to be generated and how this happens is not at all clear.

In this model, money has a role as a store of value enabling intergenerational exchange. It might be argued that this is not the most plausible way of modelling money, since its medium of exchange function is not captured at all in the approach and since money is generally dominated as a store of value. (Any asset with a positive rate of return the value of which is fixed in terms of money will dominate money as a store of value, and there are usually many such assets in an advanced economy.)

1.3 Money as a Medium of Exchange: The Kiyotaki-Wright Model

Kiyotaki and Wright (1989) (henceforth KW) use a search approach to model the role of money as a medium of exchange. The search framework means there are trading frictions, which possibly money might mitigate. Amongst their assumptions are the following (there are a number of more technical assumptions which are not given here):

1. Time is discrete.
2. There are a large number of agents, who are both producers and consumers. Agents specialise in both consumption and production. Agents produce one particular good, but consume another.
3. There are equal numbers of each of three types of agent, labelled I, II and III.

4. There are three types of indivisible goods, labelled 1, 2 and 3.
5. Agents of type i derive utility from consuming good i, but produce good i^*, where $i \neq i^*$.
6. Each agent can produce and store just one unit of her particular production good. Once the good is produced, the agent stores it until she exchanges it for another good. When she acquires her consumption good, she consumes it and then immediately produces another unit of the production good.
7. Agents can store only one unit of the good at a time. There are storage costs – good 1 is the cheapest to store, good 3 the most expensive.
8. For every period, each agent is matched randomly with another agent, and they exchange inventories if it is mutually advantageous for them to do so.

KW consider only steady-state equilibria. Specifying an equilibrium means defining trading rules – that is, whether an agent of type h with good i who meets an agent of type j with good k will want to trade – and also the steady-state distribution of inventories – that is, the proportion of agents of type h who hold good i at any particular date.

Trade will, of course, only take place if it is mutually beneficial. So it will not occur if agents of the same type meet, and will certainly take place if both agents can obtain their consumption goods by trading (e.g. an agent of type I with good 2 meets an agent of type II with good 1). What needs to be determined is whether an agent will trade to obtain a good which is not his consumption good because it will enhance his chances of acquiring the consumption good sometime in the future – for example, will an agent of type I carrying good 2 ever want to exchange it for good 3? A (pure strategies Nash) equilibrium is characterised by agents maximising their expected utilities, given that other agents also pursue their equilibrium strategies and inventories are at their equilibrium levels. Equilibrium inventory holdings are those which result from all agents adopting their equilibrium trading strategies.

In Model A ($I^* = 2$, $II^* = 3$ and $III^* = 1$, using asterisks to denote the good produced by the particular agent), it can be shown that there is – for certain parameter values – a 'Fundamental Equilibrium'. This is where agents do not exchange a lower-storage-cost good for a higher-storage-cost good unless the latter is their own consumption good. So agents need look only at 'fundamentals' – storage costs and utility values – when deciding whether to trade. However, there is also – for different parameter values – a 'Speculative Equilibrium' in which agents may acquire a higher-storage-cost good in exchange for a lower-storage-cost good because of its superior tradeability. Finally, for some parameter values, there is no equilibrium. Things are different in Model B ($I^* = 3$, $II^* = 1$ and $III^* = 2$) where there is always a fundamental equilibrium, and there is sometimes (i.e. for some parameter values) a speculative equilibrium. (So Model B can possess multiple equilibria.) KW also consider how fiat money might be introduced. In the model it is assumed that fiat money has no storage costs, is not produced or consumed by any agent (so is just held in order to facilitate trade) and (perhaps controversially) agents cannot hold money as well as a good. It can be shown that even if fiat currency exists, there are equilibria in which it is not held – if no one else wants to hold fiat currency, there is no point in holding it. However, there are other equilibria in which fiat currency is held and operates as a generally acceptable medium of exchange.

What are the welfare properties of an equilibrium? We may look at the steady-state utility levels of agents and ask if the equilibrium is optimal relative to other (non equilibrium) trading strategies. The answer is that it may not be – for example, a situation where agents always trade when they meet may make everyone better off since in deciding whether to trade or not, agents do not take into account the positive externalities they may confer on others. It can also be shown that fiat money may raise welfare – it reduces the wasteful need to incur storage costs in using real commodities as a medium of exchange.

KW is certainly an important contribution to the theory of money. However, there is much still to be done. It does not provide an account of money which enables us to understand the role of monetary policy or the way in which money may affect the price level and output. Important features are the assumptions that goods and money cannot be stored simultaneously, that goods are indivisible, that an agent can only store one unit of a good at a time and trade always takes the form of an agent exchanging all his money holdings for a unit of a good (or vice versa). The reason for this assumption is that it avoids the need for any analysis of the terms at which trade takes place – trade always consists of one agent's exchanging everything he has for everything another agent has. Obviously, relaxing this assumption is an important item on the research agenda. It may seem fairly strange to have indivisible money – however, KW argue that the fundamental property of fiat money is its inherent uselessness, not its indivisibility.

Duffy and Ochs (1999) conducted an experimental study of the KW model and found that subjects have a strong tendency to play fundamental strategies even when speculative strategies have higher payoffs.

1.4 More Recent Approaches to the Theory of Money

Of other approaches to the theory of money, that of Banerjee and Maskin (1996) deserves attention. Note that this is described as a 'Walrasian' model – it does not rely on trading frictions, as does KW. It is assumed that there is private information about the quality of commodities and this inhibits barter. (How do I evaluate the quality of the commodity someone is offering in exchange for mine?) Banerjee and Maskin argue that in such an environment a medium of exchange will emerge and, moreover, the medium of exchange will be the good for which the discrepancy between high and low qualities is smallest. So we have a reason for the emergence of a commodity money; historically, numerous commodities have been used as media of exchange – gold, cowrie shells, cigarettes in prisoner of war camps are examples that come to mind – and such an approach can explain this. However, because this good is used as the medium of exchange, an inefficiently high quantity of the good will be produced. There is a welfare improving role for fiat money – it is a 'good' for which there is no uncertainty as to its quality and it can be produced at little resource cost.

So far, we have not considered how banks might come into existence. A common account is that, in an economy where gold acts as currency, agents might deposit their gold with goldsmiths. The goldsmiths offer receipts for the gold deposited and agents come to realise that they can make many payments more easily by transferring claims to gold rather than the gold itself. Hence we see how cheques can emerge. Cheques have a number of advantages over currency; they can easily be made out for (almost) any amount, they are easy to transport and they provide a receipt.

1.5 Conclusion

Although the work reviewed in this chapter, which might be described as attempting to derive a theory of money from first principles, is extremely interesting and important, it has not so far generated insights into money and banking which are useful for monetary policy makers. However, there are two important conclusions that emerge from many of the models. The first is the importance of expectations, in the sense that for an object to function as money, it is generally necessary (and often sufficient) that agents believe that they will be able to exchange it for other assets and goods. Secondly, there is no guarantee that the monetary equilibria that might emerge in the various types of economy considered are in any sense efficient; there are numerous examples in which there can be inefficiencies, of which Samuelson (1958) is probably the starkest example. It might be hoped that further work in this area will produce more insights. In addition to those papers already cited, we might mention Shi (1997), Trejos and Wright (1995) and He, Huang and Wright (2008).

Finally, we comment on the common, but perhaps quite old fashioned, idea that money has three 'functions': medium of account, store of value and unit of account. In our view, the main function of money is that of the medium of exchange. Its function as a store of value is essentially derivative, in the sense that something which was not a reasonably good store of value would not be a very good medium of exchange since it needs to be held between transactions, and if it lost a considerable amount of its value in this time period it would not be a good medium of exchange. (One would for this reason not want to use ice cubes as a medium of exchange in a tropical or even temperate climate.) A unit of account is the unit in which prices are quoted, and there is no logical reason why the unit of account should be the same as the medium of exchange. However, if they do differ, then a calculation needs to be made when purchasing the good in question as to how many units of the medium of exchange need to be paid for a good costing a certain amount in terms of the unit of account. For example, if pesos are the unit of account, and dollars the medium of exchange, one has to multiply the peso price of a good by the relevant exchange rate between pesos and dollars to work out the number of dollars one needs to pay. Such a calculation is entirely unnecessary if the medium of exchange is the same as the unit of account. If the unit of account is just as good a medium of exchange as any other asset, it makes sense to use it as the medium of exchange as well. Occasions where the unit of account differs from the medium of exchange may occur in situations where, perhaps because of rapid inflation, the unit of account is decidedly inferior as a medium of exchange to certain other assets.

DISCUSSION QUESTIONS

1. In an economy with a commodity currency, will there always be a welfare improvement if the government replaces the commodity money by fiat currency?
2. According to Clower (1967), 'Money buys goods and goods buy money, but goods do not buy goods'. Discuss. In particular, what insights does this aphorism provide into the foundations of a monetary economy?
3. What role for government intervention, if any, do the models considered in this chapter suggest?

CHAPTER 2

Keynes, IS-LM and After

' . . . the once very popular IS-LM framework by now belongs to the history of economic thought as an unsuccessful attempt to analyze purely short-run macroeconomic events, often by means of reasonable looking behavioral relationships . . . Because none of these schedules follows from any small set of consistent axioms about rational economic behaviour, economists often say that the IS-LM structure lacks *microeconomic foundations.*'

(Azariadis, 1993, p. 46.)

' . . . the main reason for the success of the IS-LM model is indeed its versatility, the fact that it can readily be adapted to analyze a wide variety of policy and other issues.'

(Blanchard and Fischer, 1989, p. 536.)

Monetary economics and macroeconomics have an extensive history which we cannot and do not intend to survey in any detail. However, the most important event in the development of macroeconomics was undoubtedly the publication of John Maynard Keynes's path-breaking book, *General Theory of Employment, Interest and Money* in 1936 (Keynes, 1936); in fact, it can be said that this saw the birth of modern macroeconomics. What we intend to do in this chapter is to give a very brief account of the state of macroeconomics before 1936, discuss Keynes's contribution and then move on to consider some more recent developments.

2.1 Before Keynes

Whatever one's assessment of Keynes's book there is no denying its massive impact. Our interpretation of pre-Keynesian macroeconomics is undoubtedly coloured by Keynes's own characterisation of the theory he was attacking: classical macroeconomics. Undoubtedly it was a caricature, but like many good caricatures, it had an element of truth. Keynes's book was published when the world was in the midst of the Great Depression, characterised by mass unemployment. It seemed there was no satisfactory theory of how and why such unemployment could arise, or what could be done to tackle the problem; its main achievement was developing a theoretical framework that could explain, and suggest remedies for, such a problem.

The Quantity Theory of Money and the so-called (by Keynes) classical theory were perhaps the main components of pre-Keynesian macroeconomics. The Quantity Theory can be derived from the so-called 'Equation of Exchange':

$$MV = PT. \tag{2-1}$$

Here, M is the money supply, V the velocity of circulation, P the price level and T the volume of transactions in the economy. The equation is in fact an identity, something that is true by virtue of how the items in the equation are defined. The left-hand side gives how much money in the economy 'turns over' – it is the amount of money multiplied by the number of times an average unit of money is used. The right-hand side gives the total number of transactions in the economy multiplied by the average price level. So this represents the total value of transactions in the economy, and the equation can hence be interpreted as stating that the total value of transactions in the economy equals the total amount of spending in the economy, which may seem obviously true.

Identities are true by the definition of the terms they contain and do not tell us anything about the way the real world (or the economy) operates. We can, however, convert the equation into something that will make predictions if, for example, we make the following assumptions: (i) T, the volume of transactions using money in the economy, equals (or is at least proportional to) GDP (Y); (ii) T (and hence Y) is constant, or at least independent of the other variables in the equation; (iii) V is, similarly, constant or at least independent of the other variables in the equation; (iv) P is proportional to (or equal to) the GDP deflator (or some other relevant measure of the overall price level in the economy). This is quite a demanding set of assumptions! Nevertheless, suppose we do make these assumptions, then we obtain the result that

$$M = (1/V)PY = kPY. \tag{2-2}$$

Since V and Y are independent of M, it follows that changes in M, the money supply, are reflected immediately and entirely in changes in the price level, or inflation. So under these assumptions the quantity theory of money holds: inflation equals the rate of growth of the money supply. We can modify this equation in various ways. If there is trend growth in the economy, then monetary growth will equal the sum of this trend growth plus inflation, and we can also consider the implication of trend changes in velocity.

The classical theory might be interpreted as providing a reason why the volume of transactions or income is constant, or at least independent of M. Suppose wages and prices are flexible, and the economy can be described by supply and demand curves for labour and goods with conventional properties, and output and employment are related by a standard production function, then such an economy is characterised by a constant level of output. Employment will be determined by the intersection of the demand and supply curves for labour, which depend on tastes, technology and the abundance of other factors of production and are independent of the money supply (or government spending); output is then determined from the level of employment by a standard production function. How then can unemployment (by which is meant an excess of labour supply over labour demand) be explained? It might seem obvious that some sort of price rigidity must be to blame – otherwise why does the real wage not adjust to the level which ensures equality of labour supply and demand? So the classical explanation would be that wage and price rigidities are responsible for unemployment, and that the appropriate remedy would be to increase the flexibility of wages and prices.

2.2 Keynes's Contribution

The exact nature of Keynes's contribution has been the subject of enormous debate and controversy since 1936. The author's first publication (Fender, 1981) was an attempt to clarify how Keynes differed from the classical theory. Surveying the massive amount of literature on the topic is completely beyond the scope of this book and would not in any case be particularly insightful. Instead, what we shall do here is explain what the author currently believes Keynes's contribution to be; it is essentially the same as that contained in his 1981 book, although there are some things in the earlier publication that need clarification.

Keynes's contribution is essentially on the following lines: the argument that wage flexibility will ensure full employment is inconclusive as movements in the money wage may not produce the relevant movement in the real wages. This is because if prices are largely a mark up over wages, changes in money wages may be accompanied by equivalent changes in prices hence keeping real wages (approximately) unchanged. But in any case it may not be possible to induce greater downward flexibility of nominal wages – it does seem that nominal wages may be fairly inflexible downwards, and it is not clear how one would go about increasing their flexibility. So what alternative remedies are there? It is not clear. What needs to be done is to work out the way in which an economy characterised by imperfectly flexible wages and prices behaves, and once this has been done one can analyse the effects of various policy changes, as well as of changing money wage rates, on unemployment and other variables of interest. So Keynes constructs such a theory: for given money wages, output is determined by the intersection of an aggregate supply and an aggregate demand curve for output; policies work inasmuch as they affect either the aggregate supply or aggregate demand curve.

Now it can be seen that changes in the money supply, or in government spending, can affect output and employment through shifting the aggregate demand curve. The aggregate demand curve gives total demand for output as a function of output, so the appropriate equilibrium condition is that aggregate demand equals output. (This is in fact a simplified version of the Keynesian model where the aggregate supply curve is such that output is determined by demand at whatever price and wage levels happen to obtain.) The properties of the aggregate demand curve are hence of crucial importance to the behaviour of the economy. A key question is the impact of changes in income or output on aggregate demand. It is here that the celebrated 'multiplier' arises. This is related to the marginal propensity to consume, the amount of any increase in income that is spent on consumption. Suppose we assume the following relationship between consumption (C) and income:

$$C = a + b(Y - T). \tag{2-3}$$

Here, a is 'autonomous' consumption (the amount that is consumed when disposable income is zero), b is the marginal propensity to consume out of disposable income and T is taxation. The national income equilibrium condition states that

$$C + I + G = Y. \tag{2-4}$$

So, substituting (2-3) into (2-4) and manipulating, we derive

$$Y = \frac{a + I + G - bT}{1 - b}. \tag{2-5}$$

So changes in government spending, unaccompanied by changes in taxation, produce a multiplied effect on national income, since b, the marginal propensity to consume, lies between zero and unity. In fact, if b is close to unity, changes in government expenditure can produce a much greater impact on national income. If, for example, b equals 0.1, an increase in government spending of £1 produces an increase in national income of £10. No wonder the term 'multiplier' was coined. This is a radically different theory of national income determination from what preceded Keynes, suggesting that increases in government spending could be the remedy for unemployment and recession. Another result emerges when we consider a *balanced budget* increase in government spending – the increase in G is accompanied by an equal increase in T, so the government's budget remains balanced. It is straightforward to see that in this case (from (2-5)), the change in income equals the change in government spending, or the government expenditure multiplier is unity. The idea is that the increase in government spending by itself raises GDP by the same amount. However, there is no change in consumption as the effect of the increased government spending on disposable income is completely neutralised by the tax increase. If, say, G increases by £1bn, workers in the government sector have an extra £1bn in gross income, but the increase in taxes offsets this completely, and the only way in which income is affected is through the direct effect of the extra government spending.

This is of course the simplest version of Keynes's model, the so-called Keynesian cross. It is clearly deficient in many ways, one of the most important of which is its complete neglect of money and the interest rate. However, the multiplier is still one of the more important of Keynes's innovations. There has been considerable debate over the justification for the function. Why should consumption depend upon current income? It may seem to us that the answer is obvious, but this is probably because we have been immersed in Keynes's theory without necessarily realising it. If one sets up a consumer optimisation problem where the consumer can buy or sell as much as he wishes of various goods and services, his consumption of these various goods will depend basically on the relative prices he faces and on his endowments (as well as on tastes etc., which generally can be assumed constant). The concept of income does not feature in these relationships.

Things differ, however, if agents are constrained in their sales of factors. In particular, suppose a worker cannot sell as much labour as he would like to at the current wage. Then it is easy to see that the amount of labour he actually manages to sell – and hence his labour income – may well affect his consumption of goods and services. The effect may be strengthened if the worker finds it difficult or impossible to borrow on the strength of future labour income. So here we have a rigorous justification for the Keynesian consumption function – it presupposes that at least one market, the labour market, does not, or at least may not, clear – i.e. there is 'involuntary' unemployment. So this particularly innovative feature of the 'General Theory' is consequential on Keynes's considering an economy where not all markets cleared.

The assumption that investment is exogenous in the above story of course needs to be relaxed. The most obvious variable to affect investment (apart from the state of long-term expectations) is the interest rate. If one assumes the interest rate affects investment in equation (2-4) and substitutes equation (2-3) into this, then a relationship containing two endogenous variables, the interest rate and income is obtained; we write it as:

$$C(Y - T) + I(r) + G = Y. \tag{2-6}$$

This is the equation of the celebrated IS curve, telling us, for any given value of G, the values of r and Y that are compatible with goods market equilibrium. However, so far we have two unknowns and just one equation. In order to pin down these unknowns, we need another relationship. This is provided by introducing the money market. It might be supposed that the demand for money depends on both income and the interest rate. (The determinants of the demand for money will be discussed extensively later in the book). So we have the following money market equilibrium equation:

$$M/P = L(r, Y). \tag{2-7}$$

Here, M is the money supply, P is the price level and r is the interest rate. Note that what matters is the 'real' money supply (i.e. M/P or the money supply divided by the price level), not the nominal money supply. The basic idea is that if the price level doubles, but everything 'real' stays unchanged, then the demand for money should double as well – if nothing real has changed, agents should want to keep their consumption of goods and services unaltered, and therefore in order to achieve this, will need to double exactly the amount of nominal money balances they hold. Equation (2-7) combines the assumption that the money market clears (i.e. the supply and demand for money are equal) with the assumption that the real demand for money depends positively on income and negatively on the interest rate. There has been a massive amount of work trying to make more precise the relationship between the demand for money and its determinants, some of which we will review in this book. Suffice to say at the moment that if money is demanded to facilitate transactions, and transactions are positively related to income, we can justify the presence of income as an argument of the money demand function, and if we think of the interest rate as the opportunity cost of holding money (the main alternative to holding money is holding assets that pay interest) then we can rationalise the interest rate as another argument.

So equation (2-7) provides a second relationship between income and the interest rate. This represents an LM curve, telling us (for given values of P and M) the combinations of income and the interest rate that are compatible with money market equilibrium. So we now have two relationships, (2-6) and (2-7), which jointly determine these variables.

This is the famous IS-LM framework, illustrated in Figure 2.1, which even now forms a staple part of intermediate undergraduate macroeconomics, in spite of views such as those expressed in the quotation from Azariadis which starts the chapter. It allows monetary and fiscal policies to be analysed in a straightforward manner. As illustrated in Figure 2.2, monetary policy is represented by a rightward shift of the LM curve; it reduces the interest rate and this stimulates investment spending and hence national income. The power of

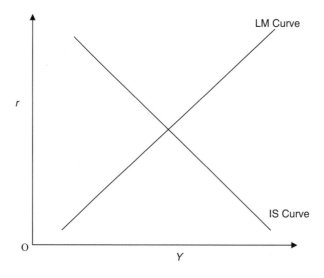

Figure 2.1   The IS-LM Framework.

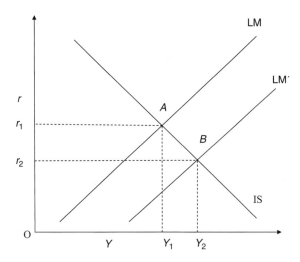

Figure 2.2   Monetary Policy in the IS-LM Framework.

monetary policy depends first of all on how much the interest rate falls when the money supply increases, and hence is *more* powerful the *less* interest elastic the demand for money is, since this means the interest rate has to fall more in response to any increase in the money supply to equilibrate the money market. Secondly, it depends on how sensitive investment spending is to the interest rate; the higher the interest elasticity of investment spending, the more powerful monetary policy will be.

The effects of an expansionary fiscal policy can be shown by shifting the IS curve rightwards; see Figure 2.3. National income tends to rise, but since the interest rate rises (unless the LM

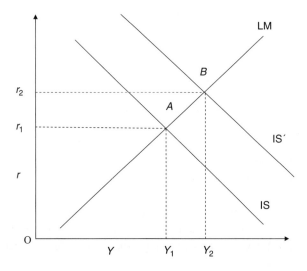

Figure 2.3   Fiscal Policy in the IS-LM Framework.

curve is horizontal) there is an offsetting effect on national income through reducing investment. This is the 'crowding out' effect of government spending. This is greater, the steeper the LM curve, which means the greater the offsetting impact on investment of any increase in government spending.

The IS-LM framework was introduced by Sir John Hicks (see Hicks, 1937); there has been some controversy over whether the framework captures what Keynes had in mind in his book; persuasive evidence that it does is provided by the fact that when Hicks sent Keynes a copy of his paper, Keynes replied that he had 'next to nothing to say by way of criticism' (Hicks, 1973, p. 9). The position taken in this book is that IS-LM is a reasonable representation of the theory Keynes had in mind. A crucial part in the theory is, of course, the LM curve, in which the dependence of the demand for money on the interest rate plays a vital role. This relationship was of less relevance for classical theory so it is not surprising that Keynes emphasised it. He developed his theory of 'liquidity preference' to explain the dependence of the demand for money on the interest rate, and uncertainty plays an important role in this.

There is much more, of course, in Keynes's 'General Theory' than what has been presented above. In particular, Keynes did analyse at some length (in his Chapter 19) the effects on output and employment of cutting money wages. The effects are somewhat complicated, but in essence are similar to those of an increase in the money supply. So if one has the choice between an increase in the money supply and cutting money wages, it might seem that one should choose the one that is easier to implement, and it is clear that increasing the money supply is much easier to implement than cutting money wages. The latter might also have some adverse effects that raising the money supply should not (such as creating expectations of further wage and price deflation), hence raising the case for using monetary policy for stabilisation purposes.

2.3 After Keynes

Keynes's contribution was indeed revolutionary, in the true sense of the term – it fundamentally altered the way economists thought about the way output and employment are determined, and about the ways in which monetary and fiscal policies operated. But this scientific revolution, as is the case with most scientific revolutions, left economists with plenty to do. (According to Kuhn, 1970, most of science is 'normal science' not 'revolutionary science' and consists of answering many of the unanswered questions that a revolutionary change in a paradigm raises.) The exact relationship between income and consumption, or between the interest rate and the demand for money, required further analysis and research. Research by a number of economists on the consumption function suggested that it may not be current absolute income that matters, but perhaps relative income, permanent income or life cycle income. Keynes's theory was extended in a number of directions, including extending the approach to an open economy. An unsatisfactory part of the 'General Theory' was its failure to explain how money wages are determined and how they change. A crucial development here was the Phillips curve, which postulated an inverse relationship between wage inflation and unemployment, implying that governments can raise output and employment by boosting aggregate demand, but at the price of higher wage inflation (which would of course feed through to higher price inflation). This led to the idea that governments needed to choose the 'best' combination of inflation and unemployment, but also to suggestions that governments should try to shift the curve, for example by using incomes policies.

But the Keynesian consensus started to break down. The co-existence of high levels of both unemployment and inflation seemed difficult to explain using Keynes's theory (or any other theory, for that matter), and led to the development of the expectations-augmented Phillips curve. Friedman's 1967 address to the American Economic Association played a crucial role in this change (see Friedman, 1968). In a few years we saw the 'rational expectations' revolution, arguing that many of the conclusions of the Keynesian revolution would disappear once account was taken of how agents formed their expectations. The idea that governments could stabilise the economy in a systematic way received a severe blow from the 'Lucas critique', according to which attempts at systematic stabilisation policy will fail as agents will come to incorporate the effects of such stabilisation policies into their expectations. (See Lucas, 1976, in particular.) There was also the development of Real Business Cycle theory, which attempted to explain economic fluctuations as efficient reactions of the economic system to various shocks, particularly technology shocks. Relevant references are Kydland and Prescott (1982) and Long and Plosser (1983).

However, starting perhaps in the 1980s, there was a Keynesian resurgence, which sought to give a more rigorous foundation to some Keynesian type views. For example, a model with menu costs and imperfect competition was argued to have many Keynesian features. We have seen the development of dynamic stochastic general equilibrium models, which (arguably) contain the best of both Keynesian and neoclassical economics, combining intertemporal optimisation with some sort of price or wage rigidity which ensure that some Keynesian effects remain.

As far as the transmission mechanism of monetary policy is concerned, the IS-LM framework emphasises that a money supply increase reduces the interest rate, and this raises investment spending, and this via the multiplier raises national income. This is still, we believe, valid as *one* possible way in which monetary policy is transmitted to income. The crucial determinants of the power of monetary policy are the interest elasticity of the demand for money, the interest elasticity of expenditure, and the marginal propensity to consume (which affects the size of the multiplier). In the next two chapters, we discuss consumption and investment, albeit briefly; discussion of the demand for money we relegate to a later chapter.

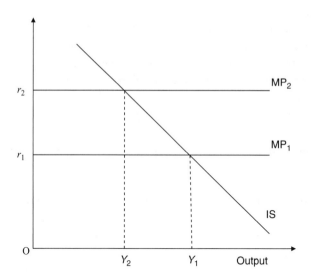

Figure 2.4   Contractionary Monetary Policy in the IS-MP Framework (after Romer, 2000).

2.4 Keynesian Macroeconomics without the LM Curve

Romer (2000) has argued that Keynesian economics should dispense with the LM curve. Instead, in a framework with the real interest rate on the vertical axis, monetary policy should best be considered in terms of the central bank following a real interest rate target. As shown in Figure 2.4, a horizontal MP curve replaces the LM curve; this shows the real interest rate the monetary authority seeks to implement. The figure shows what happens when the authority, perhaps because of worries about inflation, decides to increase the real interest rate.

Although this approach has substantial merits, it does not seem to have much impact as far as the teaching of undergraduate economics in the UK is concerned. It is certainly true that monetary policy today is better described in terms of the central bank choosing an interest rate rather than pursuing a money supply target; however, in much of the open macroeconomics literature (for example, Dornbusch, 1976) monetary policy is analysed in terms of money supply changes, and it is not clear how one would analyse policy in such models using an interest rate rule (for example, it is not clear what 'overshooting' means in an interest-rate-targeting framework). So although we would prefer to think of monetary policy as being carried out by the central bank controlling the interest rate, for some purposes it still may be appropriate to regard the money supply as the instrument of monetary policy.

2.5 Conclusion

Keynes's achievement was to develop an approach for determining the level of output and unemployment in a world of imperfectly flexible wages and prices. Much, but of course not all, subsequent work in macroeconomics can be thought of as extending and developing the Keynesian framework, and many of his insights remain relevant today. So in spite of the limitations of his theory, his achievement was immense.

DISCUSSION QUESTIONS

1. Does it matter what Keynes really meant?
2. Are there any reasons why increasing wage and price flexibility might increase output and employment in a Keynesian framework? Are there any reasons why it might decrease output and employment? Which outcome do you consider more plausible?
3. Are there any reasons why we should not adopt Romer's suggestion and dispense with the LM curve?

CHAPTER 3

Consumption

U nderstanding consumption is of major importance in understanding the transmission mechanism of monetary policy, as well as many other areas of macroeconomics, and it is not surprising that there has been a huge amount of research effort put into explaining consumption since Keynes's General Theory was published. One of the most important contributions was Friedman's permanent income hypothesis (see Friedman, 1957), which introduced the crucial distinction between permanent and transitory income. Permanent income is defined as what a household can expect to consume over a period without reducing its wealth and, according to Friedman, consumption is proportional to this. Transitory changes in income hence change consumption only inasmuch as they change permanent income. A one off payment will only affect consumption to a small degree. Closely related to the permanent income hypothesis is the life cycle hypothesis, introduced by Modigliani and Brumberg which explicitly considers a household's life time pattern of income and consumption. Typically a household will work and then retire, receiving an income that fluctuates accordingly, and hence has to decide how to allocate consumption over its life span.

In this chapter, we shall survey work on consumption, albeit very briefly; our main concern will be to understand the lessons that might be drawn for the transmission mechanism of monetary policy. We start by developing the theory of consumption in an intertemporal optimising framework.

3.1 Intertemporal Optimisation and Consumption

Suppose that a household has the following utility function:

$$U_1 = \sum_{t=1}^{N} \beta^{t-1} u(c_t).$$ (3-1)

It is assumed the household lives for N periods, has instantaneous utility function $u(.)$; c_t represents consumption at time t and β is the discount factor.[1] It also has the following intertemporal budget constraint, showing the feasible consumption paths over its life span:

$$\sum_{t=1}^{N} R^{t-1} c_t = W_1.$$ (3-2)

W_1 is the household's total wealth, and $R = 1/(1+r)$ is the real interest factor (r is the real rate of interest). We assume for the moment that wealth is independent of the real interest rate. Then maximisation of (3-1) subject to (3-2) produces the following *necessary* condition for optimality (sometimes called an Euler equation):

$$\frac{u'(c_{t+1})}{u'(c_t)} = \frac{R}{\beta}.$$ (3-3)

If we assume logarithmic utility ($u(\cdot) = log(\cdot)$) then we obtain:

$$c_{t+1} = \beta(1+r)c_t.$$ (3-4)

So consumption growth is higher, the higher the real interest rate. It is also higher, the higher the discount *factor*, which is inversely related to the discount *rate*; so the more the consumer discounts the future, the slower will be his growth in consumption. If the discount factor is less than $(1+r)$ – which means, speaking loosely, that the consumer discounts future consumption at a higher rate than the real interest rate – then consumption falls over time, but if the discount factor is greater than $(1+r)$, then consumption rises over time. We can also, by combining (3-2) and (3-4), derive the following expression for consumption in the first period:

$$c_1 = \frac{(1+r)W_1}{\{1 + \beta + \beta^2 + \cdots + \beta^{N-1}\}}.$$ (3-5)

So an increase in wealth will increase consumption, with the size of the marginal propensity to consume out of wealth depending negatively on the discount factor, and on the time horizon (N). An increase in the real interest rate will also raise consumption; in fact it acts just like an increase in wealth; it raises the household's intertemporal consumption possibilities and therefore raises its consumption in each period.

In the limit, as N tends to infinity, we obtain the simpler expression:

$$c_1 = (1 - \beta)(1+r)W_1.$$ (3-6)

---

[1] The discount *factor* should be distinguished from the discount *rate*; the two are related by the equation, $\beta = 1/(1+\rho)$ where ρ is the discount rate.

If instead we assume a constant relative risk aversion (CRRA) utility function:

$$u(c_t) = \frac{c_t^{1-\gamma}}{1-\gamma}, \text{ for } \gamma > 0, \gamma \neq 1 \tag{3-7}$$

then the Euler condition becomes

$$c_{t+1}/c_t = \{\beta(1+r)\}^{1/\gamma}. \tag{3-8}$$

So here the elasticity of substitution between consumption at any two points of time is constant and equals $1/\gamma$. If γ is close to zero, the elasticity of substitution is very high, and small changes in the real interest rate (say) can produce large changes in the rate of growth of consumption. By substituting this into the intertemporal budget constraint and solving, then we obtain, for the infinite-horizon case (the finite-horizon case is considerably more complicated and not particularly insightful):

$$c_1 = \left[1 - \beta^{1/\gamma}(1+r)^{(1-\gamma)/\gamma}\right] W_1. \tag{3-9}$$

It can easily be seen that an increase in the real interest rate now has a negative effect on consumption in period 1.

So far, however, it has been assumed that the real interest rate does not affect wealth at all. This might represent the situation of a household that has a certain amount of current wealth in the form of (say) money in a bank deposit but does not expect to receive any future income at all. Clearly, this is highly unrealistic. Suppose, instead, that the household expects to receive an income of e_t in period t, then its wealth will be

$$W_1 = \sum_{t=1}^{N} R^{t-1} e_t. \tag{3-10}$$

Now it can be seen that an increase in the real interest rate clearly reduces the household's wealth, and in this way will reduce consumption.

This framework is perhaps basic to understanding consumption, but is based on a number of restrictive assumptions. In the next section we consider the implications of relaxing some of these assumptions.

3.2 Relaxation of Key Assumptions

3.2.1 Consumer Heterogeneity

We need to move beyond the representative agent framework implicit in this framework. When we do, we may distinguish lenders and borrowers. Lenders are made better off by interest rate increases, whereas borrowers are made worse off, so the overall effects of an interest rate change on consumption may depend on distributional considerations. For example, suppose a country has fairly undeveloped capital markets and there are few private borrowers. However, suppose a large number of consumers hold short-term government bonds. Then an increase in short-term interest rates may increase households' disposable income and hence their consumption; the government is a borrower, but may not behave the same way as other borrowers when interest rates rise.

3.2.2 Imperfect Capital Markets

There is considerable evidence that many consumers are credit constrained, in the sense that they might like to consume more than they are able to, and would be willing and able to repay the borrowing they may need to undertake to carry out this consumption, but they cannot borrow, or are at least constrained in how much they are able to borrow which prevents them from consuming their desired amount. There are a number of explanations for such behaviour; borrowers may have no way of committing to repaying their loans even though they would prefer to borrow and repay the loans than not to borrow at all. The main implication of credit constraints for consumption is that we would expect the marginal propensity to consume of a credit-constrained household out of income to be high, possibly one. (If a household would ideally want to consume more than it can because it cannot borrow enough, it surely would want to consume every penny of any extra pound it happens to receive.) So the response of credit constrained households to a temporary payment may be very different from that of a non-credit constrained household; the consumption of the former will increase, most likely, by the full amount of the increase, whereas the non-credit constrained household will raise its consumption by a trivial amount, if at all.

3.2.3 Uncertainty

Uncertainty is of course pervasive in life, yet the theories developed above do not really incorporate it. If we think of the life-cycle hypothesis, we should mention that there is uncertainty about the length of life, about future income, about future consumption needs, about the returns on assets – indeed, about everything! Under the assumptions of either complete insurance markets or risk neutrality, this uncertainty does not matter, but these assumptions are very strong indeed. One cannot insure oneself (on actuarially fair terms) against many risks, and an assumption of risk neutrality is of course totally unrealistic. But then the question arises – suppose we live in a world of risk-averse agents and imperfect insurance markets, as we do – what are the implications for consumption behaviour? Here the concept of precautionary savings should be mentioned. Let us suppose that agents attach high disutility to very low levels of consumption in any state – formally, the marginal utility of consumption might tend to infinity as consumption tends to zero. Then consumers will do a lot to ensure that they never end up in such a state. This might mean, for example, that they hold 'buffer stock' savings and may be reluctant to borrow as much as they otherwise might be expected to in the face of temporarily bad times. For further discussion of precautionary savings and its implications see Carroll (2001).

3.3 Durable Purchases

We should also mention durable goods. These are goods which provide a flow of consumption services over time; examples include cars, computers, furniture, clothes, books and so forth. (Housing clearly satisfies the definition of a durable good, but it has a number of special features which mean we shall discuss it in a future chapter.) Clearly, a high proportion of a household's expenditure will often be on such durable goods. What factors affect such purchases? (Strictly, durable purchases do not count as consumption – one consumes the flow of consumption services provided by the good in question when one owns it. But it is the purchases themselves that contribute to demand for goods and services and the effect of monetary policy on these purchases is our concern here.)

Determinants of durable purchases may include the real interest rate and wealth. The existing stock of durables is probably important, as are credit-rationing effects. There might be a link with the housing market – more house buying leads to an increase in purchases of furniture and home appliances, etc.

3.4 Conclusion

We might draw the following conclusions about consumption behaviour that are relevant for monetary policy makers:

1. If the *real* interest rate falls then this will tend to induce substitution away from future consumption towards current consumption. This is the substitution effect of the change. The income effect is negative for lenders, who thus might be expected to reduce their current consumption but positive for borrowers, who might be expected to raise their current consumption. If, on average, income effects are the same for borrowers and lenders, then they cancel out at the aggregate level and we are just left with the substitution effect, and hence consumption must rise. Of course, it is highly unlikely that the income effects will cancel out in aggregate; however, for consumption to fail to rise in this framework with a fall in the real interest rate, the income effect would have to be much more powerful for lenders than for borrowers and we have no reason at all for thinking that this might be the case.
2. Inasmuch as expansionary monetary policy raises *wealth* (by raising bond, share, housing, land, gold and other asset prices), it might be expected to raise consumption.
3. There may be *expectational* effects; if an expansionary monetary policy raises expectations of future economic activity, this may mean an increase in current consumption.
4. Borrowers who are credit constrained may consume more when interest rates fall. If credit constraints are set in nominal terms, a fall in nominal interest rates may raise consumption.
5. If an expansionary monetary policy leads to a relaxation of credit constraints, there may be powerful effects on consumption – a credit-rationed borrower is likely to spend every penny of any increase in credit he can obtain. Also, consider a credit-rationed borrower

who receives an increase in income that is also an increase in permanent income. Then lenders may consider him a better credit risk because of his higher permanent income, in which case his credit limit may be raised and his marginal propensity to consume may initially exceed unity.

DISCUSSION QUESTIONS

1. Studies have shown that older retired households do not, in general, hold less wealth than younger retired households. Does this contradict the life-cycle hypothesis?

2. Consider a two-period framework where a household needs to choose between consumption today and consumption tomorrow. It receives income Y_1 today but expects to receive nothing tomorrow. It can borrow or lend at a certain rate of interest r. Derive the equation of the household's budget constraints, showing the combinations of first-period consumption (C_1) and second-period consumption (C_2) that are feasible for the household. Draw a diagram illustrating this choice. What are the effects of an increase in the interest rate? Would we expect the household to consume more or less as a consequence?

3. Carry out the same exercise as in Question (2), but this time for a household that is a net borrower in the sense that it receives no income today, but expects to receive with certainty an income Y_2 tomorrow.

Investment

I n spite of its importance, we do not seem to have a great deal of knowledge of the determinants of aggregate investment which would be useful for monetary policy purposes. We do not, for example, have a consensus on what it would be reasonable to assume about the interest elasticity of investment. In this chapter we present a simple theoretical approach to investment and some extensions; we also briefly discuss empirical work.

4.1 The DPV Approach to Investment

Let us suppose a firm is considering an investment project which is expected to produce returns for T periods and the firm estimates it will receive a net return of M_j in period j. The net return is the revenue derived from selling the good produced by the project, less all the costs associated with producing the good and involved with the project that are incurred in that year. Then we can calculate the Discounted Present Value (DPV) of the project:

$$DPV = \frac{E[M_1]}{(1+i_1)} + \frac{E[M_2]}{(1+i_1)(1+i_2)} + \cdots + \frac{E[M_T]}{(1+i_1)(1+i_2)...(1+i_T)}. \tag{4-1}$$

The interest rate for the jth period (more precisely, the interest that can be earned between time $j-1$ and j) is i_j. The DPV is, in a nutshell, what the project is worth to the investor *now*. If I expect to receive a return of M_1 next year from the project, that is worth to me $M_1/(1+i_1)$; this is the sum of money which today is equivalent to what I expect to receive next period, in the sense that by borrowing and lending operations I can transform the future amount into the current amount and vice versa. (It is assumed here that capital markets are perfect, in the sense that one can borrow or lend as much as one likes at the same interest rate.) The DPV is essentially what the project is worth to the firm. It follows that it should invest in the project if, and only if, the DPV is greater than the costs of undertaking it. So, suppose we have a large number of firms with potential projects; some of them may have DPVs greater than their costs, for others the reverse might be the case, then anything that tends to raise the DPVs will tend to raise investment, by implying that more projects will now have DPVs greater than their costs. We might draw the following conclusions:

1. Investment decisions are inherently forward looking, so expectations are important in explaining investment. Large changes in expectations can occur in a very short space of time, and these may well dwarf, in their effect on investment, any effect that even a large change in interest rates might have.

2. The interest rate, or more precisely the sequence of interest rates over the time path of the project, is also relevant; we might be tempted to argue that a fall in interest rates therefore raises investment. There is one qualification that does, however, need to be made. Suppose the last 'return' on the project is large and negative; it could be there are large exit costs; an example would be large decommissioning costs associated with a nuclear power station. Then it is possible that a fall in interest rates could actually reduce the DPV of a project.

3. The longer lived the investment, the more sensitive its present value is to changes in the interest rate. Consider an investment project the returns on which are received entirely in period j, which has a present discounted value of $M_j/(1+i_j)^j$, where i_j is the relevant interest rate and j is the date when the returns on the project are received. Then the elasticity of present value with respect to the interest rate is:

$$(\partial DPV/\partial i_j)(i_j/DPV) = -ji_j/(1+i_j). \tag{4-2}$$

The absolute value of this is clearly increasing in both j (the length of life of the project) and i_j. Since longer-term interest rates are more often than not greater than short-term rates, we might expect this elasticity to rise quite significantly in absolute value as the term of the project is extended. But before we conclude that monetary policy is more likely to affect longer-term investment projects than shorter-run projects, we should remember that the relevant interest rate for longer-term projects is the long-term interest rate, so the way in which the term structure of interest rates is determined (considered in a later chapter) may be important in explaining the power of monetary policy. The relevant elasticity (of DPV with respect to the short-run interest rate) is hence the left-hand side of (4-2) multiplied by the elasticity of the relevant longer-term interest rate with respect to the shorter-term rate.

4. Is it the real or the nominal interest rate which is relevant for investment decisions? Suppose the DPV is calculated in 'nominal' terms – i.e. future returns are calculated using the actual prices that are expected to obtain in the future, then it is appropriate that the nominal interest rate is used to calculate the DPV. However, we can transform

equation (4-1) into

$$DPV = \frac{E[R_1(1+\pi_1)]}{(1+r_1)(1+\pi_1)} + \frac{E[R_2(1+\pi_1)(1+\pi_2)]}{(1+r_1)(1+r_2)(1+\pi_1)(1+\pi_2)} + \cdots + \frac{E\left[R_T \prod_{i=1}^{T}(1+\pi_i)\right]}{\prod_{i=1}^{T}(1+r_i)(1+\pi_i)}.$$

(4-3)

Here, we define the real interest rate (r_j) for period j by $(1+i_j) = (1+r_j)(1+\pi_j)$ where π_j is the rate of inflation between periods $j-1$ and j, and we define 'real' revenue (R_j) by $R_j(1+\pi_1)(1+\pi_2)\ldots(1+\pi_j) = M_j$. Then it should be clear that provided inflation is certain, the inflation terms cancel, so the DPV calculated using nominal returns and nominal interest rates should be exactly the same as the DPV calculated using real returns and real interest rates. So, if inflation is neutral (i.e. it does not affect real values, including the real interest rate), it should have absolutely no effect on investment. Also, if one uses the expected money values of returns when calculating DPVs, that is fine provided one also uses nominal interest rates when doing the calculation; one can also use real returns provided one uses real interest rates to do the discounting, but what one must not do is calculate the DPV using real returns and nominal interest rates, or vice versa.

4.2 Relaxation of the 'Standard' Assumptions

1. Fixed capital investment has the properties of being *postponable* and *irreversible*. As a consequence, businessmen may often take a 'cautious' approach to investment in an uncertain world. For example, rumours of the introduction of an investment incentive scheme may cause investment to fall as businessmen wait to see if the scheme is actually introduced. So the predictability or unpredictability of monetary policy (and other policies) may well be an important influence on investment. Such effects were emphasised by Dixit and Pindyck (1994). An interest rate change might not have much effect if it is believed that it might soon be reversed; this is a reason for thinking that the central bank's communication strategy with the public is important. Under certain circumstances, firms may take a 'wait and see' approach to investment and increased uncertainty may well delay investment spending. Temporary tax credits may well boost investment once introduced, but if they are used too frequently, their implementation may come to be anticipated, and this may mean that investment falls as a consequence when a recession seems imminent, which is precisely the opposite of what one wants.

2. So far we have assumed that interest rates for borrowing are the same as those for lending, whereas in practice they are usually higher. This is not necessarily a reflection of capital market imperfections; it may rather be due to costs of intermediation. But this has a number of implications for investment. Presumably the firm should discount the future returns using the right interest rate – the borrowing rate if it is financing the investment by borrowing, the lending rate if it is using its own funds. But this means that internal

funds may be important. If a firm generates more internal funds by increasing its profits, the cost of investing more may decline, so investment might rise.

3. If a firm wants to borrow more, it may have to pay a higher interest rate. This again may not be a sign of capital market imperfection – instead, it may just mean that if it borrows more it is more likely to default, and this is reflected in the price. But if the firm faces an upward sloping supply of loans schedule, this again may reduce its borrowing.

4. There are numerous ways in which imperfect capital markets may be relevant. Obviously if a firm is credit constrained, this may well affect its investment. One way in which changes in nominal interest rates may affect investment spending, even in the absence of a change in the real interest rate, is through front-loading effects with capital market imperfections.

5. Taxation is almost certainly relevant for investment. It depends, though, on the type of taxation and whether it is permanent. A temporary investment tax credit may boost investment if it can be introduced unexpectedly, but if it is expected to be brought in then it may reduce investment before it is implemented.

4.3 Empirical Studies of Investment

Studies of investment suggest that the cost of capital is relevant, that the longer run effects of the cost of capital are considerably greater than the shorter run effects and that profits and cash flow may be quite significant (perhaps indicating the importance of credit rationing effects). There are a number of significant lags that may make the response of investment to changes in its determinants long and drawn out. For example, there is the lag between a change in the cost of capital and the decision to invest, a further delay as plans are drawn up, contracts signed and planning permission obtained, and there may be further delays until spending actually starts. The time from start to finish of an investment project might be quite long, often a matter of years. For this reason, there is probably not much to be hoped from changes in investment as far as the shorter term impact of monetary policy is concerned. Surveys of the literature on aggregate investment are Chirinko (1993) and Caballero (1999); studies of investment in the UK are Cuthbertson and Gasparro (1995), Carruth, Dickerson and Henley (2000) and Ellis and Price (2004).

4.4 Inventory Investment

Inventories are goods of some sort held by firms which have not been sold. We might distinguish input inventories, such as raw materials and work in progress from output inventories, which are goods that have been produced but not yet sold to final consumers. So if a car manufacturer produces 1 million cars but only sells 900,000, the difference represents an accumulation of inventories or inventory investment. Of course, it can easily be negative. Inventory investment is typically small as a percentage of GDP, but it fluctuates a great deal and often is quite important in explaining short run fluctuations in GDP. For example, if inventory investment in one quarter is $\frac{1}{2}$% of GDP (a fairly typical value for its share in GDP) but in the next quarter is $-\frac{1}{2}$%, then the change is responsible for a full 1% change in GDP. Evidence for the importance of inventory changes in economic fluctuations is provided by Ramey and West (1999), among others.

Inventory changes are quite important in the transmission of economic disturbances. If demand increases, then firms might meet the surge in demand, at least initially, by running down inventories. If they become convinced that the rise in demand is permanent, then not only do they need to increase output to meet the new higher level of demand, but they also need to raise output even further for a period of time to replenish their depleted inventories.

Explaining inventory investment has not been easy – for example, a 'production smoothing' theory of inventory holding suggests that sales should be more volatile than production, but this has not been confirmed empirically. (In fact, it seems that production is more volatile than sales, which is not easy to explain.) Evidence for the UK is provided by Cuthbertson and Gasparro (1993) and Tsoulakas (2011), who finds that a 1% rise in the real interest rate results in a fall in the stock of inventories by approximately 0.1%.

4.5 Conclusion

The direction in which a fall in interest rates affects investment is not in doubt, but the magnitude of the effect is not at all clear. Nevertheless, the effect of a sustained fall in both short-term and long-term interest rates is likely to be much greater than that of a temporary change in the short-term rate. Uncertainty may also be a major factor, as may tax policy. There seems to be quite a lot of evidence that cash flow and profits are relevant; monetary policy may of course contribute to these by reducing interest rates firms may pay on their debt.

DISCUSSION QUESTIONS

1. Why does investment fluctuate more than consumption?
2. Would a temporary tax credit to stimulate investment during a recession be a good idea?
3. Discuss the effect of inflation on investment. Does it matter whether the inflation is fully anticipated or not?

CHAPTER 5

The Demand for Money and the Supply of Money

The demand for money and the supply of money used to be central to every monetary policy course and textbook. Keynesian macroeconomics, as least as exemplified in IS-LM, stressed the importance of the income and interest elasticities of the demand for money in explaining the slope of the LM curve and the efficacy of monetary policy. Monetarism emphasised the implications of a stable demand for money and many countries adopted money supply targets. However, it will become clear in due course that the demand for money was not particularly stable and money supply targets were abandoned, or at least given less weight, by most central banks. Now, with central banks typically using interest rates as instruments and pursuing inflation targets, it might be thought that the demand for, and supply of, money are less important topics than they used to be. And it seems that this is the case as far as the economics literature is concerned – there was a huge amount of work, in particular, on estimating the demand for money in the 1970s and 1980s, but since about 1990 this work has more or less dried up. The main theoretical approaches (discussed below) to the demand for money were published between 1952 and 1966; it seems there have been no theoretical developments since 1966 in the theory of the demand for money that have made anything more than a minimal impact. Nevertheless, there are still a number of reasons for studying these topics. For example, theories of the demand for money are relevant to explaining the welfare costs of inflation and the behaviour of the money supply may be of some use in helping us understand the recent credit crunch. It is hence of some importance to study these topics.

As this is not a textbook on the history of economic thought, we do not discuss pre-Keynesian theory of the demand for money. And our discussion of Keynes's theories will be brief. But Keynes's 'General Theory' really did draw attention to the significance of the interest elasticity of the demand for money as a factor explaining the impact of monetary policy on the economy.

As is well known, Keynes distinguished between three motives for holding money: the transactions-motive, the precautionary-motive and the speculative-motive. Even more than 70 years after the General Theory was published, this is still a useful distinction. The transactions-motive is intended to capture the holding of cash by both individuals and businesses in the interval of time between their receipt of income and the spending of it. Keynes assumed it to be largely dependent on the level of money income, which was also the case with the precautionary-motive, with which it is often assimilated. The latter is intended to 'provide for contingencies requiring sudden expenditures and for unforeseen opportunities of advantageous purchases' (Keynes, 1936, p. 196). It is said that in the Soviet Union, before its collapse in 1990, people carried a great deal of money around with them. There was a chronic shortage of goods and credit facilities were non-existent. From time to time, goods that were usually hard to obtain suddenly went on sale. It would be unfortunate for a consumer if he or she were unable to avail himself of one of these opportunities for lack of cash, so this would be a reason for making sure that one was always carrying a reasonable amount of currency. This seems to be a good example of Keynes's precautionary demand for money. However, in more modern economies, with extensive credit facilities and goods shortages rarely a problem, one might expect demand for money for such purposes to be much lower. The speculative-motive occurs when an asset holder, expecting a rise in interest rates and hence a fall in bond prices, prefers to hold money rather than bonds. Although money may pay zero interest, this is better than a negative return on bonds that might result if the capital loss on bonds exceeded the interest received. This was the way in which Keynes introduced interest sensitivity into the demand for money – the lower the interest rate, the greater the likelihood of a fall in bond prices that offsets the interest on the bond, and hence the greater the demand for money for this purpose.

In the next section of this chapter we discuss some theories of the demand for money. Section 5.3 presents and discusses the well-known money multiplier model of money supply determination; Section 5.4 considers money supply determination in practice and Section 5.5 offers some concluding thoughts.

5.1 Theories of the Demand for Money

5.1.1 A Model of the Transactions Demand for Money

The transactions motive for holding cash is, quite simply the motive for holding cash in order to carry out transactions; Keynes thought it depended largely on income: 'In normal circumstances the amount of money required to satisfy the transactions motive and the precautionary motive is mainly a result of the general level of activity of the economic system and of the level of money-income.' (Keynes, 1936, p. 196). He did not rule out the possibility that the interest rate could at least have a slight effect on the transactions demand for money. Baumol's achievement (see Baumol, 1952) was to produce a model of the transactions demand for money which generates an interest-sensitive demand, whilst retaining the property that income is still of crucial importance for the demand for money. Although in some respects a very simple model, it produces some quite specific conclusions for the demand for money (for example, that the income elasticity of the demand for money is $\frac{1}{2}$ and the interest elasticity is $-\frac{1}{2}$).

The basic idea behind the model is that an individual receives income T each period which he spends during the period at a steady rate, ending the period with nothing. However, he has the option of depositing some or all of his income in an interest-bearing account, which pays interest r. There is, however, a transactions cost b (fixed irrespective of the size of the transaction) of either depositing or withdrawing money. If he deposits money, it is optimal to do this immediately (there is no point in holding money and then depositing it – this would just sacrifice interest income without reducing transactions costs). It is also optimal to withdraw the same amount each time a withdrawal is made (Tobin, 1956, showed this). It remains, then, to determine the size of each withdrawal (M). In holding more money, an individual will economise on transactions costs but sacrifice interest income. The amount of money the individual holds is derived by optimally trading off the benefit of higher money balances against the cost. We can depict the time path of an agent's money holding by a figure such as Figure 5.1 below. The only decision the agent makes is on the optimal size of each withdrawal (M^*).

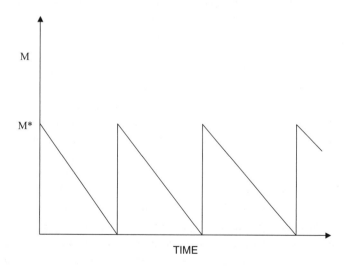

Figure 5.1   Time Path of Money Holdings in the Baumol Model.

The total number of transactions each period is T/M; this should be fairly obvious – if $T = £1000$ and $M = £250$, then the individual makes an initial deposit of £750 and three withdrawals, each of £250. Total transactions costs per period are hence bT/M; average money holdings are $M/2$; the (opportunity) cost of this level of money holding is the interest forgone in holding it, namely $rM/2$. The individual hence minimises:

$$TC = bT/M + rM/2. \tag{5-1}$$

Differentiating the right-hand side of this with respect to M and equating to zero, we derive the following first-order condition for minimisation:

$$bTM^{-2} + r/2 = 0, \tag{5-2}$$

which implies $M = (2bT/r)^{1/2}$.

So average money balances $(M/2)$ are $(1/2)^{1/2}b^{1/2}T^{1/2}r^{-1/2}$. This is the famous Baumol 'square root' formula – money holdings are proportional to the square root of income, for example. The elasticities are given by the exponents: the income elasticity of demand for money is $\frac{1}{2}$ whereas the interest elasticity of demand for money is $-\frac{1}{2}$. A number of points might be made about the analysis, simple though it may be:

1. The most important result is perhaps that it gives us an interest-sensitive transactions demand for cash.
2. Since the income elasticity of money demand is less than 1, it is sometimes interpreted as stating that there are economies of scale in money holdings: if income doubles, then the demand for money does not double, but instead rises by just over 41% (i.e. $\sqrt{2} - 1$).
3. It might be thought that if prices double, then the demand for money increases by less, and hence the basic property of homogeneity of degree one of the demand for money with respect to the price level is violated. However, this is an illusion. If all prices double, with nothing else changing, then we would expect transactions costs as well as income to both double in nominal terms (*real* transactions costs remain unchanged), and it can easily be seen that this means an increase in the demand for money of the same magnitude as the increase in prices.
4. The analysis so far has not taken the *integer-constraint* problem into account. The number of transactions has to be an integer, but in performing the minimisation exercise it has been treated as a continuous variable. However, the problem faced by the agent is still well defined. What we have done is to choose an inappropriate method of solution. What one can do is go through the different possible integral numbers of withdrawals, and calculate the costs associated with each: that is, one calculates the costs associated with zero, two, three, four transactions and so forth. (The individual might not deposit anything at all, in which case there would be no transactions; however, if he deposits anything, he will later withdraw it, so if the number of transactions is positive, it has to be at least two.) It might appear that the effects of various changes on the demand for money can be highly variable. For example, it might be that an individual is initially almost indifferent between n and $n + 1$ transactions, but chooses the lower number of

transactions and hence the higher demand for money. A small increase in the interest rate might mean that he shifts to $n+1$ transactions per period, reducing his demand for money, in which case the demand for money would appear to be highly sensitive to the interest rate. Alternatively, there might well be situations in which a change in interest rates might not change the optimal number of transactions at all, in which case it might appear that the demand for money is completely interest insensitive. However, these effects might well cancel out with aggregation.

5. It is a model of the demand for cash by households, not by firms. It might be argued that firms differ from households in having much more frequent inflows of cash, and also that uncertainty of both inflows and outflows is quite important as well. Below we introduce a model of firms' demand for cash.

6. There is no uncertainty at all; in particular, (a) expenditure, (b) income receipts and (c) interest rates are all known with certainty. The model may not be totally irrelevant for a household which receives a known monthly income and whose expenditure pattern over the month is fairly predictable. But for many households, and other agents such as firms, such an assumption may be pretty implausible. Some of the other models we look at introduce uncertainty about one (or more) of these variables.

7. For many agents, the benefits of managing their cash balances according to the Baumol rule, rather than using some rule of thumb, are trivial. If one chooses plausible values for the relevant variables, then the costs of deviating slightly from the optimal rule may be extremely small. Given that there are calculation costs in determining one's optimal money balances, it might not be worthwhile to incur these costs. However, there may be some rich individuals, and many firms and corporations with a sizeable cash flow, with low transactions costs of moving money from one account to another, for whom such calculations would definitely be profitable.

5.1.2 A Model of the Precautionary Demand for Money

A second model of the demand for money, which might be described as a model of the precautionary demand for money, is due to Miller and Orr (1966). This might be thought of as a model of the demand for money by firms, subject to stochastic inflows and outflows (whereas the Baumol model is a model of the demand for money by households). The model is characterised by the following assumptions:

1. There are two assets: non-interest bearing money and bonds which yield n per day.

2. Transfers between the two assets require a fixed cost of g which is unrelated to the size of the transaction.

3. Cash flows are random: in any short period (a fraction of a day) there is a 50% probability of an inflow of m and a 50% probability of an outflow of the same amount. There are t periods in a day.

4. Although not stated explicitly, it is assumed that there is no risk of the agent running out of resources, so if his cash balances go to zero, he can always replenish them out of bond holdings.

Analysis of the model is quite complicated, so we just present the main results here, which are as follows:

1. The optimal policy involves choosing an upper bound to money balances (h^*) and a 'return point' (z^*). There is also a lower bound of zero. When money balances reach the upper or lower bound, money holdings are immediately adjusted to the return point.

2. The optimal return point is given by

$$z^* = \left(\frac{3gm^2t}{4n}\right)^{1/3}, \tag{5-3}$$

the optimal upper bound is $h^* = 3z^*$ and average money balances are hence:

$$M^* = \frac{4}{3}\left(\frac{3gm^2t}{4n}\right)^{1/3}. \tag{5-4}$$

3. The demand for money depends on the variance of transactions (m^2t). What happens if income increases? It depends on what happens to the variance of transactions. If inflows and outflows rise by the same amount as income, then the income elasticity of the demand for money is $^2/_3$.

4. The interest elasticity of the demand for money is $-^1/_3$, rather than $-^1/_2$, as in the Baumol model.

5. Why is the return point just a third of the way to the upper bound? The explanation is that expected transactions costs over a period of time depend on the distance from the nearest bound, but interest earnings foregone depend on the distance from the lower bound, so the agent will prefer to adjust his balances to a point nearer the lower bound.

6. What happens if the price level increases? If nothing else changes, we might expect both g and m to rise by the same amount, so we have homogeneity of degree one in prices.

It seems the Miller-Orr model is a model of the demand for money by firms that captures the uncertainty of inflows and outflows; it is not entirely clear how to test it as the variance of transactions is not something that can be easily measured. It is also useful to have a model that predicts a specific value of the interest elasticity of demand for money; if nothing else, this is something that can be compared with empirical estimates and used as a plausible value of the elasticity if necessary when carrying out simulations.

5.1.3 A Model of the Speculative Demand for Money

An important model of the speculative demand for money is Tobin (1958). According to Tobin, Keynes's theory of the speculative demand for money states that individuals hold money rather than bonds if the expected return on bonds (interest plus capital gains) is negative, and bonds rather than money if the expected return on bonds is positive. (The expected return on bonds is compared with the expected return on money, which is zero.) So there is no diversification – either an all money, or an all bonds, portfolio is held.

Tobin criticised the theory as requiring (for a smooth *aggregate* relationship between the interest rate and the demand for money) that individuals hold different subjective views on the future interest rate with certainty (which means almost all will be wrong). Tobin sought to build a theory that explained portfolio *diversification*. The assumptions of his theory are as follows:

1. There are two assets: money, a riskless asset that pays a zero return and bonds, which pay a (certain) interest rate r, but there is also an uncertain capital gain g (which could be negative) on bonds.
2. A wealth holder's preferences can be described in terms of indifference curves between the mean expected return on the portfolio and the risk (measured by the standard deviation).
3. The investor is risk averse (i.e. his indifference curves are upward sloping).
4. The investor divides his wealth between the two assets in order to attain the highest indifference curve possible.

The model provides an explanation for portfolio diversification and has been the foundation for subsequent models of portfolio choice. However, risk aversion is not sufficient for diversification. In a diagram where risk is measured on the horizontal axis and expected return on the vertical axis, it is necessary that indifference curves between expected return and risk be not just upward sloping (this is risk aversion) but also concave upwards – that is, each successive increment of risk needs to be accompanied by greater increases in expected return to keep utility constant.

The substitution effect of a higher interest rate will be to induce substitution away from money towards bonds. The income effect could go in either direction, making the overall effect ambiguous. However, a positive overall effect (of the interest rate on the demand for money) would require a large positive income effect on the demand for money, which is perhaps implausible.

If the theory is taken to be one of how an individual divides his wealth between money and bonds, then it may be implicitly assuming that the wealth elasticity of demand for all assets is unity, which is perhaps implausible.

The theory has been subject to some technical criticisms. For example, an investor's preferences can be represented by indifference curves in mean-variance space only under restrictive conditions. (See Feldstein, 1969, for discussion of this point and some related issues.)

Perhaps the most telling criticism of the theory as a theory of the demand for money is that money as a non-interest bearing, capital-certain asset is dominated by other assets which are also capital certain but which pay interest (e.g. building society deposits).

It should also be pointed out that money is not a riskless asset when price level uncertainty is taken into account.

5.1.4 Further Work on the Theory of the Demand for Money

It may seem quite incredible, but there has been virtually no significant theoretical work on the demand for money since 1966. Akerlof (1979) and Romer (1986) are perhaps worth mentioning, but there is more or less nothing else. We are not including here as theoretical work on the demand for money the extremely important contribution of Kiyotaki and Wright (1989), discussed in Chapter 1, and the work it has given rise to. This work, which has attempted to explain the emergence of a medium of exchange, amongst other things, does not produce implications for the interest elasticities of demand for money, for example. There has, of course, been extensive work on asset pricing and portfolio allocation (deciding how much money to hold is presumably part of one's asset holding decision); why, then, has the demand for money been so neglected? Perhaps the answer is that it is not at all clear how to incorporate some of the crucial ingredients, in particular transactions costs, into a satisfactory theory of the demand for money.

5.2 Empirical Work on the Demand for Money

The questions that researchers have investigated are those of the interest and income elasticities of the demand for money and the stability of the demand for money function. It might be noted that virtually all the data used is time-series; there is very little cross-sectional data (across households, firms, etc.).

Prior to the mid-1970s, the following model (and variants thereon) was quite successful empirically:

$$\ln m_t = b_0 + b_1 \ln y_t + b_2 \ln r_t + b_3 \ln m_{t-1} + b_4 \ln \pi_t + u_t, \tag{5-5}$$

where m_t is real money demand in the period t, y_t is the transactions or scale variable (e.g. real GNP), r_t is the interest rate, π_t ($=(P_t/P_{t-1}) - 1$) is the rate of inflation and u_t is a disturbance term with standard properties. Data is quarterly. Note that homogeneity of degree one is assumed. It can be tested for by including a term in the price level in the equation. If homogeneity is rejected, then this is usually taken as evidence of misspecification rather than evidence against homogeneity. The short-run interest elasticity of demand is b_2, the long-run elasticity (derived by setting $m_t = m_{t-1}$) is $b_2/(1-b_3)$.

For summaries of various empirical studies, see Tables 11.1, 11.2 and 11.3 in Lewis and Mizen (2000), pp. 273, 274 and pp. 278–80.

However, after 1975, the performance of the conventional specification deteriorated sharply in both the UK and the US. The equation started to forecast poorly: there was in the US 'the Case of the Missing Money' (money demand was overpredicted between 1974:1 and 1976:2) and the 'Great Velocity Decline' (money demand was underpredicted between 1982:1 and 1983:2). In the UK, for example, the Bank of England's demand for money function seriously underpredicted monetary growth in 1971–3. There were other problems: the coefficient on the lagged dependent variable was sometimes estimated to equal (or exceed) unity, indicating a misspecified partial adjustment mechanism. Also, homogeneity was sometimes rejected. There have been numerous attempts to explain and repair these deficiencies. Some of the proffered explanations involve aggregation issues, technological progress, identification, and choice of functional form.

More recent work (see Stock and Watson, 1999, pp. 50–2), using cointegration techniques, suggests the existence of a stable long-run demand for money schedule (about which there can be considerable short-term movement); a unitary income elasticity cannot be rejected, while a figure of -0.1 emerges for the interest semi-elasticity. (The interest semi-elasticity is defined as $(dM/dr)/M$.) Another study which comes to similar conclusions is Hoffman and Rasche (1991). A more recent study by Ball (2001) concluded that the income elasticity of money demand is about 0.5 (perhaps providing support for the Baumol model) and the interest semi-elasticity about -0.05. Short-run instability cannot be ruled out, however, and should perhaps not be too surprising. The most plausible explanation is financial innovation, which may be due largely to changes in technology and regulation.

European monetary union presents some interesting issues for the analysis of the demand for money. For example, will the demand function for the euro be the aggregate of the demand functions for the currencies of the participating countries?

5.3 The Supply of Money

In this section we present and discuss the famous money multiplier approach to the determination of the money supply. The money supply (M) is, by definition, equal to deposits (D) plus currency held by the public (C_p):

$$M = C_p + D. \tag{5-6}$$

Note: currency held by the banks (C_b) is excluded from the definition of the money supply. (Otherwise there would be double counting: if someone pays £100 into his bank account, he is swapping £100 of money held as currency for £100 of money held as deposits; one would not want this transaction to increase the money supply.) We also assume it has been decided which of a bank's deposits are to be included in the measure of the money supply.

Also, by definition, high-powered money (the monetary base), H, equals currency held by the public (C_p) plus bank reserves (R):

$$H = C_p + R. \tag{5-7}$$

Reserves comprise currency held by the banks plus banks' deposits held at the central bank. Dividing (5-6) by (5-7) and dividing both numerator and denominator by D, we obtain an expression for the money multiplier:

$$M = \left[\frac{C_p/D + 1}{C_p/D + R/D}\right]H = \left\{\frac{1+c}{r+c}\right\}H. \tag{5-8}$$

The expression in square brackets in (5-8) is the money multiplier. It depends on two things: the public's currency-deposit ratio $(C_p/D \equiv c)$ and the banks' reserve-deposit ratio $(R/D \equiv r)$. Also, (5-8) is true by definition (it is derived by manipulating definitions) and therefore does not tell us anything about the determination of the money supply or anything else. In order to generate a theory, we need to say something about the determination of c and r. If c and r are constant, or independent of H, then we do have a theory: a change in H, *ceteris paribus*, generates a change in M equal to the change in H times the money multiplier. But it is surely implausible to suppose that c and r are independent of H.

Probable determinants of c include the interest rate on deposits, the size of the black economy, the degree of confidence in the banking system and the level of development of the financial and banking sector (e.g. number of branches, speed of cheque clearing, etc.). Interest rates on deposits are relevant since, given that no interest is paid on currency, they can be considered the opportunity cost of holding money. The black economy is relevant since transactions in the black economy for obvious reasons tend to be made predominantly in currency. Note that such transactions would include illegal transactions such as drug dealing and transactions that are legal but which are conducted in currency so as to avoid tax. The degree of confidence in the banking system is not something that is particularly relevant except in times of crisis when it may change dramatically, as happened in the US between 1929 and 1933. (See, for example, Chart 64 in Friedman and Schwartz, 1963.) Obviously, the more bank branches there are, the easier it will be to deposit and withdraw currency, so the lower one would expect the currency-deposit ratio to be. Generally, one would not expect these factors to change much in 'normal' economic circumstances, except possibly for changes in the rate of interest, and this is the only determinant of c which seems remotely affected by monetary policy. If the currency-deposit ratio declines with interest rates, this will tend to make the supply of money positively related to interest rates; for a given monetary base, as interest rates rise, the currency-deposit ratio falls and the money multiplier rises, hence raising the money supply.

Probable determinants of r include the required reserve ratio, interest rates on loans and other assets (non-reserve assets which may be included in banks' portfolios). The discount rate and discount policy are relevant, as is the degree of confidence in the banking system. Many of these determinants are largely independent of movements in H, except the interest rate variables. This is another reason why the money multiplier (and hence the money supply for a given monetary base) might be expected to be an increasing function of interest rates. (But note that the interest rate that might be expected to influence c is different from that which might be expected to affect r – however, if all interest rates move together, then perhaps we can talk of the money supply as a function of 'the' interest rate.)

If the money supply hence depends positively on interest rates, the LM curve becomes flatter. The LM curve would now be defined as the set of values of r and Y which equate the supply and demand for money for a given value of the monetary base, and it is monetary base changes that shift the LM curve. So this tends to weaken the efficacy of monetary policy – the reduction in interest rates tends to reduce the amount of lending banks can do as agents deposit less in the banks – whilst it strengthens the power of fiscal policy.

With this framework, we can consider various policies to change the money supply:

1. Changing Reserve Requirements

Although in principle it seems that changing reserve requirements would be a way of controlling the money supply, this is rarely done in the UK, even under monetary targeting. A reason may be that if the authorities were to attempt to manipulate reserve requirements for monetary control purposes, banks would change their reserve holding policies (accumulating reserves, for example, in anticipation of an increase in reserve requirements), and this would make the money multiplier less predictable and controllable. Note that in the above definition, r is the *actual* reserve ratio, not the legally required ratio banks may be subject to; if the reserve requirement increases, then banks might respond to this by increasing their actual reserve holdings, but our argument is that increased use of reserve requirements for monetary control purposes would make the actual reserve ratio more variable and less predictable.

Apparently China does use changes in reserve requirements for monetary control purposes, but we are aware of no other country that does.

2. Quantitative Controls on Bank Lending or Deposits

The 'corset' (or supplementary special deposits scheme), a form of quantitative control over deposits (not lending), was an example of such controls. It was abandoned in 1980 and we have not seen such controls in the UK since. Such controls may give rise to disintermediation, where transactions such as borrowing and lending which would have taken place within the financial system bypass it; there may also be inefficiencies caused by such quantitative controls, preventing relatively more efficient banks from growing at the expense of the less efficient.

3. Discount Rate/Discount Policy

By setting a high discount rate, the central bank can deter borrowing from the discount window. By its choice of discount policy, it can affect banks' lending and reserve holding policies.

4. Open-Market Operations (OMOs)

An OMO takes place when the central bank buys or sells assets (typically government bonds). For example, the Bank of England buys bonds worth £1m from a bank; it pays the bank by crediting its deposits at the Bank. This raises reserves, and the monetary base, by the same amount and hence can give rise to a multiple expansion of the money supply. Are there any reasons why the central bank cannot control the money supply using OMOs?

Controlling the money supply may involve trade-offs with other policy objectives. For example, using OMOs for monetary control purposes may have implications for interest rates. Trying to control H precisely may impart a high degree of volatility to interest rates; this, in turn, may reduce the attractiveness of holding government debt, and it may be rational for the government to try to stabilise interest rates in order to reduce the costs of servicing the national debt (on the grounds that asset holders are prepared to pay more for a less risky asset). There are a number of other reasons why the Bank of England may try to reduce volatility of interest rates. So controlling the money supply by OMOs may have trade-offs with other policy goals (as might other monetary control techniques).

5.4 Money Supply Determination in Practice

How well does the money multiplier model do in explaining the determination of the money supply in practice? The answer is – absolutely abysmally. First of all, let us mention some institutional details.

In the United Kingdom there are, strictly speaking, no reserve requirements. However, banks which report eligible liabilities of more than £500m are required to hold zero-interest bearing deposits (called cash-ratio deposits) with the Bank of England, at a rate of 0.11% of the excess of these liabilities over £500m. Such liabilities are calculated on a six-monthly basis. Table 5.1 shows the Bank of England's consolidated balance sheet for early July 2011; the total amount of cash-ratio deposits was somewhat in excess of £2bn, but these are totally dominated by reserves, which amount to over £127bn.

At the moment, figures for only one monetary aggregate, M4 are published. Figures for M0, the monetary base consisting of cash outside the Bank of England plus banks operational

Table 5.1 The Bank of England's Balance Sheet for 6/7/11.

Bank of England's Consolidated Balance Sheet for 6/7/11			
Liabilities		**Assets**	
Notes in Circulation	£54,146m.	Long-term sterling reverse repos	£10,585m.
Reserve Balances	£127,445m.	Ways and Means Advances to HM Government	£370m.
Foreign currency public securities issued	£3,815m.	Bonds and other securities acquired via market transactions	£14,004m.
Cash ratio deposits	£2,388m.	Other assets	£211,371m.
Other liabilities	£48,537m.		
Total liabilities	£236,330m.	Total assets	£236,330m.

(*Source*: Bank of England website, accessed 13/7/11)
(Note: figures have been rounded to nearest million)

deposits with the Bank of England, were published until 2006 but no longer. M4 consists of cash outside banks plus private sector retail bank and building society deposits plus private sector wholesale bank and building society deposits and certificates of deposits.

In the United States, reserves need to be held against what are called net transactions balances. For each bank, there is a lower limit (called an 'exemption amount'), which is currently $10.7m, on which the reserve ratio is zero. Above this limit, until a higher limit called the 'low-reserve tranche amount ($58.8) is reached', the ratio is 3% and above this limit the ratio is 10%.[1] Reserves are defined as 'vault cash' (i.e. currency held by banks) and balances held at the Federal Reserve. The relevant deposits on which reserves need to be held are measured over what is called a maintenance period, which in the US is two weeks. Suppose these deposits average $100m. Then we can calculate that the reserves that need to be held are $(58.8 − 10.7) × 0.03 + (100 − 58.8) × 0.10}m = $5 563 000. The bank then needs to hold reserves of at least this amount over the next two weeks' maintenance period. Once this maintenance period has started, the reserves it needs to hold over this period are predetermined; however, it does have discretion as to how it manages its holding over the period – it might hold $9m over the first week and $3m over the second week, for example, or vice versa, making average reserves holdings of $6m, implying it holds excess reserves of $437 000. Or it could do the opposite. Exactly how it manages its reserves over the period may well depend on the interest rate it could otherwise earn on its reserves or the rate of interest it would have to pay if it borrowed them. If it expects such interest rates to be much higher in the second week of the maintenance period, then it might adopt the strategy of holding much higher reserves in the first week of the maintenance period.

The European Central Bank imposes reserve requirements of 2% on deposits with a term less than two years, and nothing on deposits with a longer term. The maintenance period is approximately one month, and the appropriate reserves again need to be held during the following maintenance period. Only balances at the ECB count as reserves; cash held by banks is excluded.

It seems then that reserve requirements in these major economies are fairly modest, and very different from actual reserve ratios that banks have held in recent years. Table 5.2 shows growth in both the monetary base and the M4 measure of the money supply in recent years.

It is apparent that growth rates of the monetary base and money supply have diverged. A particularly striking instance is the year ending June 2009 where an increase of the monetary base of 130% was associated with an increase in M4 of 1.4%. The idea of a stable money multiplier relationship between the monetary base and the money supply seems

---

[1] These figures are for the calendar year 2011. The amounts are adjusted every year.

Table 5.2   Growth rate of the monetary base and of the money supply (M4) in the United Kingdom.

Growth Rates of Monetary Aggregates in the United Kingdom		
Growth rate of year ending June	**Monetary base**	**Money supply (M4)**
1990	6.4%	15.1%
1991	2%	7.1%
1992	1.6%	4.6%
1993	4.6%	3.1%
1994	6.8%	2.6%
1995	5.7%	8.5%
1996	7.4%	9%
1997	6.4%	11.5%
1998	5.5%	9.6%
1999	7.4%	3.6%
2000	7.6%	8.9%
2001	6.6%	5.9%
2002	10.1%	7.7%
2003	6.2%	9.8%
2004	6.4%	10.6%
2005	3.7%	10.9%
2006	(55.8%)	15.6%
2007	−3%	16.6%
2008	20.1%	14.1%
2009	130%	1.4%
2010	15.4%	0%
May 2011	−8.4%	−0.2%

(*Source*: Bank of England Statistics)

Note: The figures for growth in the monetary base until the year ending June 2005 are taken from figures the Bank of England published for M0. However, the Bank of England ceased publication of these figures in April 2006, and the figures for subsequent years are based on combining separate figures for holdings of notes and coins and bank reserves published by the Bank of England subsequently (author's own calculations). The figure for the change in the monetary base in the year ending June 2006 is hence particularly problematic, being based on the change in the monetary base measured in two separate ways.

completely wrong. There are many reasons for this instability. One reason, relevant for the recent credit crunch, is that (obviously) banks have decided to accumulate reserves and not lend them out. Making a loan has numerous costs associated with it; there are the initial costs of appraising the loan application and ongoing costs of administering the repayments, providing statements and so forth; there may be legal and other costs in pursuing defaulters. Expected interest payments needs to be adjusted for expected default, and the lender may be uncertain about the availability and price of the funds used to finance the loan over the time period of the loan. And a higher volume of loans may mean a lower interest rate on each. So it is not at all irrational for banks to hold reserves which pay a certain return of $\frac{1}{2}$% (and are, moreover, perfectly liquid) rather than to lend the money out with all the attendant risks and costs (including illiquidity).

5.5 Conclusion

We might ask if any of the previous analysis is relevant today, where we have interest rate targeting by the Bank of England, whereby it decides on the interest rate on banks' reserves and intervenes in the money markets to ensure that other short-term rates are in line with this rate. However, the policy of quantitative easing introduced in March 2009 is effectively the policy of conducting open market operations described in the previous section. As argued elsewhere, such policies work by changing the longer term interest rate, and are compatible with the policy of changing short-term rates. In fact, monetary policy might perhaps best be described by the Bank of England setting short-term rates, and taking actions to influence longer term rates. Such actions would comprise anything it does to try to influence expectations of future short rates, as well as purchases and sales of longer term assets.

DISCUSSION QUESTIONS

1. Suppose workers are paid more frequently. Using the Baumol model, discuss the effects of this change on the demand for money.
2. What is the effect of a successful bank robbery on the money supply?
3. What effect might you expect inflation to have on the money multiplier?

CHAPTER 6

Nominal Rigidities

I n this chapter, we discuss one of the key building blocks of much contemporary
macroeconomics, the assumption of imperfect price and wage flexibility. Since
Keynes's day there has been considerable debate over the assumption – questions
that have been asked include whether it is necessary to explain macroeconomic
fluctuations, whether it is a plausible assumption and how can such rigidities be explained?
But of course since prices do not stay constant forever, it is presumably necessary to explain
how and why prices change when they do change. In this chapter we discuss first of all
evidence for price rigidities and then possible explanations.

We should first of all clarify the definition of rigidity and distinguish between real and
nominal rigidities. As far as the definition of rigidity is concerned, saying that a price is rigid is
not the same as saying that it does not change. It might be that the reason a price does not
change is that there is no reason for it to change. Rather, price rigidity arises if a price differs
from its 'equilibrium' value, but does not change. Price rigidities in many markets seem
puzzling. Suppose there is excess demand for a particular good – that is, demand exceeds
supply at the current nominal price level. Then one would expect suppliers of the good to
have a strong incentive to raise its price. The presence of excess demand means that they can
sell at least the same quantity of goods as they are currently selling at a higher price, so they
would presumably make higher profits if they raised the price. There are a number of possible
reasons why they might not, which we will discuss in this chapter.

We should also distinguish between real and nominal rigidities. (The distinction here is
between a price relative to certain other prices being rigid and the nominal price of a good
being rigid – i.e. its price as quoted in whatever unit of account is used does not change.)

Nominal rigidities are relevant for explaining the non-neutrality of money. Also, explanations for nominal rigidities are very different, in general, from those for real rigidities.

A further issue is whether prices and wages are more rigid in a downward direction than in an upward direction. For a comprehensive recent review of evidence on price-setting behaviour, see Klenow and Malin (2011).

6.1 Are Prices Rigid?

In the last few years, there have been a number of empirical studies of price and wage rigidities, facilitated by a massive increase in the availability of information on prices and when they are changed. Some supermarkets have made available scanner data, containing information on the price of every single item which the store sold over a certain period of time. One study, for example, was based on information covering over 31 million wage changes (see Dickens *et al.*, 2007).

One conclusion that has emerged is that 'the average duration of a price spell in the euro area ranges from four to five quarters' (Dhyne *et al.*, 2006). This is higher than in the US, where according to an influential study by Bils and Klenow (2004), the median duration of price spells (i.e. periods between price changes) is 4.3 months. However, a crucial factor in generating this fairly low duration is the inclusion as price changes of prices reduced in a sale (and also, when the sale ends and the price reverts to its 'normal' level, that is treated as another price change). Whether or not sales price reductions are included has been shown to be of crucial importance in measuring the frequency of price adjustments; for example, Nakamura and Steinsson (2008) produce evidence (using US data) that the median frequency of price changes including sales items is approximately double that of price changes on non-sale items; they also show that the median duration of a price until either the regular price changes or the product disappears is between 7 and 9 months. Whether an appropriate measure of price rigidity should include sale price reductions is not clear, though, as we do not have a satisfactory account of whether the measure of price rigidity relevant for macro-economic purposes should include such price reductions.[1]

Evidence on wage changes is presented by Dickens *et al.* (2007) who provide evidence (from 15 European countries and the US) that there is some degree of downward nominal rigidity in wages, in that a frequency diagram of wage changes has a 'spike' at zero; this means there are more zero increases in wages than would otherwise be expected. However, it seems that this downward rigidity is limited, in that there do seem to be a fair number

---

[1]However in a recent paper Guimaraes and Sheedy (2011) present a model where firms have an incentive to hold sales because they have customers with differing price elasticities of demand; they conclude that it is stickiness in the 'normal' and not the sales price that is relevant for monetary policy.

of nominal wage reductions. But there are substantial differences between countries; some countries show a great deal of both nominal and real wage rigidity, others show neither, and others exhibit one without the other. The authors summarise their findings as follows: 'Across countries, we estimate that an average of 28 percent of workers are covered by nominal rigidity, in the sense that 28 percent of the wage cuts that would have taken place under flexible wage setting are prevented by nominal rigidity' (Dickens *et al.*, 2007, pp. 212–13). One important point, made by Akerlof, Dickens and Perry (1996), is that some studies, based on surveys, may overestimate the degree of downward nominal price flexibility because of measurement error. The basic point is that those who are surveyed may be asked for their current wage and what their wage was a year ago. Some respondents may misremember their former wage; some may think it was higher than it actually was and when combined with a truthful reporting of their current wage, this may give rise to a reported fall in wages when in fact no such reduction took place. Akerlof and his co-authors argue that the degree of downward wage flexibility that these studies have estimated has been significantly and wrongly increased by such measurement error.

Another important contribution is Boivin, Gianni and Mihov (2009), who produce evidence that while sectoral prices may be quite flexible in response to idiosyncratic sector specific shocks, they are quite sticky in response to macroeconomic and monetary disturbances.

Further evidence on price stickiness is provided by international data. For example, 'For anyone who looks even casually at international data, the idea that nominal price rigidities are irrelevant seems difficult to sustain' (Obstfeld and Rogoff, 1996, p. 606). There is, for example, a high degree of correlation between the nominal exchange rate and the real exchange rate for many countries. If we write SP^*/P as the real exchange rate, where S is the nominal exchange rate (domestic currency price of foreign exchange) and $P(P^*)$ is the domestic (foreign) price level, then if the real exchange rate is highly correlated with S, a fairly obvious explanation is that P and P^* are fairly inflexible compared with S.

We would conclude this section by asserting that the empirical evidence is, on the whole, not inconsistent with the contention that modern Western economies are characterised by a degree of nominal price and wage rigidity sufficient to explain significant effects of monetary policy, and other macroeconomic disturbances, on output and employment. However, exactly why there are these rigidities is not entirely clear. We turn to a review of possible explanations in the next section.

6.2 Why are (Nominal) Prices Rigid?

1. Menu Costs

'Menu costs' are defined as the costs of actually changing prices quoted for goods and services. For example, a restaurant might have to reprint its menu if it wants to change prices, and the costs of doing so might not be trivial. It is easy to see how menu costs might explain nominal price rigidity; suppose a firm with some market power is charging its profit-maximising price, and it receives a positive demand shock. In the absence of menu costs, it will (under certain conditions) raise its price; however, with menu costs, it needs to compute whether the extra profits it expects to make with a change in price exceed the actual cost of changing the price, and it is clear that for a large enough menu cost, or a small enough shift in demand, it may decide not to do so.

In Figure 6.1, a monopolist with demand curve D_1 and marginal cost curve MC produces output Q_1 where marginal revenue equals marginal cost and charges a price P_1. Suppose the demand curve shifts outwards to D_2; in the absence of a menu cost of changing price, it would charge a price P_2 and produce output Q_2. However, if there is a menu cost of changing its price, then it has the possibility of producing output Q_3 at an unchanged price of P_1. It then needs to compare the profits it receives from this choice, with those it obtains if it does indeed charge the profit maximising price, but pays the menu cost as well.

One common reaction to the menu cost explanation of price stickiness is that menu costs are too small to give rise to price rigidities sufficient to explain the monetary non-neutralities which many economists believe exist. However, the magnitude of menu costs is surely an empirical issue, and it can also be argued that although menu costs are small, this does not mean they cannot have significant macroeconomic effects (e.g. Mankiw, 1985). There have been some studies that have attempted to measure menu costs; this is not easy to

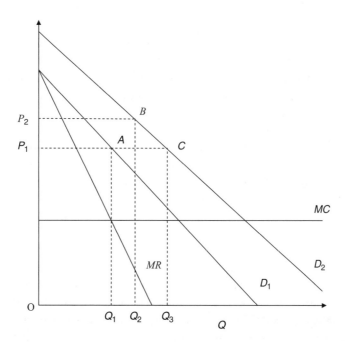

Figure 6.1 The Effect of a Menu Cost on a Firm's Pricing and Production Decisions.

do. One study found that for some large American supermarket chains, the total costs incurred in changing prices were 0.70 per cent of revenues (Levy *et al.*, 1997). One cost that came to light was that of rectifying mistakes that were occasionally made when changing prices. If the price charged erroneously is too low, then the firm suffers a loss of revenue and profits and if the price is too high, there may be a loss of consumer good will and consumer complaints which may be quite costly to the firm.

One application of the menu cost approach is to explaining the effects of the introduction of the euro (see Hobijn, Ravenna and Tambalotti, 2006). In January 2002, when euro notes and coins were introduced in the euro zone, there was a significant upward jump in restaurant prices, although there was no significant increase in the overall price level. This is readily explained by the menu cost approach. Suppose there is a moderate level of inflation – perhaps in the order of 2–3% – and in this environment restaurants will typically raise their prices once a year by about the rate of inflation. The introduction of the euro meant that they had to post new prices in January 2002; essentially this is the same as their being able to adjust their prices without incurring a menu cost at this point of time. So what did restaurants do? Those that might have otherwise increased their prices shortly before the transition to the euro may decide to wait until the introduction of the euro before increasing their prices. If a restaurant typically increases its prices every year on 1 October, it will usually have a year to reap the benefits of such a price increase; but with the euro being introduced on 1 January 2002, it would have been able to obtain these benefits for only three months if it increased its prices in 2001, so may decide it is not worth incurring the costs of changing its prices on 1 October 2001, but might instead wait until 1 January 2002 to do so. But also, restaurants that did increase their prices in the year prior to the introduction of the euro would expect these prices to be in force for less than a year and to increase them again earlier than they otherwise would have; this means that the price they would set, being some sort of average of the optimal prices over the period for which the new price would be in force, would be lower than it otherwise would have been. As a consequence there was some bunching of price increases in January 2002 and that prices immediately before the change were lower than they otherwise would have been.

2. Costs of Gathering and Processing Information

When firms contemplate changing their prices, how do they know which new prices to set? Information about the factors relevant for their pricing decision may not be easy to obtain, and once gathered, may not be easy to interpret. Firms may need to devote considerable resources to obtaining and processing this information; given these costs, it may not be sensible to gather and interpret the information continuously; instead, it may be a good idea to make price decisions periodically, which may enable them to economise on these costs.

It seems that many firms go through a complicated process of gathering and processing information in order to make pricing decisions, and for that reason adjust prices infrequently and at set intervals. A model with these characteristics is presented by Maćkowiak and Wiederholt (2009), who consider firms faced by both idiosyncratic and aggregate shocks. Under certain conditions, firms pay almost all their attention to idiosyncratic shocks, meaning that prices may react strongly to such shocks, and hardly at all to aggregate shocks. In particular, a period when there are small aggregate shocks may mean that firms give even less attention to such conditions in their pricing decisions, making monetary policy even more powerful. However, should aggregate shocks increase, firms may pay more attention to them in their pricing decisions, hence making prices more responsive, and output less responsive, to monetary policy, and so on. Another important paper is Zbaracki *et al.* (2004), which documents the managerial and customer costs of adjusting prices. These costs include the considerable costs of gathering relevant information and of the various meetings at which prices would be determined. The customer costs including those of persuading disgruntled customers that the price increases are indeed justified. It turns out that these costs are by no means negligible. One interesting result is that many of these costs increase more than proportionately with the size of the price increase. It may be that customers accept small price increases without a murmur, whereas large increases generate complaints which require considerable expenditure of resources to deal with. This is of course very different from the standard assumption of lump-sum menu costs.

Often, a distinction is made between state-dependent and time-dependent pricing models. In a state-dependent pricing model, prices are adjusted if the cost of the deviation of a price from its optimal level grows too large (i.e. is exceeded by the benefits of changing the price). In a time-dependent model, prices are adjusted at regular intervals. The most popular time-dependent models are those of Taylor (1980) and Calvo (1983). In Taylor's model, price setters are divided into groups who change prices at different times, but all keep prices fixed for the same period of time. So his model would be consistent with price-setters' changing prices annually, but at different times during the year. In Calvo's model, firms are allowed to change their prices only when they receive a 'signal', which they receive randomly and, independently of the time they have kept the price constant. Taylor's approach seems more realistic and, is consistent with the argument that firms only choose new prices infrequently because of the costs of acquiring and processing information. However, it might be suggested that firms may not apply such adjustment rules rigidly. For example, a firm that receives a large shock some time before it normally reviews its prices may decide to review and adjust them in response to the shock. So, we would expect that price adjustment in reality contains both time-dependent and state-dependent elements.

3. Disruptive Effects of Frequent Price Changes

Frequent price changes by a firm may be quite disruptive. If customers anticipate the firm might raise its prices soon, they may bring forward the purchases they were planning to make, and they may postpone purchases if they anticipate price reductions, so that a firm that is known to adjust its prices frequently may face more volatile demand. As a consequence, it may be more difficult for the firm to plan its production and holding of inventories. It might also need to hold more inventories, which will be costly. A retailer may find it more difficult to cope with more variable purchases, for example, if it only has a certain number of check-outs (and check-out operators). Volatility in sales may mean long queues at tills at certain times, and empty stores at others. More technically, we might say that the marginal costs of selling goods rise rapidly with the level of sales within a particular period, and there may be considerable costs in being able not to process sales rapidly, in terms of customer good will.[2]

While this seems a plausible explanation of why some firms, particularly retail outlets, do not adjust their prices frequently, there does not seem to be a formal model that captures this idea.

4. Interdependencies between Price Setters

Oligopolistic behaviour may give rise to price rigidities under certain circumstances. One early example of this was the 'kinked-oligopoly demand curve' (the original reference is Sweezy, 1939) according to which firms assumed that if they cut their prices, competitors would follow suit, whereas if they raised them, their competitors would leave their prices unchanged, hence giving firms a strong incentive not to change their prices. There has been a considerable amount of further work in industrial organisation exploring this possibility, which we do not intend to review; however, the idea that oligopolistic interdependence may generate price rigidity seems eminently plausible.

A related idea is that price rigidities for some goods may increase price rigidities for other goods; a firm which faces highly variable input prices may feel it has no alternative but to change its prices frequently, but if the prices of its inputs are fairly stable it may keep its prices fairly stable.

5. Some Slightly Offbeat Explanations for Nominal Price Rigidities

    i. Indivisibility of the Unit of Account

        The unit of account is not perfectly divisible; in the UK, for example, the price of a good must be an integral number of pounds and pence. So even if the optimal price of a good moved continuously, its actual quoted price has to move discretely, and this would involve periods when it is unchanging.

    ii. Salience

        It has been observed that many prices end in the digits '9' or '5'. This might be for a number of reasons. Psychologically, a price of £9.99 may seem much lower than one of £10 even though the actual difference is trivial. There may be other reasons why some prices might be preferred to others. For example, some prices may be easier to remember than others; also, some may enable retailers to economise on their holdings of small change. For example, a good costing £9.99 may typically be purchased with a ten-pound note which would imply giving only a penny in change, whereas a good that costs £9.57 would require much more change to be given in exchange for a ten-pound note. These costs may have changed with developments in payment technology (e.g. they do not seem to be relevant for purchases made by credit or debit card) but may still be relevant for some transactions.

---

[2]This idea is perfectly compatible with firms holding sales. Retailers may attract to their sales customers who they otherwise would not attract, induced to come by the lower prices and not (sufficiently) deterred by having to queue to make their purchases. The retailers also decide when their sales take place, and by hiring more sales staff and in other ways reduce the costs of making a high volume of sales in a short period of time.

iii. Investment in Information about Prices by Consumers

If a supermarket does not change its prices often, consumers who visit the store may gather information about prices that does not decay too rapidly. They may visit the store to find out how much an item is priced, then do some comparison shopping and, if the item is indeed cheapest at the store, then they may go back and purchase it there. Such a strategy may not be so profitable if the store changes its prices frequently.

So it might be the case that certain prices might, for these reasons, offer firms slightly but discretely higher profits than other neighbouring prices. If the firm's profit function, abstracting from these factors, is continuous with a unique maximum, as would be suggested by standard microeconomics, then it may be almost indifferent between prices in the vicinity of its profit-maximising price, and hence these other factors might induce it to choose the particular price it does. To give an example, on the basis of conventional profit maximisation, a firm's profit maximising price might be £A, but the profit function might be sufficiently flat in the vicinity of this price that the firm is almost indifferent as to where it prices in the range £$[A - \varepsilon, A + \varepsilon]$, where ε is a fairly small, but not negligible, number. If one of the prices in this range has greater salience or is more profitable for the firm for one of these additional reasons, then this may give the firm a reason to choose this particular price, and perhaps to keep it constant even though the profit-maximising price (abstracting from this particular factor) might change.

6.3 Wage Rigidities

Rigidity of nominal wages is often believed to underlie Keynesian economics. We have already discussed some of the evidence for nominal wage rigidity above. As far as explanations for such rigidities are concerned, some of the explanations given for nominal price rigidity can also be used to explain nominal wage rigidity, but it might be thought that the main reason for changing wages infrequently is not so much the costs incurred by the personnel department in changing the amount they pay workers, but rather information gathering and bargaining costs, which make it optimal to change wages infrequently. Both workers and firms may find it easier to plan if wages are constant for significant lengths of time. Also real wage rigidities may reinforce nominal wage rigidities; if a firm does not wish to change the real wage it pays in response to a shock, it may not change its nominal wage either, particularly if there are at least some costs of doing so. A basic explanation for real wage rigidity, known as the efficiency wage hypothesis, is that firms may not cut the wages they pay workers even if there is excess supply of labour because it may not be profitable for them to do so; workers may become less productive if employers cut their wages, and the costs of workers being less productive may exceed, in their effect on profits, firms' savings in paying lower wages. One reason why workers' productivity may fall when wages are cut is that they have an increased incentive to shirk (see Shapiro and Stiglitz, 1984); a lower wage means they have less to lose if they are fired, so have less incentive not to shirk; there are several other explanations for efficiency wages as well.

6.4 Conclusion

On the basis of the existing evidence, it seems reasonable to conclude that many modern economies possess a significant amount of nominal price and wage rigidity, sufficient to explain real effects of monetary and other disturbances. We do not fully understand the reasons for such rigidities, but the various explanations that are reviewed above do go a long way towards explaining them. Given these rigidities, monetary policy affects output through changing aggregate demand, and much of this book is devoted to studying such effects. Of course, prices do not stay constant forever; we also need to understand how prices change in response to various economic forces, and this is something we consider in the next chapter.

DISCUSSION QUESTIONS

1. Does the existence of menu costs imply that money is always non-neutral?
2. It is usually assumed that menu costs are lump sum – i.e. independent of the size of the price change. What reasons are there both for and against this assumption? What would be a plausible alternative?
3. Are menu costs too small to explain price rigidities of the magnitude needed to explain monetary non-neutralities of the size typically observed in advanced Western economies?

CHAPTER 7

Inflation and Unemployment

I nflation, by which is meant a persistent upward movement in prices, has been one of the major economic concerns of many UK governments since the early 1960s. However, inflation has not always been a problem. Table 7.1 shows the price level in the UK between 1750 and 2010 and Figure 7.1 shows levels of inflation over shorter periods between 1750 and 1998.

It is apparent that the price level was lower in 1900 than it was in 1800, so that on average the nineteenth century was a century of disinflation. However, as shown in Figure 7.1, inflation was highly variable in the nineteenth century, although this variability seems to have tailed off somewhat in the latter part of the century. Inflation was much higher in the twentieth century; the price level rose 266% between 1900 and 1950; between 1950 and 2000 it rose about 1780%, so that over the century as a whole, prices were 68.8 times higher at the end than at the beginning. This means that a pound lost over 98% of its value in the twentieth century, which saw an average annual rate of inflation of about 4.3%. In the first half of the century the annual rate of inflation was about 2% on average; in the second half, it was just under 7%.[1]

Unemployment was, of course, a major problem in the UK throughout the interwar years and it was in this environment that Keynes's 'General Theory' was published. The postwar

---

[1] There are of course, non-negligible problems in constructing price indices and making comparisons over long periods of time. The bundle of goods consumed by households changed enormously over the period in question and there have almost certainly been major quality improvements in goods which may not have been captured in the data. The figures should be regarded as no more than indicative of general trends over the periods in question. Some information is given about the measurement of inflation in the Appendix to the chapter.

Table 7.1 The Price Level in the United Kingdom between 1750 and 2010.

1750	5
1760	5.5
1770	6.1
1780	6.2
1790	7.4
1800	13.3
1810	14.2
1820	11.5
1830	9.7
1840	10.9
1850	8.2
1860	9.1
1870	9.3
1880	9.2
1890	8.6
1900	9
1910	9.4
1920	24.8
1930	17
1940	20
1950	32.9
1960	46.4
1970	68.2
1980	243
1990	458.5
2000	619.2
2010	813

(*Sources*: the figures for 1750 to 1990 are those contained in Twigger (1999). The figures for 2000 and 2010 are calculated by using figures for the RPI produced by the Office for National Statistics to update Twigger's. The price level is measured such that the price level for 1974 is 100.)

period from 1945 to 1973 or so is generally considered to be a period of full employment, but rising inflation levels forced policy makers to adopt disinflationary policies, resulting in high unemployment levels in much of the 1970s and 1980s. The last years of the 1980s saw the so-called 'Lawson' boom and entry into the Exchange Rate Mechanism of the European Monetary System in October 1990. There followed a major recession, but also a rapid decline in inflation. In September 1992 the pound was ejected from the ERM and there followed a

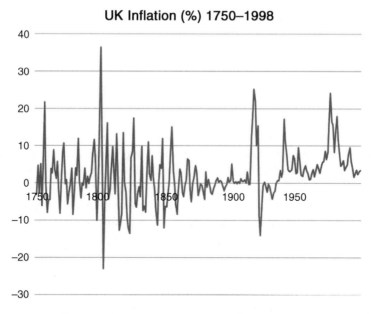

Figure 7.1   UK Inflation, 1750–1998 (*Source*: Twigger, 1999).

period of reasonable stability, at least as far as inflation and unemployment were concerned. The term the 'Great Moderation' was coined to describe this period, which lasted until the onset of the worldwide credit crunch in 2007. (It hardly needs to be pointed out that this was not a period of stability as far as asset prices and levels of debt were concerned.) Figure 7.2 shows unemployment levels in the UK for the last 40 years.

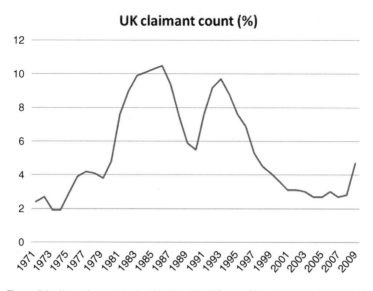

Figure 7.2   Unemployment in the UK, 1971–2009 (*Source*: Office for National Statistics).

In this chapter we review, briefly, some of the literature on the relationship between inflation and unemployment.

7.1 The Phillips Curve

One of the most important and influential papers ever published in macroeconomics was Phillips (1958), which introduced the idea of the Phillips curve, an inverse relationship between money wage inflation and unemployment. This was postulated on the basis of a statistical study of wage inflation and unemployment for the United Kingdom between 1861 and 1957. If there is a stable relationship between wage inflation and price inflation given by the rate of increase of productivity, so that, for example, if productivity is increasing by 2% a year, increases in wages of 5% will generate an increase in prices of 3%, then one can derive a relationship between unemployment and price inflation, giving rise to the idea that policy makers need to choose a point on the Phillips curve. Presumably the point they should choose is the 'best' combination of inflation and unemployment that is feasible (i.e. lies on the relevant Phillips curve). Formally, one can show this by supposing that society has downward sloping indifference curves between inflation and unemployment, and the optimal choice is the one that lies on the indifference curve that is nearest to the origin – i.e. the indifference curve that is tangential to the Phillips curve. See Figure 7.3, where IC_1 represents an indifference curve and PC_1 a Phillips curve. The point of tangency is A.

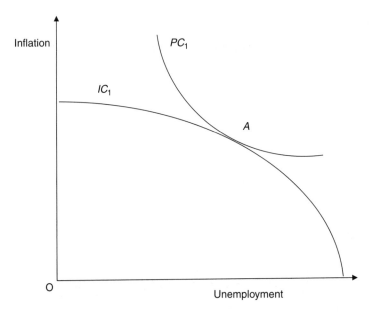

Figure 7.3   The Simple Phillips Curve and the 'Optimal' Combination of Inflation and Unemployment.

Of course, policy makers might also consider the possibility of shifting the Phillips curve in a favourable direction (i.e. one that reduces inflation for any given level of unemployment) and to this end labour market policies (training, improving labour mobility and the like) might be used. Increasing the rate of increase of productivity should – provided it does not shift the relationship between wage inflation and unemployment – shift the relationship between price inflation and unemployment in a favourable direction. Perhaps more controversially, encouraging immigration may improve the trade-off. If there is excess demand for labour in a particular labour sub market, then improved immigration opportunities may mean that immigrants flow in to alleviate the excess demand without much increase in wages, whereas with restrictions on immigration wages may be forced higher.

The Phillips curve soon came to be widely accepted among economists. A rationale for the relationship is that the price of a good might be expected to rise in proportion to the excess demand for that good (the difference between the amount demanded and the amount supplied at any given price); in the case of labour, unemployment is negatively related to excess demand for labour (alternatively, unemployment might be thought of as 'excess supply of labour'), so higher unemployment is associated with lower wage inflation, and so forth. Algebraically, we can write it as

$$\dot{W}/W = f(U). \tag{7-1}$$

Here, W is the money wage and $\dot{W}$ $(= dW/dt)$ is its rate of change. U is unemployment, and we have $f'(U) < 0$. It is sometimes forgotten that Phillips did make a number of qualifications in his article. He suggested that the rate of change of unemployment (as well as its level) might be a factor in influencing wage inflation, in the sense that if unemployment is falling, wage inflation might be higher than otherwise expected and vice versa if unemployment is rising. He also found that there could be wage-price spirals due to rapid increases in import prices. It is also sometimes forgotten that Phillips concluded: 'These conclusions are of course tentative. There is need for much more detailed research' (Phillips, 1958, p. 299).

Ten years after Phillips published his paper, the idea of a stable inverse relationship between unemployment and inflation was effectively demolished by Milton Friedman in his famous Presidential address to the American Economic Association in 1967 (Friedman, 1968), which argued that although there might be such a trade-off in the short run, the trade-off disappeared in the long run.

7.2 The Expectations-Augmented Phillips Curve and the Natural Rate of Unemployment

Friedman criticised the simple Phillips curve for ignoring inflationary expectations. Suppose the government decides to reduce unemployment and is willing to accept a higher rate of inflation as a price worth paying. The reduction in unemployment raises wage inflation; this feeds through to price inflation, and, if it is expected to persist, raises expectations of inflation. But higher expected inflation may cause wages to rise faster than they otherwise would. If employers expect inflation to be one percentage point higher than previously over the period over which they will be paying a wage they are currently negotiating, then they will, *ceteris paribus*, be willing to offer a wage increase of one per cent extra over that period. One would expect workers to demand a larger increase in wages over that period as well. Putting the point in a slightly different way, for any given state of the labour market, the level of inflationary expectations will raise wage inflation one-for-one. This gives rise to the so-called expectations-augmented Phillips curve:

$$\dot{W}/W = f(U) + \pi^*, \tag{7-2}$$

where π^* is expected inflation. It follows that there can be no long-run trade-off between inflation and unemployment, provided that expectations of inflation adjust to actual inflation. If $\pi = \pi^*$ and wage inflation and price inflation are related by an equation such as $\dot{W}/W = \pi + q$, where q is the rate of increase of productivity, then by substitution we obtain $\dot{W}/W - \pi = q = f(U)$ and the solution to the latter equation gives us the so called 'natural rate of unemployment'. This is the only rate of unemployment consistent with anticipated inflation. So unemployment cannot be reduced permanently below this level; if it is reduced temporarily below the natural rate, then inflation will accelerate, and sooner or later unemployment must return to its natural level. The natural rate terminology is perhaps somewhat unfortunate; and it has sometimes been supplanted by the term 'non-accelerating inflation rate of unemployment' or NAIRU. It might be thought that this gives policy makers a more complicated policy choice. If inflation is high, then in order to reduce it, assuming they cannot act directly on inflationary expectations, they have to accept a temporarily higher level of unemployment. However, there is still the question of how much unemployment needs to be raised and for how long; policy makers are subject to a complicated intertemporal maximisation problem. But also, a policy of reducing the natural rate of unemployment might be contemplated as well; the measures we mentioned earlier (labour market policy, improving labour mobility and the like) might be thought of as policies designed to reduce the natural rate of unemployment. Of course, not all policies that might reduce the natural rate are necessarily desirable; for example, reducing unemployment benefits might possibly reduce the natural rate but not be something one would want to implement.

The expectations-augmented Phillips curve quickly seemed to be accepted, although generally with misgivings. One observation is that we do not seem to have a very satisfactory account of how the natural rate is determined, or a plausible account of why it has changed. For example, unemployment was low in the United Kingdom in the 1950s and 1960s, but much higher in the 1980s. It is not at all clear why this happened, if these differences were largely differences in the natural rate. There do not seem to be any really satisfactory theoretical models that generate an expectations-augmented Phillips curve. Perhaps the best attempt to construct underpinnings was Phelps (1970), which attempted to derive Phillips curves (inter alia) on the basis of models containing search frictions, but the approach did not generate widespread acceptance, and there were some unresolved problems with the approach. For example, the theories did not explain involuntary unemployment.

7.3 The New Keynesian Phillips Curve

The next important theoretical development was perhaps the so called New Keynesian Phillips curve (NKPC). It can be derived in the following way. First of all, let us suppose the economy is populated by a large number of imperfectly competitive firms, each of whom follows what are known as time-contingent adjustment rules. This means that firms can only adjust their prices at particular times. The well-known Calvo (1983) assumption is that opportunities to adjust prices arrive randomly. Let us suppose that each period, a fraction λ of firms are given the opportunity to adjust prices. We now need to determine what new price a firm will choose if it is allowed to change its prices. To do so, it is useful to define, first of all, the ideal price that a firm might set in each period if it were allowed to choose its price freely in every period. This might be given by

$$p_t^* = p_t + \alpha y_t. \tag{7-3}$$

This states that the firm's ideal price depends on the overall price level and its own output. It would be possible to derive this equation on the basis of profit maximisation by monopolistically competitive firms, as in Blanchard and Kiyotaki (1987). The parameter α is related in some way to the elasticity of demand facing firms.

When firms obtain the opportunity to change their prices, they must take into account the fact that they may not receive another opportunity to do so for some time, so they need to set the price that maximises their discounted expected profits over the period, which is of course of uncertain length, until their next price change. It seems reasonable to suppose that this price is a weighted average of the current and future ideal prices. So we have the following equation:

$$x_t = \lambda^* \sum_{0}^{\infty} (1 - \lambda^*)^j E_t p_{t+j}^*, 0 < \lambda^* < 1. \tag{7-4}$$

The left-hand side, x_t is the price set by the firm at time t if it has the opportunity to set its price at time t, sometimes called the 'new' price. The right-hand side gives the new price as the weighted average of all future ideal prices. The weights, $(1 - \lambda^*)^j$ decline with j; the further in the future the ideal price is, the lower weight it will have in the determination of the current new price, for two reasons: the further in the future any date is, the more likely the firm is to have changed its price by then (meaning that optimal prices after that date will have no relevance for setting the current price), and also because the firm is assumed to discount the future. Note that although equation (7-4) seems reasonable, it is directly postulated, not derived.

To complete the model, we need an expression for the overall price level, which is a weighted average of all the new prices that firms have set in the economy:

$$p_t = \lambda \sum_{j=0}^{\infty} (1 - \lambda)^j x_{t-j}. \tag{7-5}$$

By expanding this expression, we can gain some insight into why it holds. In period t, a proportion λ of firms will choose a price; each charges x_t; in period $t-1$, there will be a proportion $\lambda(1-\lambda)$ of firms that were given the opportunity to change their prices in that period without being offered the opportunity to reset prices in period t; such firms will have set the price x_{-1}, so the contribution of such prices to the overall price index will be $\lambda(1-\lambda)x_{-1}$; continuing this logic we derive expression (7-5), which might be regarded as a definition of the current price level (i.e. it is not a behavioural equation).

It is now straightforward to derive a NKPC. From equation (7-4) applied for both x_t and x_{t+1}, we can derive:

$$x_t = \lambda p_t^* + (1 - \lambda^*)E_t x_{t+1}.$$ (7-6)

Similarly, from (7-4) we can derive

$$p_t = \lambda x_t + (1 - \lambda)p_{t-1}.$$ (7-7)

We can solve for x_t to obtain $x_t = p_t/\lambda - \{(1 - \lambda)/\lambda\}p_{t-1} = \pi_t/\lambda + p_{t-1}$, where $\pi_t = p_t - p_{t-1}$ is the rate of inflation at time t. Substituting this and the equivalent expression for x_{t+1} into (7-6), we obtain:

$$\pi_t/\lambda + p_{t-1} = \lambda^* p_t^* + (1 - \lambda^*)E_t[\pi_{t+1}/\lambda + p_t].$$ (7-8)

Now using (7-3) to eliminate p_t^*, we obtain

$$\pi_t = \frac{\lambda\lambda^*\alpha y_t}{1 - \lambda} + \frac{1 - \lambda^*}{1 - \lambda}E_t\pi_{t+1}.$$ (7-9)

This is an example of a NKPC. It may be compared with the equation on p. 1299 of Mankiw and Reis (2002), for example. It may be noted that the coefficient on expected inflation will only equal unity if $\lambda = \lambda^*$. If $\lambda^* > \lambda$, the coefficient on expected inflation is less than unity, implying that an increase in expected inflation *ceteris paribus* produces a less than equivalent increase in actual inflation.

We can argue that λ^* should indeed be greater than λ. Consider a situation where λ is 0.5 (i.e. half of all firms are given the opportunity to reset their prices every period). Then it follows from equation (7-5), as well as being obvious, that the current new price has a weight of 50% in the determination of the current price level. As far as the setting of the new price is concerned, firms will expect that, with 50% probability, they will get the opportunity to reset their price next period, in which case the optimal new price to set is the ideal price for the current period. With a 25% probability, firms expect that they will not be able to change their price next period but will be able to set their price the period after that, in which case the optimal new price to set should be a weighted average of the ideal prices for the two periods, i.e. $\{p_0^* + \delta p_1^*\}/(1 + \delta)$, in which case the current ideal price should have a weight of at least one-half, because of positive discounting, and so forth. Thus we can argue that the current ideal price should have a much greater weight in the determination of the new wage than the weight the current new price should have in the determination of the current price index (i.e. $\lambda^* > \lambda$).

7.4 Inflation Persistence

Since an important paper by Fuhrer and Moore (1995), there has been extensive discussion of the fact that a NKPC fails to exhibit the type of inflation persistence that is typically found in the data. The failure of the NKPC to exhibit inflation persistence can be illustrated as follows: suppose we rewrite the NKPC as

$$\pi_t = \beta E_t \pi_{t+1} + \gamma y_t, \qquad (7\text{-}10)$$

then, by continual substitution (i.e. substitute the corresponding equation for π_{t+1} into (7-10), and then the relevant equation for π_{t+2} into the equation thus derived and so on indefinitely) we derive the following equation for current inflation:

$$\pi_t = \gamma[y_t + E_t\{\beta y_{t+1} + \beta^2 y_{t+2} + \beta^3 y_{t+3} + \ldots\}]. \qquad (7\text{-}11)$$

In deriving this equation, it is crucial that $\lambda^* > \lambda$, as argued in the last section. We have also used the 'law of iterated expectations' which states that the expectation of a future expectation of something is the same as the (current) expectation, or $E_t[E_{t+n}\{x_{t+m}\}] = E[x_{t+m}]$ for all $m > 0$, $n > 0$ and $m > n$. Equation (7-11) implies that inflation has no backward looking component; it depends entirely on current output and on expected future outputs, each of which enters the equation with a declining weight. This is equivalent to saying that inflation has no persistence – past values of inflation play no role in the determination of current inflation. However, there has been extensive empirical work (starting with Fuhrer and Moore, 1995) testing the NKPC, and a common result is that the data usually show a substantial amount of persistence, at least for post war US data. Moreover, it can be shown that a formulation such as (7-10) implies that it is possible to reduce inflation at little or no cost in output (in contrast with empirical work such as Ball, 1994b, that shows that disinflation is often very costly). In fact, Ball (1994a) showed that with a monetary sector added to the NKPC, a fully anticipated monetary disinflation should cause a boom. Further empirical work has investigated the question of persistence at greater length; relevant examples are Rudd and Whelan (2005 and 2006), Sbordone (2007), Cogley and Sbordone (2008) and Benati (2008). The prevailing consensus is that explaining inflation persistence is still a puzzle, although some progress has been made. One suggestion is that relaxing the assumption of rational expectations might be a promising direction to explore.

Several other contributions are worth noting: Ascari and Rankin (2002) show that Ball's result that a perfectly credible disinflation is expansionary disappears in a model with properly specified microfoundations, and Mankiw and Reis (2002) present a model based on 'sticky information', that explains inflation persistence by firms often not updating the information upon which they base their pricing decisions for a considerable period of time. Sheedy (2011) shows that if instead of the Calvo assumption that the probability of a firm being allowed to change its price is independent of the time the price has remained fixed, it is assumed that a firm is more likely to be able to change a price the longer it has remained fixed, then persistence may be explained.

7.5 Conclusion

It seems that the NKPC is an accepted part of contemporary macroeconomic modelling in spite of the fact that its empirical performance has been somewhat mixed. There does not seem to be any plausible alternative, but it might be suggested that appropriate incorporation of various frictions into well specified dynamic general equilibrium models might well be the way to generate a more satisfactory explanation of the dynamics of inflation and unemployment.

Appendix

The Measurement of Inflation and Unemployment

Inflation is generally defined as a sustained rise in the general level of prices, but then the question arises as to how this level is calculated. In the UK at the moment, there are two main measures of 'the' price level, the Consumer Prices Index (CPI) and the Retail Prices Index (RPI). Both indices measure the cost of a basket of representative goods and services purchased by households; the indices are compiled each month. Around 120 000 separate price quotations are used to compile the indices, with there being about 650 goods and services included in the indices.

Within each year, each index can be described as a fixed quantity (Laspeyres) index, giving the cost of a fixed basket of goods and services. However, every year the items covered by the index and the weight that item is given in the index are updated. New items may be added, and the weight given to existing items may be changed to reflect changing expenditure patterns. So the indices can be 'chain linked' to give some idea of the longer term trend in the price level.

There are several differences between the two indices, of which the following are the most important:

1. The RPI is an arithmetic average of the relevant prices included in the index, whereas the CPI is a geometric average. This means that if the items in the indices and the weights are the same, increases in the CPI will tend to be lower than increases in the RPI. A simple example illustrates this: suppose there are two goods in the economy, with prices P_1 and P_2. Let the RPI be

$$P_R = \alpha P_1 + (1 - \alpha)P_2 \qquad (A7\text{-}1)$$

and let the CPI be

$$P_C = P_1^{\alpha} P_2^{1-\alpha}. \qquad (A7\text{-}2)$$

Then if P_1 increases by 10% and α is 0.5, the RPI will increase by 5% but the CPI will increase by about 4.88% $((1.1)^{0.5} - 1)$.

It seems that, over the last few years, this factor has been responsible for the CPI increasing by between $\frac{1}{2}$% and 1% less than the RPI.

2. A number of items relating to owner-occupied housing costs, including mortgage interest payments and depreciation costs are included in the RPI but excluded from the CPI. This can lead to big differences in the rates of inflation measured by the two indices if, for example, there are large changes in mortgage interest rates. This happened in 2009, when because of the large reduction in interest rates in late 2008, the annual increase in prices as measured by the RPI was actually negative.

There are a fair number of other differences between the two indices, including technical differences and some additional differences in the items covered.

The CPI is the index upon which the inflation target given to the Bank of England is based. A number of contractual payments have been linked to the RPI but the government recently announced that from April 2011 they would be linked to the CPI.

A variant of the RPI, RPIX, defined as the RPI without mortgage interest payments, was used as the price index in terms of which the inflationary target given to the Bank of England was defined until December 2003.

There are two main measures of unemployment. One is the so-called 'claimant count', based on the proportion of the labour force receiving Job Seekers' Allowance. The second is based on the Labour Force Survey.

Further information about measuring both inflation and unemployment can be found on the Office for National Statistics (ONS) website.

DISCUSSION QUESTIONS

1. Must a reduction in unemployment below the natural rate always raise inflation?
2. Can inflation decline without a rise in unemployment?
3. Explain how each of the following would affect the trade-off between inflation and unemployment:
    a. a reduction in the benefits received by unemployed workers;
    b. tighter restrictions on immigration;
    c. a faster rate of technological progress;
    d. an increase in monopoly power throughout the economy.

CHAPTER 8

Time Inconsistency: Theoretical Foundations for Independent Central Banks?

T he topic of time inconsistency is of central importance in explaining many of the institutions of policy making. The idea of time inconsistency can be explained quite simply. Suppose at time 0, a policy maker decides on and announces the policy he is going to carry out in the future. He could, for example, decide upon an interest rate i_1 for time 1 and i_2 for time 2, and so forth. Then suppose at time 1, when the time has come to decide upon an interest rate for that particular period, he instead chooses a different interest rate from the one announced the previous period. Suppose, moreover, that nothing unexpected has happened that should cause policy to differ from what had been announced. Then the initially chosen policy is *time-inconsistent*: the policy maker does not have an incentive to carry out the policy that he had previously announced. It is essentially the same as saying the policy is not credible.

There are many examples of time inconsistency, both in economics and in life. In economics, it may be optimal for a government to announce a policy of low monetary growth so as to reduce inflationary expectations (and hence inflation). However, once inflationary expectations have been reduced, the government may have an incentive to inflate at a faster rate in order to boost output and employment, so that the initially announced policy is not time consistent. Another example is where a government has an incentive to announce low taxation on capital to encourage saving and investment. But once the investment has taken place, it may then have an incentive to impose high taxation – after the capital has been installed, there may be nothing the owner can do to avoid paying the tax. Outside economics, it might be optimal for a decision maker to promise draconian penalties for certain offences. But when the time comes to implement these penalties, it may no longer be in the best interest of the decision maker to do so.

It is generally assumed that time-inconsistent policies will not be pursued – agents will not believe they will be pursued, so there is no point in announcing them. So policy makers are constrained to pursue time-consistent or credible policies. But this creates the problem that many optimal policies may be time inconsistent, so that the outcome will be inferior to that which would be obtained were the policy maker able, in some way, to pursue the optimal (albeit time-inconsistent) policy. There are a variety of ways in which society has sought to make optimal policies time consistent. In this chapter, we first of all present the Barro-Gordon model, which provides a neat exposition of the time-consistency problem. We then discuss some of the remedies for the time-consistency problem that might be suggested in the light of this model. We then move on to consider the case for and against central bank independence, and try to relate it to the time consistency question.

8.1 The Barro-Gordon Model

In this section we present a version of the Barro-Gordon model, which provides a simple yet tractable framework for thinking about the time-consistency problem in the context of monetary policy.[1] Suppose that a policy maker has the following single-period loss function over output (y) and inflation (π):

$$L(\cdot) = a\pi^2 + (y - ky^*)^2, \tag{8-1}$$

where $a > 0$, $k > 1$ and y^* is the 'natural rate of output'. ky^* may be thought of as the 'target' level of output. It is implicit in (8-1) that the optimal rate of inflation is zero. A more general formulation, allowing for the possibility of a non-zero optimal rate, would replace the first term on the right-hand side of (8-1) with a term in the divergence of inflation from its optimal rate. The symbol a denotes the relative weight the authorities put on inflation (as opposed to output) in the social loss function – the higher it is, the more the authorities consider inflation undesirable relative to deviations of output from its target level. That k is greater than 1, implying that the 'optimal' level of output is higher than the natural rate, is necessary (as we shall see) if there is to be a time-consistency problem; one justification is that tax distortions or imperfect competition cause the natural rate of output to be too low. An expectations-augmented Phillips curve (or a Lucas surprise supply function) relates inflation

---

[1] The relevant papers are Barro and Gordon (1983a) and (1983b). In our exposition we will follow, at least initially, the excellent treatment of the issue by Fischer (1990).

and output:

$$y = y^* + b(\pi - \pi^e). \tag{8-2}$$

Here b is the slope of the curve, indicating how responsive output is to inflation surprises; π^e is anticipated inflation, chosen by the public. (An alternative interpretation of the framework is that π^e is the wage rate, chosen by a monopolistic trade union.) According to (8-2), output can only rise above the natural rate if inflation is greater than expected (a number of rationales can be given for such a relationship; we reviewed some possible explanations in the previous chapter).

We have a game between the policy maker and the public, with the public first of all choosing π^e, the government then chooses inflation, π, these values (and the corresponding level of output) are then realised and the game ends. We suppose the authorities can control inflation perfectly. Obviously this is an extreme and unrealistic assumption, but as is standard practice within economics, we need to see how a model behaves with a fairly simple assumption before exploring the complications that moving in the direction of greater realism makes. An alternative would be to assume that the authorities control the money supply, and this is related to inflation in some way, but this would introduce complications we do not want to get into at the moment. The framework is also, as it stands, a one-period framework; we shall later extend the approach to multiple periods.

To work out what happens in this game, we first of all analyse the policy maker's decision, taking the public's decision as given. We then consider how the public make their choice; they choose, knowing how the policy maker will behave once they have made their decision. So, the policy maker minimises (8-1) subject to (8-2) taking inflationary expectations as given. Formally by substituting for y from (8-2) into (8-1), taking the first-order condition and solving for π, we obtain the following expression for the policy maker's choice of inflation:

$$\pi = (a + b^2)^{-1} b[(k - 1)y^* + b\pi^e]. \tag{8-3}$$

This might be described as the policy maker's reaction function; that is, it gives their choice of π given any value of inflationary expectations chosen by the public. We now need to consider how π^e is determined by the public, and thus we need to consider how the public make their decision. Suppose they wish to minimise the difference between π and π^e. (If we adopt the trade union interpretation of the public, think of the union as having a target real wage.) Then the public can calculate from (8-3) the inflation rate the policy maker will choose for any given π^e; the public will therefore choose a value of π^e such that the authorities, reacting as in (8-3), choose exactly the same value of π. To determine π and π^e, we therefore substitute $\pi = \pi^e$ into (8-3) and solve to obtain:

$$\pi_d = a^{-1} b(k - 1)y^*, \tag{8-4}$$

where subscript d stands for discretion. This is the only rate of inflation which, if anticipated, will induce the authorities to produce exactly the same rate, and this is what the public will choose. We hence have a positive theory of inflation: inflation is higher, the greater the slope of the Phillips curve, the lower the social cost of inflation (as might be expected) and the greater the divergence between the target level of output and the natural rate. The value of the loss function under discretion (derived by substituting (8-4) and (8-2) into (8-1), with $\pi_d = \pi^e = \pi$) is hence

$$L_d = \{(k-1)y^*\}^2(1 + b^2/a).$$ (8-5)

A possibly surprising implication of this equation is that a reduction in the social costs of inflation (a) raises the value of the loss function – i.e. is socially costly. This is so even though it reduces the social cost of any given rate of inflation. The explanation is that it raises inflation so much that the increase in inflation generates sufficient extra costs to outweigh this effect.

However, suppose the policy maker could credibly commit himself to zero inflation (so $\pi = \pi^e = 0$), then it is easy to see that the value of the loss function becomes:

$$L_c = \{(k-1)y^*\}^2.$$ (8-6)

The crucial point is that L_c (subscript c for commitment) is less than L_d, so discretion is suboptimal. But a zero inflation rate is not credible under discretion – were the policy maker to announce his intention to produce zero inflation, he would not be believed, since the public realises that were they to set inflationary expectations to zero, the policy maker would inflate. However, it would be optimal for the government to commit itself credibly to zero inflation, if it could do so. The government faces a *time-consistency* problem. Are there any remedies? In the next section we consider some possible solutions to the problem that have been proposed.

8.2 Possible Solutions to the Time-Consistency Problem

8.2.1 Reputation

Perhaps the government can acquire a reputation for generating zero inflation – it may then have an incentive to continue to generate zero inflation in order to maintain its reputation. The above analysis is of a one-shot game – to analyse reputation we clearly need to bring in intertemporal considerations. Accordingly, suppose the authorities seek to minimise the following intertemporal loss function:

$$M_t(\cdot) = \sum_0^\infty (1+\delta)^{-i} L_{t+i}(\cdot),$$ (8-7)

where δ is the discount rate and subscripts refer to time periods. We need to specify how expectations are formed (and revised). Let us assume that if the policy maker has never inflated, he is expected to continue to produce zero inflation. However, once he has inflated, his reputation is destroyed and he is expected to generate the discretionary rate of inflation forever. Again, this is an extreme assumption, but it enables us to capture in a tractable way the assumption that cheating destroys reputation. By 'cheating', the government can generate a one-period gain, but thereafter there is a loss as, since the government has lost its reputation, it can do no better than revert to the discretionary inflation rate. To analyse this, we first of all need to work out what happens if the policy maker 'cheats': that is, creates positive inflation when the public expects zero. From (8-3) we obtain the inflation rate the policy maker would set in these circumstances:

$$\pi_f = b\left(a + b^2\right)^{-1}(k - 1)y^*,\tag{8-8}$$

where subscript f is used to denote 'fooling'. From (8-2) we derive the level of output the policy maker can obtain when he cheats:

$$y_f = \left(\frac{a + kb^2}{a + b^2}\right)y^*.\tag{8-9}$$

It might be noted that this level of output is higher than the natural rate but less than the 'optimal' level of output (ky^*); the idea is that in cheating, the policy maker raises output above the inefficiently low natural rate towards its optimal level, but not all the way, as there is an inflation cost of doing this. By substituting (8-8) and (8-9) into the loss function and manipulating, we obtain the following expression for the loss function under cheating:

$$L_f = \frac{ab^2}{(a + b^2)}\{(k - 1)y^*\}^2 + \left\{\frac{a + kb^2}{a + b^2}y^* - ky^*\right\}^2.\tag{8-10}$$

Further manipulation establishes that

$$L_f = (1 + \theta)^{-1}L_c, \text{where } \theta \equiv b^2/a.\tag{8-11}$$

(L_c is defined in (8-6)).

So the one-period gain from cheating is

$$L_c - L_f = \theta L_c/(1 + \theta).\tag{8-12}$$

This gain needs to be offset against the loss, which stems from the fact that, as the policy maker's reputation is destroyed by cheating, he has to accept the discretionary rate of inflation and its accompanying loss function every period thereafter. The per-period loss is

$$L_d - L_c = \theta L_c.\tag{8-13}$$

The Present Discounted Value of this is (it is a loss which continues indefinitely):

$$\theta L_c(1 + \delta)/\delta.\tag{8-14}$$

However, the loss from cheating takes place one period after the cheating occurs, so (8-12) needs to be compared with the present value of (8-14) expected next period:

$$\theta L_c / \delta. \tag{8-15}$$

Cheating will take place if (8-12) is greater than (8-15), or hence if $\delta > 1 + b^2/a$. The incentive to cheat is greater (i) the greater the discount rate, (ii) the lower the slope of the short-run Phillips curve (b) and (iii) the greater the relative weight the decision maker puts on inflation in the social loss function (a). (i) is fairly obvious: the greater the discount rate, the more likely it is that the immediate benefit from cheating exceeds the longer term costs of the loss of reputation. But (ii) and (iii) may seem paradoxical. After all, a fall in b (rise in a) reduces the immediate gain from cheating (any given increase in π raises output less, etc.). However, the long-term costs of cheating also fall – see (8-14) – and this second effect outweighs the first.

So, it seems that reputation *may* solve the time-consistency problem of monetary policy – it depends on a parameter condition which may or may not be satisfied. Nevertheless, some questions do arise about this analysis. Firstly, it has not been explained at all how reputation is established in the first place. Secondly, it is not at all clear how robust the approach is to the introduction of uncertainty. For example, suppose, realistically, that the central bank cannot control inflation directly; instead, it controls the growth of the money supply, which equals inflation plus or minus a random term, i.e. $\pi = \mu + \varepsilon$, where μ is the growth of the money supply and ε is the error term. Assume that the public cannot observe monetary growth but instead has to draw whatever inferences it can from the inflation rate it observes. Then the question that arises is the following: suppose the public observes a high value of inflation. How do they know whether the explanation is that the government has cheated (i.e. generated a high rate of monetary expansion deliberately) or is it that the government has adopted the monetary policy consistent with the discretionary solution, but an exceptionally large value of the error term has generated the inflation?

8.2.2 A 'Conservative' Central Banker

Another possibility (suggested by Rogoff, 1985) is to appoint a 'conservative' central banker to run monetary policy. By 'conservative' is meant having a higher aversion to inflation (higher a) than the policy maker or public. In the Barro-Gordon model presented above, appointing a central banker with an infinite aversion to inflation to control inflation would solve the problem; such a central banker would just set inflation to zero, regardless of whatever else happens in the economy (and, in particular, independently of inflationary expectations formulated by the public).

However, this conclusion presupposes that the only problem is the time-consistency problem facing policy makers. The economy may be subject to real disturbances which monetary policy can be used to combat (and it might be optimal to use it for such purposes). In this case there is a trade-off between reducing inflation and giving the central banker the appropriate incentives to react to real disturbances (which he will not do if he has an infinite aversion to inflation). If inflation can occur by accident, an arbitrarily high value of *a* will certainly not be optimal. Analytically, these shocks can be represented by adding a disturbance term to the right-hand side of the surprise supply function (8-2), with the public making its choice before the value of the disturbance is realised, with the policy maker acting afterwards.

8.2.3 An Exchange-Rate Mechanism

It has often been argued that a fixed exchange rate regime may be useful to combat inflation. It was an argument frequently heard before the time-consistency literature formalised the concept of credibility – instead, it was presented as an argument that a fixed exchange rate regime imposed the appropriate 'discipline' on policy makers. From the perspective of the time-consistency literature, we might say that the argument is that a monetary policy maker with a time-consistency problem can solve the problem by 'importing' the optimal rate of inflation.

One formal analysis of this argument is Giavazzi and Pagano (1988) who consider whether by joining the Exchange Rate Mechanism (ERM) of the European Monetary System (EMS), a country could in such a way make itself better off. They conclude that such a system may, but not necessarily will, raise a country's welfare. However, there are several qualifications that need to be made to their analysis:

1. Let us suppose that monetary policy in the fixed exchange rate system is determined by what we shall call the dominant central bank (or DCB) of the system. Then for the argument to work, the DCB must have solved the time-consistency problem discussed above. The Bundesbank in the EMS may have solved the problem, but this may not always be the case. For example, in the Bretton Woods system, the Federal Reserve Board of the US was effectively the DCB of the system, but it is not clear that it had solved the time-consistency problem, as is evidenced by its policies in the late 1960s and early 1970s that (arguably) led to the breakdown of the system through excessive monetary expansion.
2. The existence of the system may change the incentives of the DCB; for example, currency depreciation, relative to the countries in the system, will no longer follow monetary expansion, so may change (weaken) the incentives for the DCB to pursue the optimal policy. This in fact may explain the breakdown of the Bretton Woods system.
3. The optimal monetary policy for the country contemplating joining the system may not be the same as that pursued by the DCB. Optimal inflation rates may differ between countries. For example, inflation is, in part, a tax on the black economy, so the optimal rate of inflation for a country with a large black economy may well exceed that of an economy with a small black economy. The determinants of the optimal inflation rate are discussed in greater length in Chapter 9. So the monetary policy a country imports may not be the best one for that country.

4. We would expect the DCB to react to real country-specific shocks in the country in which it is located; if they do this, they may well impose an inappropriate monetary policy on the other countries in the system. For example, in the early 1990s, because of the inflationary consequences of German reunification, the Bundesbank pursued a contractionary monetary policy. This may have been appropriate for the recently reunited Germany, but not for the rest of the countries in the ERM (certainly not for the United Kingdom), which experienced the deflationary consequences of the policy.

5. There is also the opposite risk to that described under (iv): real shocks in a country in which the DCB is not located may not lead to the appropriate change in monetary policy, since the DCB only reacts to shocks affecting the country in which it is located. We might here note a difference between the Bundesbank in the EMS and the European Central Bank (ECB) in the current eurozone. The Bundesbank would react to shocks just in Germany, whereas the ECB should react to shocks in all the countries of the eurozone, at least to some extent, since all the member countries are represented on the board of the ECB.

6. Fixed exchange rate mechanisms are subject to speculative attacks. So the relevant comparison is not between a floating exchange-rate regime and a regime where the exchange rate never changes. It needs to be taken into account when entering a fixed exchange-rate system that the country might be forced to abandon the regime if it does face a sufficiently fierce speculative attack. Obstfeld and Rogoff (1995a) discuss problems of this kind associated with fixed exchange rates.

The above points should make us extremely sceptical about the case for entering into something on the lines of the EMS in order to combat a monetary policy time-inconsistency problem. An alternative might be that of adopting a common currency; the European single currency comes to mind as an obvious example. We would note that (on the plus side) some of the above problems are mitigated or solved. For example, with a single currency there cannot of course be a speculative attack which leads to a collapse of the system.[2] Also, the DCB, now the European Central Bank, presumably takes conditions in all countries in the system into account when making its decisions, not just those in which it is located, hence mitigating, but not solving, the problems referred to in (iv) and (v) above. There may be other advantages of adopting a common currency, such as the abolition of transactions costs for currency exchange. However, there is the big disadvantage that there may be no satisfactory adjustment mechanism when a country's costs and prices get out of line with those elsewhere in the system. It is not intended to pursue a more thorough discussion of the pros and cons of monetary union in this book. Readers might consult De Grauwe (2009) if they are interested in this issue.

---

[2]However, recently a number of countries in the eurozone – specifically Greece, Ireland and Portugal – have experienced what might be described as 'debt default' crises, where expectations that the country might default on its debt leads to selling of the country's debt, reducing its price and increasing the costs of funding its deficit, and so forth. However, it is not clear that these crises have any intrinsic connection with membership of a common currency area.

8.2.4 Optimal Contracts for Central Bankers, and other Solutions to the Time-Consistency Problem

Walsh (1995) makes the following point. Suppose the central banker, who would otherwise share society's preferences, is given a contract linear in inflation, so that his preferences are now represented by

$$L(\cdot) = a\pi^2 + (y - ky^*)^2 + 2\chi\pi. \tag{8-16}$$

Then, carrying out the optimisation as before (i.e. the central bank governor minimises (8-16) subject to (8-2), and the rate of inflation is determined by equating actual and expected inflation), we obtain the following expression for the discretionary rate of inflation:

$$\pi = a^{-1}\{-\chi + b(k-1)y^*\}. \tag{8-17}$$

It follows that by setting $\chi = b(k-1)y^*$, the government can induce the central banker to produce the optimal (commitment) rate of inflation, zero. A further attraction of this proposal is that when we introduce a possible stabilisation role for the central bank à la Rogoff, the governor has the appropriate incentives to stabilise the economy as well. So it might seem that this is the ideal solution.

However, such a solution would be extremely difficult to implement. It is not clear how one would ascertain the preferences of the central bank governor. The prospect of having to pay a large sum of money if inflation misses its target (which could of course happen by accident and be nothing to do with the governor's actions) might deter suitable candidates for the position from wanting the job. Alternatively, one could give the central bank governor a large salary, but reduce it by a certain amount according to how much inflation deviated from its target. But in this case, the possible political repercussions might not be too palatable; one might imagine the storm that would be created if the governor was rewarded with a large salary for having met the inflation target if he did this by causing a large rise in unemployment.

Svensson (1997a) has suggested another way in which central banks can be given appropriate incentives. The loss function (8-1) assumes that the optimal rate of inflation is zero. A more general formulation of the loss function would be to replace π^2 in (8-1) with $(\pi - \pi^*)^2$ where π^* is now the optimal rate of inflation. This represents society's preferences. Now the central bank can be given an objective function with the inflation term $(\pi - \pi^b)^2$, where π^b is the inflation target. Svensson shows that by appropriate choice of π^b, the central bank can be induced to produce the commitment equilibrium, without prejudicing its ability to react appropriately to shocks. Such an idea is of obvious contemporary relevance, given the prevalence of inflation targets in a number of countries, including the UK, where the Bank of England is given an inflation target, but is allowed to choose the appropriate policy to achieve that target. Svensson also examines the case where there is persistence in employment; in our formulation, this would be captured by rewriting (8-2) as

$$y_t = \rho y_{t-1} + y^* + b(\pi_t - \pi_t^e), \tag{8-18}$$

where y_t is output as time t, etc.

Elsewhere, Svensson (1997b) has argued that, because of the lag (18 months to 2 years) before monetary policy actions affect inflation and because of the many other factors that can affect inflation over this horizon, inflation targeting should be replaced by inflation-forecast targeting. It is left to readers to contemplate the merits and demerits of this idea.

There are a number of other suggested solutions to the time-consistency problem. Romer (1993) has argued (and presented evidence) that more open economies experience less inflation. This has stimulated a certain amount of further work and discussion.

Much discussion of solutions to the time-consistency problem has centred round the idea that central bank independence will solve, or at least hugely mitigate, the time-consistency problem. We consider some of the relevant issues in the next section.

8.3 Central Bank Independence as a Solution to the Time-Consistency Problem

Since the mid 1980s or so, there has been a trend throughout the world towards greater central bank independence. The question whether central banks should be independent of government has been discussed extensively in the literature. It is impossible to do justice to this discussion in the space we have available. Instead, we shall just make a few relevant points:

1. Independence is a matter of degree. There will never be a completely independent central bank. Central banks are always subject to some legislative requirements. For example, the Federal Reserve Act obliges the Federal Reserve, one of the most independent central banks in the world, to seek 'maximum employment, stable prices and moderate long term interest rates' although it does not specify how it should behave when these objectives conflict. Also the head of the central bank is appointed by a political process, and may under certain circumstances be eligible for re-appointment.
2. There are different types of independence. For example, operational, goal, legal, and financial independence have all been distinguished in the literature. The Bank of England has operational independence, but not goal independence: it is given an inflation target by the government, but is allowed to use monetary policy as it sees fit to achieve that target.
3. Even if the central bank is given a high degree of independence of some sort, it is always possible for the executive to pass legislation to curtail its freedom. The executive may be able to change the behaviour of the central bank, perhaps by hinting that it may, at some future stage, seek to reduce its independence.
4. In empirical work, it is necessary to have some measure of central bank independence. A large number of measures have appeared in the literature, including legal indices derived from the charters of central banks, questionnaire-based indices, the turnover of CB governors and the fraction of political transitions that are followed by the replacement of the central bank governor within six months. It is not difficult to think of criticisms of

these measures. For example, the turnover of central bank governors is generally considered a symptom of a lack of CB independence, but there are ways in which it might indicate the reverse. For example, it might be the case that high turnover reflects the fact that job opportunities outside the central bank are quite abundant, and central bankers may therefore not object too much if politicians oust them, so they can, if they wish, act fairly independently while in office. On the other hand, if turnover of central bank governors is low, this may reflect the fact that a central bank governor cannot find a similarly attractive job outside the bank, so is willing to do the politicians' bidding to avoid being dismissed.

5. Initial empirical analysis (e.g. Alesina and Summers, 1993) was quite supportive of the beneficial effects of central bank independence: within industrial countries, inflation was negatively related to legal independence whilst average real growth rates were unrelated to legal central bank independence. This led to the idea that central bank independence was some sort of 'free lunch', in that it reduced inflation without having any adverse effects at all. However, the results were perhaps less supportive of beneficial effects for less developed countries, with there being no relationship between inflation and legal independence although there was a positive relationship between inflation and governors' turnover.

   More recent empirical work has perhaps been somewhat less supportive of the idea that central bank independence is beneficial. Acemoglu *et al.* (2008), for example, argue that whether central bank independence has desirable effects may well depend on the underlying constraints preventing politicians from pursuing optimal policies in the first place. They argue that central bank independence is most likely to be effective when such constraints are intermediate, and that it has little or no effect when these constraints are strong or weak. A sceptical analysis of the relationship between central bank independence and inflation is Klomp and de Haan (2010). Crowe and Meade (2007) is a useful article that reviews some of the relevant issues. A somewhat different test of the effects of central bank independence looks at the effects of the surprise decision of the incoming UK government to give operational independence to the Bank of England in May 1997. According to Chadha, MacMillan and Nolan (2007), the announcement led to a decline in medium and long-term interest rates of about 50 basis points, something which they interpret as indicating a sharp increase in the policy maker's aversion to inflation.

6. Acemoglu *et al.* (2008) also raise the possibility that with an independent CB an imperfect institutional framework may result in these imperfections manifesting themselves in other ways elsewhere in the economy. For example the central bank independence may eliminate the inflationary dangers of a budget deficit, so budget deficits might be higher with an independent central bank.

7. It is not at all clear whether any of the models of central bank behaviour we discussed earlier in the chapter explains central bank behaviour in practice at all well. For example, if independent central bankers act as Rogoffian conservative central bankers, then it is difficult to see why independent central banks cause greater variability of real output as well as reducing inflation. And it is very difficult to believe that the reason for the success of independent central banks is that they are subject to the optimal contracting solution propounded by Walsh. It seems then that, although the theories that have been developed have given considerable insights into their behaviour, and time inconsistency of some sort

will almost certainly be an important ingredient of a satisfactory theory, we do not as yet have such a theory independent central banks.

8.4 Conclusion

Central bank independence has usually been rated a success in countries that have introduced it. For example, it is widely regarded as one of the best decisions of the Labour government that assumed office in the United Kingdom in 1997, and the new government that came to power in May 2010 seemed to accept the operational independence of the Bank of England. Nevertheless, the fact that there is no fully satisfactory theoretical explanation of why central bank independence is successful must be a cause for concern, as must the fact that the empirical evidence for the success of central bank independence in combating inflation must be described as mixed. It might also be the case, as suggested by Acemoglu *et al.* (2008), that the distortions that produced higher inflation before central bank independence might show up in other ways under central bank independence (for example, it might lead to higher government spending and a higher budget deficit) even if it does reduce inflation. A further point is that while it is generally agreed that there was a marked improvement in US monetary policy in 1979, the Federal Reserve has always been independent, so independence is certainly not the only thing that matters for good monetary policy. This is an area in which more research is needed.

DISCUSSION QUESTIONS

1. Is there any way in which central bank independence might be harmful?
2. Explain why a lower discount rate makes the reputation solution to the time-consistency problem easier to maintain. Would it therefore be appropriate to delegate monetary policy to a central banker with a long term in office who therefore has an incentive to establish and maintain a reputation for low inflation?
3. Why might it not be desirable for an economy with an excessive rate of inflation to appoint a central banker with an infinite aversion to inflation, even if this is the only feasible remedy to the inflation problem it is suffering?

CHAPTER 9

The Social Costs of Inflation

C ontrolling inflation is now the stated goal or objective of monetary policy in the UK; the Bank of England is given an inflation target by the government which it is expected to meet. We might ask why this is the case. One answer is that inflation is socially costly, and that monetary policy is an appropriate tool for controlling it. In this chapter we discuss the first half of this answer, i.e. why inflation may be socially costly. The second half of the answer, why monetary policy might be particularly appropriate for combating inflation is discussed elsewhere in this book, although we note that this is not a view that has always commanded universal consent – sometimes it has been thought that other policies, such as incomes policies, should be employed against inflation.

Although it is now generally agreed that inflation is undesirable, this view is not unanimous, and sometimes it has been thought that there may be some benefits from inflation. The precise reasons why it might be desirable or undesirable have not always been clear. In this chapter we discuss a number of reasons why inflation may have either benefits or costs. There are several related questions. One is that of the optimal rate of inflation, and whether this is positive, negative or zero. Another question that arises is whether, if inflation is indeed costly, it might be possible and/or desirable to make changes which reduce these costs so that any given rate of inflation is less socially costly.

In the first section that follows, we discuss the various costs and benefits that have been mentioned in the literature. We concentrate on the steady-state effects of inflation – that is, suppose we could change the steady-state rate of inflation, what would the costs and benefits of doing so be? In Section 9.2 we briefly discuss indexation and Section 9.3 discusses transitional issues – i.e. if the current rate of inflation is not the optimal rate, what considerations and problems are involved in moving to such a rate? We emphasise that it will be possible only to discuss a tiny fraction of the enormous amount of literature that has appeared on the topic. For further reading, readers are invited to consult Fender (1990), Woodford (1990), Bakshi, Haldane and Hatch (1997), Sinclair (2003) and Schmitt-Grohé and Uribe (2011).

9.1 The Benefits and Costs of Inflation

9.1.1 Inflation as a Tax on Real Money Balances

Unless we state otherwise, we shall assume inflation is fully anticipated. According to the Fisher effect, the real interest rate is constant in the face of changes in expected inflation, so higher inflation raises the nominal interest rate by the same amount. There are a number of reasons why the Fisher effect might not operate, including taxation, but we would still expect a rise in inflation to have at least some positive effect on the nominal interest rate. Assuming this happens, it reduces the incentive to hold (non-interest-bearing) money. Holding such money conveys benefits, as agents incur costs to hold it (they could hold interest-bearing assets instead) and the interest rate can be regarded as a measure of the marginal benefits of holding money. Assuming the social cost of creating real money balances is (almost) zero, this means that inflation involves sub-optimal holding of money; in fact, one can go further than this and argue that any rate of inflation or deflation that involves a positive nominal interest rate is sub-optimal for this reason. With a positive nominal interest rate, agents attempt to reduce their real money holdings and resources are used up in doing this. But although there are private benefits to reducing one's money holdings in such a way, there are no social benefits, only social costs as wasteful transactions costs (such as those considered in Baumol, 1952) are incurred. One can draw a number of conclusions:

i. The optimal rate of inflation equates the nominal interest rate to zero (this implies a rate of *deflation* equal to the real interest rate, the so-called Friedman Rule).

ii. It is possible to derive a 'consumer surplus' measure of the costs of inflation – see Figure 9.1.

The loss in consumer surplus in going from an inflation rate which implies a zero nominal interest rate to one which implies a nominal interest rate of OA is given by the area OABD; however, this is reduced by an 'inflation tax' (or seigniorage) of OABC, giving a total welfare cost of BCD. Hence, with a linear demand curve for money, the welfare costs of inflation are given by $\pi^2 \partial(M/P)/\partial \pi$, so that with such a demand curve for real money balances, the quadratic cost of inflation function used extensively in the economics literature is justified. It also means that the costs of inflation are greater, the more sensitive the demand for money is to the interest rate, which accords with optimal tax theory – a tax is more distortionary, the more elastic the tax base.

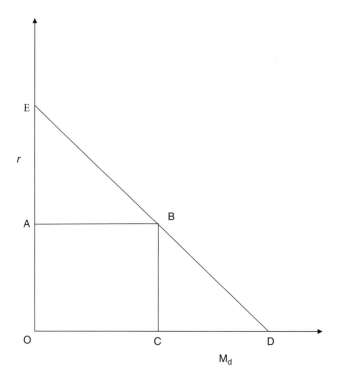

Figure 9.1   The Welfare Costs of Inflation.

We can use the Baumol formula developed in Chapter 5 to derive an explicit formula for these costs of inflation. By substituting the expression for optimal money holdings into the total cost function, the following expression for the total costs of inflation due to its interference with money's role as a medium of exchange can be derived:

$$TC = \sqrt{2bT(\rho + \pi)}, \qquad (9\text{-}1)$$

where we use the Fisher relationship that the nominal interest rate (r) equals the sum of the real interest rate (ρ) and the rate of inflation (π). It is clear that this is minimised when inflation equals minus the real interest rate, supporting the Friedman rule. However, this 'costs of inflation' function is very different from the quadratic function typically assumed in macroeconomics. The function is a concave function of inflation, and would seem to imply that the marginal cost of deviating from the Friedman rule is infinite! However, we should remember the integer constraint point, which we discussed in Chapter 5 – if the rate of inflation is initially such that the nominal interest rate is zero and holdings of real money balances are maximised, a small increase in inflation would almost certainly not cause individuals to hold less money – for that to happen, the increase in inflation would have to be such that the benefits of holding an interest-bearing alternative to money for a period of time (i.e. the extra interest) would have to exceed the transactions costs of swapping money for the asset and back again and interest rates would almost certainly have to rise by a non-negligible amount above zero before reduced money holding is worthwhile given plausible parameter values. This point is developed by Mulligan and Sala-i-Martin (2000), who present a model where households need to pay an adoption cost before holding any interest-bearing assets at all; at low rates of inflation a substantial fraction of households choose not to hold such assets, and inflation has no effect on these households providing they maintain their decision not to hold any interest-bearing assets. They conclude on the basis of their calibrations that the welfare costs of inflation are low when inflation is low.

Lucas (2000) has estimated that the benefits from enhanced holdings of real money balances derived by reducing inflation so that interest rates fall from 14% to 3% are about 0.8% of real income. The further benefits to be derived from going to the Friedman rule (reducing the nominal interest rate to zero) depend on whether one adopts a log-log specification for money demand (the logarithm of the real demand for money depends linearly on the logarithm of the nominal interest rate) or a semi-log specification (the logarithm of the real demand for money depends linearly on the nominal interest rate). With a log-log specification, the further benefits (i.e. of reducing inflation so that nominal interest rates fall to zero from 3%) are about 0.9% of GDP, whereas with a semi-log specification, the benefits are less than 0.1% of GDP. With the dearth of evidence on the effects of interest rates less than 3%, it is difficult to ascertain which is the more relevant specification. Lucas's estimates are for the US. Chadha, Haldane and Janssen (1998) give some estimates for the UK. Ireland (2009) presents some more recent evidence for the US, coming down strongly in favour of the semi-log version, and his estimates suggest that the welfare costs of a 2% inflation (compared with adopting the Friedman rule) are less than 0.04% of income. Whether the costs identified by Friedman are the most important costs of inflation is a controversial topic; however, they are certainly the most discussed and analysed costs of inflation.

An important point is that these costs can be avoided if interest is paid on money, and reduced if interest can be paid on part of the money supply. The money supply consists of currency and deposits; although it is probably impossible to pay interest on money it is perfectly possible to pay interest on deposits.[1] So the costs should relate specifically to suboptimal holdings of currency due to inflation. One way of looking at these costs is as follows. Suppose someone receives a net income of £2000 once a month, spends this steadily during the month, ending the month with nothing, at which time he is paid again, and so forth (as in the Baumol model). He need incur no transactions costs at all from his asset management if he holds just cash for the entire period, which means that his average cash holdings over the month are £1000. Then consider a one-percentage point change in the

---

[1] Whilst paying interest on deposits is straightforward, it is not clear how paying interest on currency could be achieved. One idea might be to pay holders of bank notes (and coins) a certain amount, proportional to their holdings of cash, on specific dates. One can imagine the enormous practical problems in doing this, as well as the incentive for hoarding currency as the payment date approaches. For these reasons, we feel justified in assuming that paying interest on currency is impossible.

interest rate, from (say) 2% to 3%. The extra loss in potential interest earnings if he holds average cash balances of £1000 is £10 over the year; over a month it will be about 83p. This is an upper bound of the transactions costs that might be saved by reducing the rate of inflation and interest rate by one percentage point – but this is just 0.04% of annual income, and an upper bound! This argument suggests that moderate changes in inflation are unlikely to have large costs when inflation is initially low for this particular reason.

The costs of inflation due its erosion of money's function as a medium of exchange can be very high, though, at high rates of inflation. One need only read accounts of hyperinflation to realise this. For example, at the height of the German hyperinflation in 1923, workers were paid several times a day, and they (or their families) immediately rushed to spend the money before it depreciated further in value.

9.1.2 Menu Costs

The higher the rate of inflation, the more often prices are changed, and hence the more resources are involved in changing prices. It would seem to follow that zero inflation is optimal (unless there is an asymmetry in price adjustment costs), and that the costs of inflation due to menu costs depend on the deviation of inflation from zero – in either direction. How large are menu costs? A study of US supermarket chains (Levy *et al.*, 1997) estimated menu costs to be 0.70% of revenues (but it is not clear how these change with inflation). Although higher inflation means that prices are changed more frequently, it is also likely that each individual price increase will be greater, and hence, given non-synchronised price changes, relative price variability will increase with inflation (when there is no reason why increased relative price flexibility would be desirable). This may be costly, if resources are misallocated as a consequence of the relative price changes. For example, suppose in a time of 2% inflation, a firm raises the price of a good once a year so that, assuming it has no desire to change its relative price, it increases its nominal price by 2% annually. If inflation is constant throughout the year, the real price of the good increases by 2% immediately after the price increase, and will steadily decline throughout the year until it is increased again. Now let us suppose that inflation rises to 10%, and the firm decides to change the price twice a year, each time by (approximately) 5%. Then the real price rises abruptly by 5% twice a year, but returns to its original level by the time of the next price increase six months later. So relative price variability has increased. We might expect economic behaviour to change as well – perhaps demand will rise immediately before the price increase, and slump immediately afterwards. But this involves some inefficiencies if there is no reason why the 'optimal' price charged by the firm should change (e.g. people may be induced to distort their intertemporal time profile of consumption). This distortionary effect on economic activity of the relative price variability due to inflation is another cost of inflation, consequent upon the fact that it is costly to change prices.

A firm faces a trade-off in a time of inflation between, on the one hand, changing its prices more frequently (and incurring higher menu costs) in order to keep its prices closer to their optimal levels and, on the other, changing prices less often, reducing the total menu costs it incurs, but this means its prices will often be further away from their optimal levels, and this is also costly to the firm. A formal analysis of a firm faced with this problem is contained in Fender (1990), pp. 41–46; this in turn develops a model presented by Mussa (1977). The main conclusion of the analysis is that in such a situation, the frequency of price changes should be proportional to the two-thirds power of the rate of inflation, as will be the total costs due to inflation. The result that the frequency of price changes, and the welfare costs of inflation due to menu costs, are less than proportionate to the level of inflation, can be given a straightforward explanation. If inflation doubles, then a firm can ensure that it incurs exactly the same costs due to its price being away from its optimal price by changing prices twice as often – if it changes prices once a year if inflation is 5%, then if inflation rises to 10%, and if it changes price twice a year, by 5% (approximately) on each occasion, its price still rises by 5% each time the price is increased and the costs over the course of the year of the price being away from the optimal price stay the same. So the total costs due to 'menu costs' (the menu costs themselves and the costs due to prices being further away from their optimal levels) incurred when the inflation rate doubles, increase by less than twofold if the firm increases prices twice as fast; the distortionary costs of prices being away from their optimal levels stay the same and the menu costs themselves double. But the firm is almost certainly not optimising if it behaves this way – it is in fact optimal for the firm to increase prices less frequently than this, which is another reason why these costs rise less than proportionately with the rate of inflation.

This particular type of loss function means that if inflation is initially 3%, then it would have to rise to between 8% and 9% for the frequency of price changes, and for the costs of inflation, to double. According to Levy et al. (1997), menu costs incurred by a number of supermarkets at a time of about 3% inflation were about 0.70% of revenues. If we regard this as indicative of the order of magnitude of menu costs in the economy, then an increase in inflation that doubles the frequency of price changes will increase the 'menu costs' cost of inflation by about 0.7 % of GDP. This would seem roughly comparable with, or even greater than, the costs due to the erosion of money's role as a medium of exchange, referred to above. If inflation rose to 27%, then these costs of inflation would rise to about 3% of GDP whereas with inflation at 64%, these costs would come to about 5.4% of GDP. These numbers do not seem grossly implausible. There are a number of reasons why these costs might, in fact, be underestimated:

1. Levy et al. admit (1997, p. 809) that their measures of menu costs do not incorporate a number of costs which really should be included under menu costs (e.g. costs of informing consumers of the new prices);
2. the costs reported by Levy et al. are given as a fraction of revenues, not valued added; there might well be menu costs incurred for the goods in question at other stages of the supply chain which are not taken into account at all;
3. the estimates measure just the actual costs of changing the prices, not the costs of the prices being away from their optimal levels, which are of course an important component of costs due to 'menu costs'.

Going in the other direction, we might ask whether there are any reasons why these costs are overestimates. One point is that many price changes are due to real factors, rather than inflation. The above analysis abstracts from the real factors that may induce agents to want to change prices. Introducing such real factors, as shown by Mussa (1977) may dramatically change the shape of the social loss function. In the absence of real factors, no agent will want to change his relative price, so zero inflation will be optimal for all agents. But with reasons for changing relative prices, most sellers will over time want to either increase or reduce their relative prices. If inflation is positive, then sellers who wish to reduce their relative prices will have at least some of this reduction done automatically by inflation, which means that they may need to adjust their prices by less under inflation, and possibly not at all. Inflation also means that a firm whose optimal relative price is declining over time suffers less if it does not change its price. So small deviations of the inflation rate from zero have minimal effect on aggregate 'menu costs' costs incurred – firms which need to raise their relative prices incur more menu costs and greater costs because of the deviation of their prices from their optimal levels but these costs are largely offset by the lower such costs incurred by firms that wish to reduce their relative prices. However, for higher rates of inflation, fewer and fewer firms will ever wish to reduce their nominal prices, and the menu costs of inflation rise.

9.1.3 Calculation and Accounting Costs

Even if perfectly anticipated, higher inflation involves greater calculation and accounting costs. Intertemporal price comparison becomes more difficult. For example, suppose one wants to know whether a good one is contemplating buying is cheaper 'in real terms' than one bought five years ago. If prices have been stable since then, all one need do is remember the price one paid five years ago, but in a time of inflation one needs also to find out the rate of inflation over the last five years and perform the relevant calculation. Similar problems may emerge when one is trying to ascertain whether one's standard of living has increased (and by how much). It is not easy to put a magnitude on these costs. One would guess they are small, but not completely insignificant. It is also necessary to include not just the costs themselves but any costs consequential on these costs being higher – for example, people may make mistakes more often for this reason.

9.1.4 Inflation with Incomplete Adaptation of the Tax System

The tax system is, of course, imperfectly adapted to inflation. A rise in nominal incomes will push some non-taxpayers above the crucial threshold and they will start paying tax even if there is no change in their pre-tax real incomes. There are perhaps three problems due to the incomplete adaptation of the tax system:

    i. Failure to adjust brackets and thresholds.

    ii. Taxable income or profits can differ significantly from 'true' income or profits (which should be the tax base) in inflationary conditions.

    iii. Real interest rates faced by economic agents may be distorted considerably by inflation.

The first is not too serious a problem, as it is relatively straightforward to adjust thresholds, etc. when prices and wages rise. The second may mean that agents are not taxed on 'true' income, and firms not taxed on 'true' profits. For example, inflation may exaggerate profits by regarding nominal capital gains on inventories (which take place just because prices are rising) as a component of profits and through not adjusting depreciation allowances for inflation (which means that in a time of high inflation, depreciation allowances will be far below what would be needed to reflect 'true' depreciation requirements). There may be a number of consequences of such arrangements; some firms may be particularly prone to liquidity squeezes in a time of high inflation and investment decisions may be distorted (for example, the way depreciation allowances are calculated may bias firms against long-term investment decisions in a time of inflation.)

The third is perhaps the most serious problem. An example is the treatment of interest income – suppose pre-tax real interest rates are 3%, and invariant with respect to inflation. If inflation is zero, and the tax rate on nominal interest income is $1/3$, then the after-tax real interest rate is 2%. If inflation rises to 12%, then the pre-tax nominal interest rate rises to (about) 15%, but since a third of this goes in tax the post-tax nominal interest rate is 10% so the post-tax real interest rate is minus 2% (and the effect is reinforced if the pre-tax nominal interest rate does not fully adjust). So relatively modest changes in the rate of inflation can significantly affect the return to saving and hence distort saving decisions.

So when the tax system is not adjusted to take account of inflation (which is usually the case), inflation can have large effects by distorting investment and savings decisions and hence, over time, considerably affecting both the level and composition of the capital stock. There are of course distributional consequences of such changes as well – for example, recipients of interest income will suffer from a fall in real post-tax interest receipts because of inflation.

It is plausible to contend that these factors are an important reason why inflation was considered such a concern in much of the post-war period in the UK (and in some other countries). It is difficult to believe that an annual inflation rate of (say) 12% should be particularly harmful if the main reasons for concern about inflation are menu costs and the erosion of money's function as a medium of exchange. But such an inflation rate may cause considerable harm if it changes the real interest rate faced by economic agents (as illustrated in the example above) from a positive rate of about 2% to a negative rate of 2%. And the damage from such distortions may be cumulative if these effects persist over a number of years.

What is the optimal rate of inflation if the aim is to minimise these costs of inflation? As far as the distortion of 'true' profits and income is concerned, it might be argued that the optimal rate of inflation is zero; falling prices would also distort the measurement of profits and income. But as far as the distortion of the real interest rate faced by agents is concerned, it seems that the distortion would be minimised if the nominal interest rate were zero, or hence if the Friedman rule were adopted. It should be stressed that this presupposes that there is nothing that can be done about the fundamental cause of the distortion, namely that it is nominal but not real interest that is taxed. This issue is considered below.

9.1.5 Inflation and Liquidity Constraints

Borrowing constraints are often set in nominal terms. Consider a credit-constrained individual who has borrowed £10 000, the maximum amount lenders will allow. Then if interest rates are 3% and inflation zero, his interest payments are £300. If inflation now rises to 12%, and interest rates to 15% (so real interest rates are unchanged), his interest payments jump to £1500. If he cannot borrow any more in nominal terms, he presumably has to reduce his current consumption by £1200, which may not be painless. In the absence of other real effects of inflation, he will be able to consume an extra £1200 (in present discounted value) later, but, given that he was originally credit constrained, this will make him worse off. So there may be significant effects of inflation on the well being of liquidity-constrained borrowers, who are forced to reallocate their consumption over time in a welfare-decreasing way. There may also be implications for decisions financed by debt, such as many corporate investment and private house purchase decisions. So inflation may reduce both the level and type of investment; more of the investment that is done may have a payoff over a fairly short term, for example.

9.1.6 Inflation and Asset Prices

Much inflation is unanticipated, in the sense that contracts are outstanding which were signed before the inflation became anticipated. Consider the holder of a 3% perpetuity, bought at par at a time of zero inflation. Suppose now inflation rises to 12% and nominal interest rates to 15%, then the price of the bond falls to one fifth of its purchase price!

Inflation (more strictly, changes in the rate of inflation) may also have large effects on real asset prices because different assets may be taxed in different ways and their relative tax treatment may change because of inflation. Owner-occupiers may not be liable for higher real taxes on the return on their houses when inflation is higher, but owners of other assets may pay higher real taxes because, as mentioned above, it may be real and not nominal interest that is taxed, so the relative attractiveness of holding each type of asset, and hence their relative price, may change. There may well be distributional consequences of such a change in relative asset values; there may also be efficiency consequences, although it is not easy to say what these are. (One possibility is that if real equity prices are especially depressed for this reason at a time of high inflation, worthwhile projects financed by equity may not be undertaken.)

9.1.7 Inflation and Monopoly

Inflation undoubtedly has numerous other effects. For example, Diamond (1993) presents an ingenious model in which a moderate rate of inflation can be beneficial because (in a world where price adjustment is costly) it reduces firms' monopoly power. The basic idea is as follows: with positive costs of changing prices, a firm will typically keep the nominal price of the product it sells constant over a period of time. But if inflation is positive over this period, this means that the real price it charges will decline between price changes. How does the firm choose this nominal price? Presumably it will choose the price to maximise the discounted present value of its stream of profits over this period; with positive discounting it will give more weight to profits earned earlier in the period rather than later. Since the real price is higher earlier in the period, this is a force tending to reduce the real price in the first half of the period over which the price is constant. The higher the rate of inflation, the greater this force, and hence the lower the markup and degree of monopoly. A similar argument has sometimes been made in models of overlapping wage contracts: higher inflation leads to lower real wages and hence higher employment (in a model where employment is demand determined); there is hence a positive long-run relationship between inflation and employment. There are a variety of other models in the literature which predict a negative relationship between the markup and inflation. There is some empirical support for such an effect; for example, Banerjee and Russell (2004) show that there is a negative long-run relationship between inflation and the markup in post-war US data.

It does not necessarily follow that if inflation reduces the markup that inflation is desirable, at least for this reason. For one thing, costs may be higher (in real terms) if inflation is higher, hence offsetting the benefits of the lower markup. The issue really needs to be explored in a model that explains the markup; one would guess that there are a number of reasons why the markup declines with inflation, and the welfare effects of higher inflation may depend on the underlying cause.

9.1.8 Inflation as a Tax

If the inflation tax revenue (seigniorage) is used to offset distortionary taxes elsewhere, then this reduces the welfare costs of inflation. We should be clear how inflation enables other distortionary taxes to be reduced. We can write a simple version of the (consolidated) government budget constraint as follows:

$$\dot{M}/P + T = G. \tag{9-2}$$

Here, M is the amount of (high-powered) money in the economy, so the first term of the left-hand side of (9-2) represents the resources that a given increase in the money supply can generate for the government. We let G denote government spending and T tax revenue; if G is given, then it might appear that by increasing monetary expansion the government can secure a reduction in tax revenues. But we need to be careful with this argument, since it is not clear what happens to the price level (P) if monetary expansion changes. We can rewrite (9-2) as

$$\frac{\dot{M}}{M}m(\pi) + T = G, \tag{9-3}$$

where $m = M/P$ and $m(\pi)$ shows the dependence of real money balances on inflation. Naturally, m is a decreasing function of inflation. In the steady state with no productivity growth, we might have $\pi = \dot{M}/M$, the rate of monetary expansion, so we can write the first term on the left-hand side of (9-3), which we might describe as the inflation tax term, as πm (π). As long as increasing inflation increases this term, then higher monetary expansion can, in the steady state, be used to reduce the amount of tax revenue that needs to be collected and hence the distortionary costs of taxation.

A basic principle of optimal taxation is that the marginal distortionary costs of each form of taxation employed be equated; since there are no non-distortionary taxes (given that lump-sum taxes are not used), a rate of inflation that involves a positive inflation tax is optimal. This was an argument propounded by Phelps (1973). It should be pointed out that this is not (necessarily) an argument for positive inflation, but for a positive inflation tax – i.e. a positive nominal interest rate, which could still involve deflation. It has also been quite difficult to establish the proposition that such tax considerations do in fact require a positive inflation tax – it is possible to find literature in which these distortionary costs exist, but in which the Friedman rule still holds.

A related argument is that inflation might also be a way of taxing the 'black economy'. Inflation is effectively a tax on the holding of cash, and as the underground economy typically and for obvious reasons tends to use a lot of cash, this might be a reason for a certain amount of inflation. It may mean that in economies with a large underground economy, the optimal rate of inflation is higher than in one with a much smaller black economy. One paper that considers this issue is Nicolini (1998).

9.1.9 Inflation and Stabilisation

It is clearly important to be able to use monetary policy for stabilisation purposes. If a central bank wants to stimulate the economy, the usual way in which it does so is to reduce the short-term nominal interest rate. But if the economy has adopted the Friedman rule, then nominal interest rates will be zero, and hence it will be impossible to reduce interest rates any further. Therefore, it might be argued, it is not desirable to reduce steady-state interest rates to zero, in order to preserve some freedom for monetary policy to be able to stimulate the economy in response to negative demand shocks.

This benefit of being some distance away from the Friedman rule has become very clear in the recent credit crunch and recession, with the Bank of England, for example, reducing interest rates from 5% in early October 2008 to just 0.5% in February 2009. It is too early to judge how successful this reduction has been, but it is reasonably safe to suppose that things would have been far worse if in such circumstances the Bank of England had not been able to reduce nominal interest rates. The Bank of England has resorted to other measures, such as quantitative easing, which are not subject to such a 'lower bound constraint'. Fiscal policy may well be used in such circumstances. However, it would be extremely risky to seek to adopt a lower steady state rate of inflation (and correspondingly lower interest rate) on the grounds that were anything like the crisis of 2007–2009 to recur, these alternative techniques could be used. The short-run interest rate is an extremely valuable instrument of economic policy and it would be quite foolish to lose control of it. This would seem to be an important argument for a positive inflation target. Whether it implies that the target (2%) adopted since 2003 is too low is another matter which we will consider later.

This argument can be reinforced if we consider what would happen if the economy were to adopt the Friedman rule on a permanent and credible basis. Then not only would current short-term interest rates be zero, but future short-term interest rates would be expected to be zero as well. It is not clear exactly what would happen to long-term interest rates (this depends on how the term structure of interest rates is determined, something considered in Chapter 12), but it is reasonable to suppose they would be pretty low. Hence, if a need for monetary stabilisation suddenly arose, not only would the central bank be unable to reduce the short-term interest rate but it would also not have much capacity for reducing long-term interest rates. It would seem to follow that the lower the inflation target, the lower the ability of the authorities to reduce both short-term and long-term interest rates in response to a crisis. For further discussion of the 'zero lower bound problem' see McCallum (2000) and Eggertsson and Woodford (2003).

9.1.10 Inflation and Economic Growth

Barro (1995) has studied the link between inflation and growth, concluding that inflation of 10% reduces growth (of per capita real GDP) by 0.2% to 0.3% per year (compared with zero inflation). Cumulated over long periods of time, there can be very significant effects on GDP. Barro suggests that the permanent effect of 10% inflation (compared with zero) might be to reduce UK GDP by between 4% and 7%. The explanation for this might well be that inflation reduces investment because of the tax induced distortions mentioned earlier.

9.1.11 Inflation and Steady-State Unemployment

Since Milton Friedman's celebrated address to the American Economic Association (Friedman, 1968), which we have discussed in more detail elsewhere in this book, economists have typically believed there to be no long-run trade-off between inflation and unemployment. However, in two important papers (Akerlof, Dickens and Perry, 1996 and 2000), George Akerlof and his co-authors have argued that while the absence of a long-run trade-off is correct for moderate and high rates of inflation, it is in fact not the case for low and negative rates of inflation; in fact, they argue that there will be a significant trade-off between inflation and unemployment at such rates of inflation. Note that the trade-off is between *steady-state* inflation and unemployment. In their 1996 paper, the explanation revolves around downwardly rigid wages.

Consider, first of all, an economy with numerous sectors, buffeted by sector specific shocks which hence require adjustment in each sector. With flexible wages and prices, there is no problem – in response to a negative demand shock in a particular sector, wages and prices there fall and hence adjustment takes place in the standard microeconomic way. However, let us suppose that there is downward nominal wage rigidity. Then if inflation is high enough, adjustment can take place without any problem – if, for example, adjustment in a particular sector requires real wages there to fall by 2%, then if inflation is 5%, that is achieved by nominal wages rising by 3% and downward nominal wage rigidity is no problem at all. But suppose that inflation is zero, then with downward nominal wage rigidity real wages cannot fall by 2%; the most they can fall by is zero, meaning that real wages stay unchanged and adjustment has to take place through increased unemployment. So downward nominal wage rigidity impedes sectoral adjustment when inflation is low and the effect is greater, the lower is inflation. According to a simulation exercise performed by Akerlof *et al.* (1996), these effects may be quite dramatic: suppose the equilibrium unemployment rate when inflation is high is 5.8%; at 2% inflation it rises to 6.1% whereas price stability means an equilibrium unemployment rate of 7.6% which rises to 10% for 1% deflation.

The second paper by Akerlof and his co-authors (Akerlof *et al.*, 2000) emphasises the idea of 'near rationality'. This is the idea that under certain circumstances, the loss from departing from fully rational behaviour may not be too high and can be trivial. Since behaving in a fully rational way may be costly, in that it involves calculation costs, it may be rational for agents to use a rule of thumb. An example is provided by the Baumol model of the demand for money. It can be shown that, under plausible parameter values, the benefits of following the Baumol rule as opposed to a 'rule of thumb' may be quite trivial and outweighed by the calculation costs of behaving fully rationally. However, the overall macroeconomic implications of agents following a rule of thumb may be very different from those of agents behaving in a fully rational way. Akerlof and his co-authors apply this idea to inflation; for example, agents may be happier when their nominal wages rise, not realising that wages and prices elsewhere may have risen. In an efficiency wage context, firms may be able to exploit this near rationality by reducing wages and hence employment rises. A slightly different way in which lower rates of inflation may make a real difference is as follows: suppose (average) productivity is rising by 2%, so average real wages should be able to rise by 2% a year and compare a situation of 2% inflation with one of 3% deflation. In the former, if wages are increased once a year, workers will receive a 4% nominal wage increase annually; at the time it is awarded, workers' real wages will also increase by 4% (assuming a fairly steady rate of inflation over the year), but the rise in prices will reduce the increase to 2% by the time of the next increase. On the other hand, with 3% deflation, workers would need to receive a 1% nominal wage decrease once a year, which at the time awarded would also be a real wage decrease, although over the course of the year the fall in prices would transform this into a 2% real wage increase. Although both scenarios involve workers getting a 2% annual real wage increase, one can imagine workers being much happier with the former, where their real wages initially increase by 4% and are then gradually eroded, rather than with the latter, where they receive a 1% reduction in real wages, which is gradually translated into a real wage increase through deflation. If this is the case, then firms may be able to exploit this by offering slightly lower real wages over the course of the year in the positive inflation case and this would mean higher employment.

Akerlof *et al.* (1996) calculate that these effects might be quite important and that there may be a positive rate of inflation which minimises steady-state unemployment; in the model they calibrate, this rate of inflation is 2.6%. Departures from this inflation rate in either direction will considerably increase steady-state unemployment.

9.1.12 Redistributive Effects of Inflation

Inflation may have significant redistributive effects. The reasons for this are that much inflation is unanticipated, that inflation may have large effects on asset prices and rates of return, and that the tax system is by no means neutral with respect to inflation, which are effects already discussed elsewhere in this section.

9.2 Indexation

Since it can be argued that the most important costs of inflation are (at least at moderate rates of inflation) due to imperfect institutional adaptation and indexation (particularly of the tax system and in the capital markets) can remove the causes of the problem, this might seem an attractive solution. But there are a whole number of reasons for rejecting such a suggestion:

1. Indexation may raise inflation significantly – indeed, to such an extent that welfare actually falls. The effects of indexation may be represented as reducing a in society's loss function (as in Equation (8-1) in Chapter 8.) This raises the rate of inflation – see Equation (8-4); moreover, substitution of (8-4) back into (8-1) shows that the reduction in a actually raises the value of society's loss function. Of course, this presupposes that the government has not found any way of solving the time-inconsistency problem that means that a suboptimal rate of inflation is chosen.
2. Indexation (e.g. of certain parts of the tax system) may sometimes not be easy to implement.
3. Perfect indexation is impossible (it is impossible to protect everyone's real income from a negative supply shock, for example), and partial indexation may make matters worse. For example, a borrower may not want to take on indexed liabilities if his assets are not indexed.

4. There are, of course, problems such as the choice of an appropriate index.
5. Indexation may transfer risk rather than eliminate it. Suppose most agents in the economy have indexed incomes, but some do not. An adverse economy-wide real income shock will thus reduce the real incomes of just the non-indexed agents, which means that the impact on these agents is magnified. This may not be desirable, particularly if these agents have not chosen to be unindexed.
6. There are some costs of inflation that indexation cannot remedy or reduce. Examples are the erosion of money as a medium of exchange and 'menu cost' costs.

9.3 Transitional Considerations

According to the expectations-augmented Phillips curve, if it is not possible to act directly on inflationary expectations, deflation (i.e. raising unemployment temporarily) may be necessary to reduce inflation. Such a rise in unemployment and the associated fall in output are, of course, socially costly and can be justified only if there are offsetting gains. The following considerations may be relevant in deciding the correct policy:

1. The speed of deflation should be chosen optimally – but is a gradual deflation or a 'cold turkey' approach preferable?
2. If there is 'hysteresis' in unemployment (i.e. a temporary rise in unemployment raises the natural rate), then an attempt to raise unemployment temporarily to reduce inflation may in fact raise unemployment permanently, so that it is no longer the case that just a temporary rise in unemployment will produce a permanent reduction in inflation. The idea of hysteresis was suggested by Blanchard and Summers (1986) in the context of the European unemployment problem. There are a number of possible explanations; one is that workers who become unemployed lose job-related skills through unemployment and hence become less employable.
3. There may be costs associated with deflation apart from unemployment – as argued above, a reduction in inflation may be associated with real asset price changes which have adverse distributional and other consequences.

9.4 Conclusion

Deciding on the optimal rate of inflation is extremely complicated. There are a large number of different models, each, generally, producing different conclusions. Presumably the optimal rate of inflation is a weighted average of the optimal rates generated by each of these models. But the optimal inflation rates suggested by these models depend on parameters whose values we do not know; it is not clear what the weights should be and there may well be additional considerations which are ignored by the models.

However, there are two models which produce unambiguous answers – the Friedman 'money under the demand curve' model, according to which deflation at the real interest rate is optimal, and the menu costs approach, which suggests that zero inflation is optimal. However, there are several approaches which suggest that there may be considerable costs of reducing inflation below 2–3%. One is the 'stabilisation' argument, and the other two are those by Akerlof and his co-authors, one based on downward nominal wage rigidities and the other based on 'near rationality'. There are several other arguments that positive inflation may be optimal – especially the inflation tax and monopoly arguments, and also the argument based on the zero lower bound to nominal interest rates that the higher nominal interest rates and inflation, the greater the ability of the central bank to reduce real interest rates if it needs to for stabilization purposes. Moreover, there are reasons for thinking that modest increases in inflation from initially low levels do not increase either the 'menu costs' costs or 'area under the money demand curve' costs of inflation significantly. It would seem, then, that a case can be made that the optimal rate of inflation, and hence the appropriate rate to target, is of the order of 2–3%. It would certainly be very dangerous to reduce the inflation target to anything much below this at the moment. It may be that the reasons for thinking that reductions in inflation have these costs are not valid, or that the economy would adjust were a lower inflation target to be adopted – for example, perhaps nominal wage and price rigidities would disappear were a determined attempt made to implement a zero or negative inflation target. But we just do not know whether this would be the case. It would be extremely risky to try to reduce inflation in these circumstances.

A further point is that when inflation is at a moderate level (e.g. 1–3%) it seems to disappear from public discussion – very few people mention it as an item of major concern, as opposed to the situation when inflation is high. On the basis of the discussion in this chapter I would conclude that there is no persuasive case for reducing the inflation target below its current level. Some authors have argued that a higher inflation target might be appropriate. The main reason seems to be a desire to enhance the possible stabilisation role of monetary policy. But there are a number of arguments against such a conclusion. The policy would involve accepting permanently higher distortionary costs from a higher average rate of inflation; the benefits would only accrue if the economy experienced a really severe downturn which requires a large cut in interest rates to offset it. But there are other policy tools, quantitative easing and fiscal policy, which can be used in such circumstances even if nominal interest rates cannot be reduced any further. Also, there are costs of changing the inflation rate, and one may not want to change the inflation target too readily, in case one might generate expectations that it might be changed more often again in the future.

One major uncertainty relates to the costs of inflation when the tax system is not fully indexed (see Section 9.1.4). We just do not know how large these costs are, or how these costs change with inflation. It is reasonable to conjecture that these costs are already quite high for rates of inflation that might be called 'moderate' (e.g. of the order of 5–10% a year). This is an area which future research should concentrate on.

In any case, there is no plausible theory of the costs of inflation which suggests that inflation significantly above 3% is optimal. A continuation of the 2% inflation target in the UK would seem appropriate. A timelier question is whether the inflation targeting framework is at all appropriate – or should central banks have other targets which they attempt to meet as well as their inflation targets? This is a question which we will discuss later in this book.

DISCUSSION QUESTIONS

1. Divide the various costs of inflation into those that suggest that negative inflation is optimal, those that suggest that zero inflation is optimal, and those which suggest that positive inflation is optimal. Are there any costs which you find it difficult to categorise in this way? Explain your answers.
2. Taking all the above considerations into account, what do you consider to be the optimal rate of inflation?
3. Suppose inflation is considerably above its optimal level, how fast is it optimal to reduce it to its optimal level?

10

Financial Intermediaries, Credit Market Imperfections and their Relevance for Monetary Policy

F inancial institutions are of crucial importance for the functioning of any advanced economy as well as playing an important role in the transmission mechanism of monetary policy. Unfortunately, though, much discussion and analysis of monetary policy completely omits the role of financial intermediaries. For example, a standard textbook account of the transmission mechanism of monetary policy in the IS-LM framework involves an increase in the money supply reducing interest rates, and the reduction in interest rates stimulating investment spending, but there is no mention of banks or financial intermediaries in this account at all. The basic question is what difference such institutions make to the transmission of monetary policy. In this chapter we discuss some of the relevant literature and issues. But it is useful first of all to discuss why there should be financial institutions at all.

10.1 Why Financial Intermediaries? And Why Banks?

We might start by thinking about an intertemporal economy where there are some agents who currently wish to spend more than their current resources (called deficit units) and others who do not wish to consume all their current resources now (called surplus units), and would prefer to defer some of their consumption. A typical deficit unit might be an entrepreneur, wishing to set up a business; a typical surplus unit might be a household wishing to save for their retirement. An obvious solution would be for the surplus unit to transfer resources to the deficit unit, in exchange for a binding promise that the deficit unit transfers a certain quantity of resources to the surplus unit at a specific date in the future. But it is easy to see that there might be problems with such an arrangement. Is there a way in which the borrower can make a binding promise? What happens if the borrower cannot deliver on his promise? What happens if the lender wants to consume before the borrower is able to transfer him the resources? And so forth. The latter problem might be mitigated if the borrower could finance himself by issuing bonds, which could be sold by a lender if he wishes to consume earlier than the borrower wishes to redeem them; but then there is still the problem of what happens if the borrower is unable or unwilling to redeem the bonds at the appropriate date in the future or make whatever interim payments he might be committed to pay. Of course there are also many potential borrowers who cannot finance themselves by issuing bonds.

It seems then, that there are some major problems in relying on direct finance – that is, where ultimate borrowers borrow from ultimate lenders without using an intermediary. Of course, there is much direct finance in most economies, but if this were all that were available to finance borrowing, there are many potential borrowers and lenders who would be unable to borrow or lend, and many mutually beneficial loans that would not be made. It is here that financial intermediaries, who borrow from ultimate lenders, and lend to ultimate borrowers, have a role. The reasons why they do have a role might be summarised in the words *asset transformation*, *asymmetric information*, *economies of scale*, *transactions costs*, *pooling* (*risk-sharing, insurance*) and *reputation*. We discuss each in turn:

1. *Asset transformation.* Borrowers may often wish to borrow for a long time without being under any obligation to repay the loan early; lenders may wish to lend on a fairly short-term basis, or at least have the option to obtain command over what they have lent at short notice. Financial intermediaries can accommodate both these preferences. They can make long-term loans to entrepreneurs, for example, financed by shorter term deposits; there will be continual inflows into, and outflows from, these deposits, but the financial intermediary should learn over time how to manage its reserves and lending so as to be able to have enough resources to meet the normal demands of its depositors to withdraw their funds at any particular time without imperilling its ability to make these longer term loans.

2. *Asymmetric information.* By this we mean a situation where one agent knows something that another does not. In financial transactions, as in many other areas of life, asymmetric information may be a problem. If I am considering lending to a potential entrepreneur, I may not know how risky the project really is or how hard the entrepreneur is prepared to work. A financial intermediary can mitigate these problems. For example, a bank may consider lending to its current account customers. By thus having information on their financial transactions over a period of time, banks may have information about a

potential borrower's credit worthiness that other potential lenders do not. Also, investigating credit worthiness may have a fixed cost component, be subject to learning by doing and may require specific skills, so may better be done by specialists.

3. *Transactions costs and economies of scale.* It might be quite costly if a borrower needed to make contracts with a large number of individual lenders; there could be considerable transactions costs involved in negotiating each individual contract; although these could be reduced if the borrower borrowed from just one large lender, there might be few direct lenders able and willing to lend the total amount sought by the borrower. A better option might be for the borrower to borrow from one large financial intermediary. Transactions costs often have a fixed cost component which gives rise to economies of scale. There might be no problem if transactions costs were proportional to the size of the transaction; if so, a borrower would incur the same transactions costs in borrowing £1m from one lender as borrowing £1000 from each of 1000 lenders, but this seems absurd. One important reason for economies of scale is the existence of monitoring costs (emphasised by Diamond, 1984). Lenders may need to monitor borrowers, to ensure they are observing any conditions imposed on them by the lenders and that they are acting in ways which mean they are likely to repay the loan. Since borrowers may often behave in ways that are inconsistent with the lenders' interests, they may well need to be monitored and constrained. But if a borrower borrows from a large number of lenders, then it would seem inefficient for each lender to monitor – this would involve wasteful duplication. On the other hand, if the results of monitoring can be ascertained by other lenders at minimal cost, this may give rise to a free-rider problem and not enough monitoring may take place. The solution may be for the borrower to borrow from one lender who does the monitoring, but this in many cases may give rise to the need for a large lender. (The lender may need to be large in order to lend not just the necessary amount to this particular borrower, but also to achieve a sufficient degree of diversification.)

4. *Pooling (risk-sharing/insurance).* Lending is often risky, so a lender who lends to just one borrower may be taking a huge risk. He might prefer to lend instead to a large number of borrowers; even if each of them has a non-negligible probability of default, he will reduce his risk considerably by doing this provided that the risks are not highly correlated. This will often be the case, but a drawback of lending to a large number of borrowers will be that, as discussed above, there may be considerable transactions costs in so doing. Again, a better solution may be for the borrowers to borrow from a financial intermediary; lenders instead obtain their insurance by lending to the intermediary rather than by diversifying.

5. *Reputation.* A lender's main concern when he makes a loan is almost certainly whether he is likely to get his money back. There may be limitations to relying on legal remedies to enforce repayment; it may be costly to enforce repayment this way and sometimes the borrower may be unable to pay. Collateral may be used in certain circumstances to increase the probability of repayment, but this may not be feasible for all types of lending or all types of borrowers. So a potential borrower may find it much easier to borrow if he has a reputation for repaying his debts. However, many of those who wish to borrow may not have such a reputation and may not be able to establish one, and this may make direct

finance infeasible. Lenders may therefore lend to a financial intermediary which has an established reputation for repaying rather than to smaller borrowers with dubious reputations, who might seek instead to borrow from a financial intermediary. Of course, the financial intermediary will then have the problem of extracting payment from those to whom it has lent, but a large lender may have certain advantages in this respect compared with much smaller lenders. There may well be, for example, economies of scale in becoming familiar with and applying legal methods of inducing repayment. Also, a borrower may be interested in borrowing again from the same lender sometime in the future, and this may be an inducement to repayment – this is less likely to be a factor when borrowing from a fairly small lender.

So there are a number of reasons why there are financial intermediaries, and why these intermediaries are often large. Banks are a particular type of financial intermediary, the distinguishing feature of which is that they perform liquidity transformation, creating liabilities that act as means of payment for those who own them. They are, of course, of particular relevance for monetary policy. In the next section, we consider a model of a bank in some detail.

10.2 Bank Runs: Theoretical Models and the Role of Regulation

Ultimately, a good theory of money should explain the emergence of banks and bank deposits as a medium of exchange. We are some way away from explaining such things in terms of a random matching model at the moment (see the discussion in Chapter 1); however, there are a number of insightful models of banks in the literature. One important and influential model which explains the emergence of bank deposits as a way of providing liquidity transformation is that of Diamond and Dybvig (1983). In their model there are three periods (zero, one and two) and agents have a long-term investment project which they wish to undertake. This involves investment at time 0 and the return on the project is received at time 2. Agents can finance the investment project themselves. However, there is some chance that they will need to consume before the project comes to fruition (i.e. in period 1), which may involve liquidating the project if they finance it themselves. Ideally, they would like to buy insurance to protect themselves against the possibility that they may need to consume early but they cannot do this, as such shocks are private information. However, Diamond and Dybvig show that a bank deposit arrangement can achieve the full-information solution (i.e. what would happen if agents could insure themselves against shocks). Agents deposit their initial endowments with a 'bank' in period zero; in the first period, they can withdraw from their deposit account if they wish to, being paid a certain rate of interest, provided the bank has sufficient resources to pay for withdrawals. Those wishing to withdraw are subject to a sequential service constraint ('first come, first served'). In the second period, the bank pays out its remaining resources to its remaining customers (it is effectively a mutual bank).

Diamond and Dybvig show there is an equilibrium which duplicates the full-information solution. Agents only withdraw from the bank in the first period if they experience a taste shock implying positive utility of first-period consumption; otherwise, they wait until the second period when they receive what is due to them from the bank and consume. However, there is also another equilibrium where all agents attempt to withdraw in the first period (a bank-run equilibrium). This is clearly also a Nash equilibrium; if all other agents are intending to try to withdraw their deposits in the first period, it will be rational for the remaining agent to attempt to do so as well. (He would receive nothing if he waits until the second period, since it is costly for the bank to liquidate resources to pay depositors in the first period, and it will run out of resources if nearly all customers withdraw their money in the first period.) A bank-run equilibrium is inferior to the full-information equilibrium (in the sense that everyone is worse off); it is also inferior to the equilibrium that would have obtained had agents not deposited at all, which would have guaranteed one unit of the good in the first period for every unit deposited; however, in the bank-run equilibrium, although agents expect to receive a unit of the good for every unit deposited, some receive more while others receive nothing; with risk aversion, this is inferior.

Why, then, do agents make deposits if there may be a bank run? Obviously, they will not if they expect a bank run with a high enough probability. However, if there is only a small probability of a bank run, it may be still rational to make their deposits – the expected gains from making the deposits outweigh the expected costs.

A further contribution of Diamond and Dybvig (1983) is to show that a government deposit insurance scheme may eliminate the bank-run equilibrium. If agents know they will not lose their deposits whether or not they attempt to withdraw, there is no reason for them to attempt to withdraw their deposits in the first period unless they have a relevant taste shock. Such a government insurance scheme is backed by the government's powers to tax.

So, the Diamond-Dybvig model has (or may have) multiple Pareto rankable equilibria, but also shows that government policy may eliminate the undesirable equilibria, hence ensuring that the best equilibrium is chosen. Note that a government insurance scheme need not actually be observed to work to be effective; what is crucial is that agents believe insurance will be paid to depositors if banks fail, and therefore bank runs do not take place.

Morris and Shin (2000) argue that the multiple equilibrium result collapses when the common knowledge assumption is relaxed. Suppose, for example, that depositors receive a noisy signal of the return on bank assets (which is stochastic). They show that there is a critical value of this return (a fundamental) which triggers a bank run. However, a small movement in a fundamental (perhaps in the banking context it could be the expected return on the bank's portfolio of assets) could result in a jump from a no-bank-run equilibrium to a bank-run equilibrium, so that a change in fundamentals can be regarded as the 'proximate cause' of a bank run.

It seems, then, that these models give considerable insights into the role of banks in the economy and the role of regulation. But they focus on the liability side of a bank's balance sheet. There are important issues that arise relating to the asset side as well. For example, if a bank's deposits are insured, it may not have a sufficient incentive to avoid making excessively risky loans since if it does so, and the bank fails, the managers of the bank (or whoever makes the decision to make the loans) do not bear the full cost. Also, if depositors are insured, they will not have an incentive to withdraw their deposits if they suspect the bank is indulging in irresponsible lending behaviour. In the next section, we consider some of the problems that may arise relating to the asset side of banks' balance sheets.

10.3 Credit Rationing and the Role of Financial Intermediaries in the Transmission of Monetary Policy

What implications does the existence of financial intermediaries have for the transmission of monetary policy? Discussion of the question has usually centered around the so called 'credit channel' of monetary policy transmission, which in turn can be divided into a 'balance sheet' channel and a 'bank lending' channel (see, e.g. Bernanke and Gertler, 1995). However, it might be appropriate first of all to mention the topic of 'credit rationing' and consider its relevance for the transmission of monetary policy.

It has often been suggested that banks ration credit, in the sense that there is excess demand for credit at the interest rate on loans charged by lenders to borrowers. This immediately raises the question why they do this – surely lenders could make themselves better off in such a situation by raising the interest rates they charge on loans? (Excess demand means they can offer the same quantity of loans and raise the interest rate on each.) The standard explanation is that an increase in interest rates may not in fact raise the lender's expected returns, as it may increase the probability of default sufficiently to reduce the lender's expected profits. There are two basic reasons why an increase in interest rates may raise the probability of default. The first is an *adverse selection* explanation: if the interest rate increases, safer borrowers may drop out of the market, leaving just riskier borrowers wanting to borrow. The second is a *moral hazard* explanation: if the interest rate rises, borrowers may act in a riskier fashion, hence again raising the probability of default. The outcome may be that the profit-maximising interest rate for lenders is such that there is excess demand for credit at that interest rate. So the lender will set the interest rate at that level and not lend any more, even though there are borrowers who would be willing to borrow more at that interest rate. Figure 10.1 illustrates; the horizontal axis measures the interest rate charged by the lender and the vertical axis his expected return. Initially, increases in the interest rate charged by the lender raise his expected return – the relationship between them is positive. But as default rises with a higher interest rate, the slope of the curve relating these variables flattens, reaches a maximum and then starts to decline. Clearly the lender will choose the interest

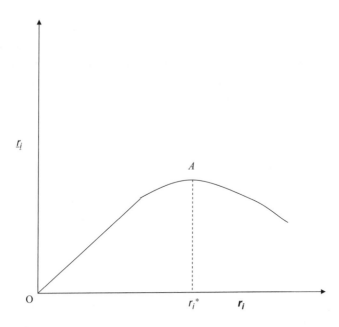

Figure 10.1   A Possible Relationship between the Interest Rate Charged by Lender and Expected Return.

rate, r_i^*, that maximises his expected return; this is so even if there is excess demand for loans at that interest rate.

How does the existence of credit rationing affect the transmission of monetary policy? Assume that a lender can divide its potential borrowers into a number of groups. In each group i, the actual interest rate it charges is r_i and its expected rate of return is $\underline{r}_i$. There may be no strict relationship between r_i and $\underline{r}_i$ – borrowers to whom it charges a high interest rate may in fact generate a low expected return, and vice versa. Suppose the lender has an opportunity cost of the funds it might lend out – say, it could otherwise place the money in a safe security with a certain rate of return (r). Then it might be expected to lend to all those potential borrowers for whom $\underline{r}_i \geq r$. Now suppose there is a fall in r. This may mean that there are more borrowers to whom the lender will want to lend – those for whom the expected return lies between the old and new interest rates. Then the lender might be expected to lend to these borrowers as well, spending will go up and this can be regarded as a consequence of the expansionary monetary policy. But the actual average quoted interest rate on loans (which is presumably what is observed) may not in fact go down; it could in fact increase, if the new borrowers to whom loans are made pay a higher quoted interest rate than 'old' borrowers. So there might be no observable relationship between interest rates on loans and spending even though it is a reduction in (other) interest rates that causes the increase in spending. A second way in which monetary policy may affect lending is through affecting the relationship between the expected return and the actual interest rate on the loan (in terms of Figure 10.1, it could shift the curve OAB upwards for at least part of its length if expected default falls because of the lower interest rate), and this could induce the lender to lend more.

In related work, some authors have identified what has been labelled a bank lending channel of monetary policy transmission (see e.g. Kashyap and Stein, 1994). There are two necessary conditions for there to be such a channel: first of all, borrowers must not be able to substitute other forms of finance for bank loans costlessly (otherwise they could offset a decline in the supply of bank loans by, say, increasing their supply of commercial paper) and secondly, that the central bank must be able to affect the supply of intermediated loans offered by the banking system. Both assumptions are plausible. For example, banks may have a considerable amount of private information about the firms to which they lend, and in the absence of such information other lenders may be unwilling to lend to such firms. There has been a considerable amount of work testing such a relationship. For example, Gertler and Gilchrist (1994) produce evidence that small firms disproportionately (compared with large firms) reduce their borrowing when the Federal Reserve implements a contractionary monetary policy. Their interpretation of these results, which seems reasonable, is that smaller firms are much more reliant on bank loans than large firms, who may be able to offset a decline in bank loans by tapping other sources of funding. One survey article concludes: 'the evidence for the *existence* of a lending channel is already quite strong . . . this evidence comes from a number of sources, uses both aggregate and cross-sectional data, and for the most part produces results that complement each other' (Kashyap and Stein, 1994, p. 253).

The so-called balance sheet channel of monetary policy transmission is slightly different, yet complementary. There may be a safe interest rate at which firms can lend internally generated funds; presumably this is the relevant interest rate the firm should use when contemplating an investment project financed internally. However, if it needs to use external funds to finance its investment it will generally need to pay a higher interest rate. The difference between this rate and the safe rate is sometimes called the external finance premium, and it reflects the transactions costs of making the loan plus an allowance for risk. The basic idea behind the balance sheet channel is that the external finance premium may decline if the firm's balance sheet improves; an improvement in the firm's balance sheet means that it is less likely to default on the loan and if it does default, the lender may be able to recoup more of what it has lent. Furthermore, a decline in interest rates may improve firms' balance sheets. There are perhaps two main mechanisms: firstly, the decline in interest rates should boost asset values (as discussed elsewhere in this book) and inasmuch as firms hold these assets, their balance sheets should improve. Secondly, if interest payments decline on firms' borrowings, this should improve their balance sheets over time. Of course, in addition, if the expansionary monetary policy creates an expansion of economic activity, firms' profits may increase and this may improve their balance sheets with a consequential further increase in borrowing.

10.4 The Role of Regulation

All firms in a modern market economy are subject to a certain amount of regulation. Reasons for regulation include protecting consumers, promoting competition and combating fraud. However, financial institutions, including banks, are typically subject to greater regulation than most other firms. For example, they are usually subject to capital requirements – they are obliged to hold at least a certain fraction of their assets as capital. Why are financial intermediaries subject to such regulations? The first part of an answer to that question is that they may well have an incentive to take excessive risk; the second part of the answer is that the consequences of the failure of financial intermediaries can be severe and possibly catastrophic for the rest of the economy. For this reason banks will often be rescued rather than allowed to fail, and even if they do fail, the cost to the bank's management may be considerably less than the actual costs incurred. If a banker makes a bad decision, usually the worst that can happen to him is that he is fired; even though he may have been responsible for huge losses, he is not going to have to repay these. Also, bank shareholders are in essentially the same position; whatever debts a bank leaves behind when it fails, shareholders do not have to pay any of these because of limited liability. So a banker, in making a risky loan, may get the reward if the project is successful, but not incur any personal cost if the loan is not repaid. Regulation is therefore necessary to combat the excessive incentives to risk taking that are inherent in banking. Moreover, bailing out financial institutions can be extremely expensive for the tax payer, and if financial institutions fail – or if a risk of failure emerges – this can lead to a collapse of confidence with potentially catastrophic consequences, as happened in the aftermath of the collapse of Lehmann Brothers in September 2008. Deposit insurance is a further reason why a bank might take excessive risks – if they do so, insured depositors do not have the incentive to withdraw their funds if they suspect a possible bank failure as a consequence of the bank's actions; they do not even have an incentive to monitor banks' behaviour in the first place.[1]

It is not entirely clear how regulation will affect the transmission mechanism of monetary policy. It has been suggested that capital requirements should be countercyclical – i.e. they should be raised in a boom and cut in a recession. If this happens, lending will presumably rise by less than it otherwise would during a boom, so such a proposal is effectively a way of introducing a countercyclical monetary policy. There is, of course, the question of how one knows the economy is in a boom or recession. It perhaps would be preferable, given the various lags involved, to raise capital requirements if one anticipated the economy to be about to enter a boom (etc.), but this then raises the question of how one ascertains that a boom or recession is imminent. In the UK, decisions about whether it is appropriate to change monetary policy are delegated to the MPC of the Bank of England, so it might be thought that this is the appropriate body to decide on whether to raise or reduce capital requirements.

10.5 Conclusion

The banking system is undoubtedly important in the transmission mechanism of monetary policy. However, perhaps more important are shocks to the banking system in generating

---

[1] Dow (1996) provides some arguments for regulation of the banking system. For an account of bank regulation in practice (but before the 2007–2009 credit crisis) see Heffernan (2005), Chapter 5.

fluctuations in aggregate demand. Unfortunately we do not as yet have many satisfactory macroeconomic models which incorporate a banking system which we can use for analysing these questions. Developing such models is an important priority for research.

DISCUSSION QUESTIONS

1. Are there any reasons why the regulation of banks should be any different from the regulation of car manufacturers or supermarkets?
2. Explain why deposit insurance prevents bank runs in the Diamond-Dybvig model. Does deposit insurance have any possible adverse consequences that policy makers should be aware of?
3. Do banks have an essential role in the transmission of monetary policy?

11

Monetary Policy in an Open Economy

I n most of this book so far, we have ignored the fact that the economy is open, that it trades with the rest of the world and lends to, and borrows from, other countries. Clearly, this is a major omission. The fact that the economy is open is extremely relevant for the transmission of monetary policy as well as for many other issues in economics. In this chapter we seek to remedy this deficiency. In the first main section, we discuss the ways in which economies are linked to each other, in Section 11.2 we present one of the most common open economy macroeconomic models, the Dornbusch overshooting model and in Section 11.3 we discuss the international transmission of monetary policy, which we illustrate with a simple model. Section 11.4 considers more recent literature briefly, and Section 11.5 draws some conclusions about monetary policy in an open economy.

11.1 How Monetary Policy Works in an Open Economy

In an open economy, there is an additional way in which monetary policy may affect economic activity, namely by impacting on the exchange rate. An exchange rate change will typically change relative prices; a depreciation of the exchange rate may reduce the foreign currency price of exports; if other foreign currency prices are not altered as a consequence, exports are relatively cheaper, so foreigners buy more of them and exports rise. The depreciation may also raise the domestic currency price of imports; inasmuch as this means the relative price of imports rises, consumers may switch away from foreign goods to domestic goods, and imports may fall. In what follows in this section, we will make these mechanisms more precise.

One basic concept in open economy macroeconomics is the law of one price (LOOP) which states that a homogenous good will sell at the same price everywhere:

$$P_i = EP_i^*. \tag{11-1}$$

Here P_i is the price of good i in domestic currency terms; P_i^* is its foreign currency price and E is the exchange rate, defined as the number of units of domestic currency per unit of foreign currency, e.g. the number of pounds per dollar. This means that if E increases, this is a *depreciation* and the domestic currency is cheaper in terms of the foreign currency.

For there to be real effects of a depreciation, there needs to be some sort of domestic price rigidity, but in discussing price rigidity in an open economy context, it is important to specify which price is rigid; clearly if equation (11-1) holds then both the foreign and domestic prices of the good in question cannot both be rigid. A commonly made assumption is that the price of exports is constant in domestic currency terms, in which case a depreciation means a fall in the foreign currency price of exports. Assuming foreigners have a price-sensitive demand for our exports, this means demand for, and output of, exports rises, hence raising aggregate demand.

As far as imports are concerned, a common assumption is that their foreign currency price is given, in which case a depreciation raises their domestic currency price by the full amount of the depreciation – i.e. a depreciation of 10% raises their price by 10%. There may be some domestically produced goods in the economy, the prices of which do not change when the depreciation occurs, so the depreciation raises the relative price of imports. This reduces consumption of imports for the usual reason; inasmuch as consumers switch to domestic goods, there is a rise in aggregate demand. So, basically, a depreciation raises the demand for domestically produced goods by reducing their prices relative to foreign produced goods. In practice, a depreciation of the exchange rate raises the prices of goods which are generally regarded as tradeable by a much lower percentage; an explanation for this is that many ostensibly tradeable goods have many nontradeable inputs included in their price – these may include insurance, transport, advertising, storage, retailing services and the like.[1]

An important concept is that of exchange-rate pass-through, which may be defined as the effect of an exchange-rate depreciation on the domestic price level. Empirically, it seems to be the case that pass-through is generally far less than unity, although positive; there is also often a considerable lag before exchange rate changes affect domestic prices.

---

[1] One paper that documents the possible magnitudes of these effects is Burstein, Eichenbaum and Rebelo (2005).

Monetary policy may result in a depreciation of the exchange rate and this is arguably the main reason why it has many of its effects in an open economy. We shall go into some detail into how and why this may happen later in this chapter. A simple explanation can be based on the well-known uncovered interest parity condition:

$$i = i^* + E[de/dt]. \tag{11-2}$$

This is another key relationship in open economy macroeconomics, stating that the domestic interest rate equals the foreign interest rate plus the expected change in the exchange rate. This means that expected rates of return are the same regardless of the currency in which the relevant asset is denominated. So if one country's interest rate is higher than another's, the explanation must be that its currency is expected to depreciate vis-à-vis the other country's. It will hold if there are enough agents who are 'risk-neutral'; empirical evidence on the relationship has not been unambiguously supportive, but we would point out that the same argument would go through if the relationship contained a risk premium independent of the other terms in the equation.

Suppose that Equation (11-2) holds, with the expected rate of depreciation equal to zero, and now the home country unexpectedly reduces its interest rate. What happens? If the country is small, which means that it cannot affect the foreign interest rate, it must mean the exchange rate is expected to *appreciate*. How and why does this happen? Let us suppose that in the longer run the exchange rate reverts to a new steady-state level, involving a depreciation relative to its initial level, then the only way an appreciation can be rationally anticipated is if the exchange rate depreciates immediately beyond this new steady-state level, and then is expected to appreciate back. Even if there is no change in the longer-run expected exchange rate, then a lower interest rate must be accompanied by expectations of appreciation, which means that the exchange rate must depreciate instantaneously.

This argument is somewhat informal; in particular, to work out what actually happens we need an account of how the steady-state exchange rate to which the exchange rate might adjust is determined. Also, if the interest rate in (11-2) is reduced permanently, then, with an unchanged foreign interest rate, there cannot be a new steady state – instead the exchange rate will be expected to appreciate indefinitely. It is somewhat easier to consider a once and for all increase in the money supply, which will imply a reduction in the interest rate, but this reduction is only temporary, and the economy does approach a new steady state over time. The Dornbusch model, which we analyse in the next section, models this adjustment process rigorously.

11.2 The Dornbusch Overshooting Model

This model has been hugely influential in open economy macroeconomics. It provides an explanation of why in a world of flexible exchange rates we see highly volatile exchange rates. The version of the model presented here differs from the original (published in the *Journal of Political Economy*, 1976) in assuming rational (instead of adaptive) expectations. It also simplifies the expression for aggregate demand. It might be noted that in the basic Dornbusch model, output is exogenous, even in the short run. An important extension (contained in the Appendix to the original article) considers how an assumption of endogenous output (where output is demand determined) changes its conclusions.

11.2.1 A Basic, Simplified Version of the Dornbusch Model

The model is as follows:

$$dp/dt = \pi(y^d - y), \tag{11-3}$$

$$y^d = \delta(e - p) + g, \tag{11-4}$$

$$m = p + \varphi y - \lambda i, \tag{11-5}$$

$$i = i^* + de/dt. \tag{11-6}$$

Notation is as follows: p is the price of the one good produced domestically, e is the exchange rate, y^d is output demanded, y is output produced, g is government expenditure, m is the supply of money, i the domestic nominal interest rate and i^* the foreign interest rate. All the variables except the interest rates are in logs. Note that y is given whereas y^d is endogenous. Also, g, i^* and the parameters λ and φ are all exogenous.

Equation (11-3) states that adjustment in the price level depends on the difference between the amount of output demanded and the (exogenous) level of output supplied: excess demand for output leads to the price of output rising, and so forth. Equation (11-4) is the equation for output demanded (or aggregate demand). This depends on two things: the real exchange rate $(e - p)$ and government spending (g). It simplifies the expression in the original Dornbusch model by assuming no interest rate effect on aggregate demand. It does include government spending, which can easily be interpreted as a shift term. Note that in defining the real exchange rate as $e - p$, we have normalised the foreign price level to unity, so that its logarithm is zero and does not enter into the equation. Equation (11-5) combines an assumption that the money market is in equilibrium with an entirely conventional demand for money equation, given by the right-hand side of (11-5). The demand for money equation is homogenous of degree one in prices (i.e. a doubling of the price level doubles the nominal demand for money, or leaves the real demand for money unchanged). The income elasticity of the demand for money is φ (remember that m and y are the logarithms of money and income, respectively), and λ is the interest-rate semi-elasticity of the demand for money ('semi-elasticity' since i is the actual interest rate, and not its logarithm). Equation (11-6) is the uncovered interest parity condition (introduced earlier) combined with the assumption of short-run perfect foresight – that is, that the actual change in the exchange rate in the next 'instant' equals its expected change.

The first step in solving is to reduce the system to two dynamic equations in e and p. By combining (11-5) and (11-6) and re-arranging we obtain:

$$de/dt = \{p + \varphi y - m\}/\lambda - i^*. \tag{11-7}$$

This is one of the two key equations of the model. Also, combining (11-3) and (11-4) generates:

$$dp/dt = \pi[\delta(e - p) + g - y]. \tag{11-8}$$

This is the second key equation of the model, which is hence characterised by the two dynamic equations (11-7) and (11-8). The basic idea behind analysing the system is that for any given values of e and p, (11-7) and (11-8) tell us the change in both e and p. We can thence work out (speaking loosely), where these variables will be the 'next' moment in time, and so on. We can then trace out the whole time path that these variables will take if we know where they are at any point in time. So there remains the question of determining where the system is at some point in time. Here terminal (and initial) conditions are relevant. How they are relevant will be explained below.

In more detail, the procedure for analysing the system is as follows (this is a method that can be used to solve other systems of dynamic equations in two variables):

1. Firstly we derive the equations of the 'stationaries': the sets of values of e and p such that $de/dt = 0$ and $dp/dt = 0$, respectively. From (11-7), $de/dt = 0$ implies

$$p = \lambda i^* - \phi y + m \tag{11-9}$$

From (11-8), $dp/dt = 0$ implies

$$\delta e = \delta p + y - g. \tag{11-10}$$

2. We now depict these stationaries graphically. These are shown in Figure 11.1, with e on the horizontal axis and p on the vertical.

    Specifically, the $de/dt = 0$ stationary is a horizontal line: there is just one value of p which is consistent with an unchanging value of e. The $dp/dt = 0$ locus is upward sloping: specifically, as can easily be checked from (11-10), it has a slope of unity. Its slope is due to the fact that the interest rate does not enter into the aggregate demand equation. Were it to do so, an increase in the price level would, by reducing real money balances, tend to increase the interest rate and hence reduce aggregate demand. In the absence of such an effect, an increase in the price level needs to be accompanied by an equal increase in the exchange rate to keep the real exchange rate, and hence the level of aggregate demand, constant.

3. We now can use Equations (11-7) and (11-8) to calculate the direction of motion of the system out of the steady state; this is illustrated by the arrows of motion shown in Figure 11.1. To analyse, for example, what happens above the $de/dt = 0$ locus, note that if we start off with a value of p on the $de/dt = 0$ locus and raise it, then it follows from Equation (11-7) that the right-hand side of the equation rises and hence de/dt becomes positive, explaining the arrow pointing rightwards. Similarly, if we are below the $dp/dt = 0$ locus, Equation (11-8) can be used to show the price level must be rising; in this case, there is excess demand for output (the real exchange rate is too high) and this gives rise to upward pressure on the price level. The other arrows can be similarly explained.

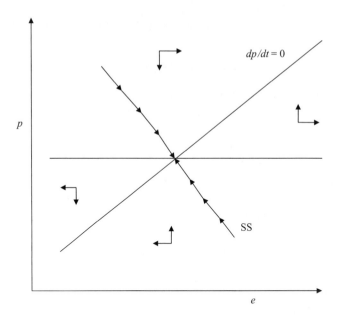

Figure 11.1 The Dornbusch Overshooting Model.

4. Generally the dynamic paths are divergent; that is, they lead to ever increasing or decreasing values of p and e. However, there is an exception, known as the *saddlepath* and labelled SS in the figure. This is the dynamic path that converges to the steady state. It can be seen that there must be such a path. For example, suppose we choose an initial combination of p and e such that the resulting dynamic path takes us to the left of and below the steady state; now suppose we increase the initial value of e, keeping p constant. It can easily be seen that by doing this, we shift the resultant dynamic path to the right; a large enough increase in e will mean that the dynamic path now goes to the right of the steady state; it should be obvious if there is an increase of just the right amount this will give a dynamic path that takes us to the saddlepath exactly (this follows from continuity).

5. We usually assume that the system follows the saddlepath to the steady state, or in other words follows a convergent dynamic path. Why should this be the case? This is a complicated and controversial topic on which there is a considerable amount of literature. The question is discussed further in the Appendix, where it is argued that an assumption of long-run perfect foresight may be sufficient to justify such an assumption. The next question is how does the system get to the saddlepath if it is not on the saddlepath already? The answer is as follows. We assume one variable (e) is a 'jump' variable (that is, it is not constrained to move in a continuous fashion) and the second variable (p) is instantaneously sticky (that is, it has to move continuously). This enables us to determine how the system moves to the saddlepath immediately. If the system is not initially on the saddlepath when a shock hits the economy (and if no further shock is anticipated), then the system must move horizontally to the saddlepath, and it then follows the saddlepath until it reaches the steady state.

11.2.2 Effects of an Unanticipated Increase in the Money Supply

A standard exercise we perform in macroeconomics is that of considering the effects of a completely unanticipated permanent increase in the money supply. Elsewhere in this book we have argued that the instrument of monetary policy is the interest rate. However, it is tricky to carry out the analysis of this chapter in a framework where the interest rate is the instrument of monetary policy; a permanent reduction in the interest rate would be incompatible with the system ever reaching a steady state, so we would need to consider a non-trivial interest rate adjustment rule. Moreover, the analysis in the original paper and in much of the literature is conducted in terms of a change in the money supply, and the whole concept of overshooting does not really make sense in an interest rate-targeting framework.

So, we assume the economy is initially in a steady state, and then the money supply completely unexpectedly increases, and is expected to stay at its new higher level forever. No change in any other policy variable or parameter is expected either. How does the system behave?

Algebraically, it is helpful to calculate the steady-state values of e and p (from (11-9) and (11-10); using 'overbars' to denote steady-state values, these are given by

$$\bar{p} = \lambda i^* - \varphi y + m. \tag{11-11}$$

$$\bar{e} = \lambda i^* + \{(1/\delta) - \varphi\}y + m - \gamma/\delta. \tag{11-12}$$

It is apparent that we have steady-state monetary neutrality – that is an increase in m produces an equivalent increase in the steady-state levels of e and p.

So, if there is an unanticipated increase in the money supply, the steady-state values of both the exchange rate and price level increase by the same proportionate amount. But although e can jump in response to the increase, the price level cannot. What happens? If we calculate the new saddlepath corresponding to the new value of the money supply, we find that it lies to the right of the initial saddlepath. In accordance with the above analysis, the system must hence jump to this new saddlepath, and then follows it, with p rising and e falling until it reaches the new steady state. The interest rate falls; this implies, from the uncovered interest parity condition that the exchange rate must be expected to appreciate, and this entails, because of the perfect foresight assumption, that it must actually appreciate. The fall in the interest rate would in most models increase aggregate demand, but not in this version of the Dornbusch model, as we have assumed no interest rate effect on aggregate demand (see Equation (11-4)). Since the exchange rate depreciates but the price level does not change when the money supply is increased, there is a depreciation of the real exchange rate, and it is this that causes excess demand for goods and price increases as the economy moves to the new steady state along the saddlepath.

The most important thing to note is that the exchange rate *overshoots* in response to the permanent, unanticipated increase in the money supply: the initial change in the exchange rate exceeds the steady-state change. So a 10% increase in the money supply means a greater percentage depreciation in the exchange rate, perhaps 15%. Why does this overshooting occur? The basic idea is that the money supply increase means that both the steady-state level of e increases but its rate of change (de/dt) must fall. How is an increase in the (steady-state) *level* of a variable compatible with a decline in its *rate of change*? The only possible answer is that by overshooting the exchange rate jumps beyond its new steady-state level and then moves back to this level.

It is easy to see why the Dornbusch model quickly became popular – it provided an explanation for the volatility of exchange rates in the years immediately after the collapse of the Bretton Woods system in 1971 and the introduction of flexible exchange rates among the major economies of the world.

11.2.3 Effects of Fiscal Policy

It is straightforward to analyse fiscal policy using the model. It can be seen from equations (11-7) and (11-8) that an unanticipated, permanent increase in government spending (g), shifts the $dp/dt = 0$ leftwards but leaves the $de/dt = 0$ locus unchanged. So the steady-state price level remains unaltered, although the steady-state exchange rate falls. So there is no need for any period of adjustment; the economy jumps immediately to the new steady state. The appreciation of nominal the exchange rate means a real exchange rate appreciation which exactly offsets the effect of the increased government spending on aggregate demand. This is exactly the same as happens in the Mundell-Fleming model with perfect capital mobility.

It is not difficult to see limitations of this analysis of fiscal policy. How the increase in government spending is financed is not specified. Also, the appreciation of the exchange rate presumably means a permanent deterioration of the balance of trade, something which might be expected to be incompatible with an appropriate intertemporal budget constraint.

11.2.4 An Anticipated Increase in the Money Supply

Suppose that at time t_0 it becomes perfectly anticipated that at some future time t_1 the money supply will increase by a certain amount and stay at that new higher level indefinitely. Moreover, no changes in any of the parameters or other exogenous variables of the model are anticipated at all. What happens? It should be clear that, if we do assume that the system will converge to the steady state associated with the new value of the money supply, that the system should be on the new saddlepath at time t_1. But before time t_1, the system is moving in accordance with the laws of motion of the 'old' dynamic system – i.e. the one associated with the original value of the money supply. It follows that at time t_0, there must be a jump depreciation of the exchange rate which puts the economy on a dynamic path associated with this system which reaches the new saddlepath at time t_1. The system then follows the new steady state to the new saddlepath. One point of interest is that between times t_0 and t_1, the exchange rate is depreciating and the price level rising, which is the opposite of the relationship between the price level and the exchange rate on the saddlepath. So we should be wary of statements to the effect that the Dornbusch model predicts that the exchange rate and price level always move in opposite directions. It does not, unless it is also assumed that the economy is always on the saddlepath.

11.2.5 Dornbusch Model with Endogenous Output

If output is determined by demand in the short run, then overshooting may not occur: the idea is that monetary expansion causes the exchange rate to depreciate and output to increase; in order to preserve money market equilibrium the increase in income may be sufficient without a fall in the interest rate; indeed, it is possible that the interest rate may need to *rise* (not fall), and this means overshooting need not occur (since the exchange rate now needs to depreciate further after the initial monetary expansion). In the exogenous output case, the only way that an increase in the money supply can be absorbed is through a decline in the interest rate and this necessarily implies overshooting. But with endogenous output, now output can adjust (as well as the interest rate) to absorb the extra money, and it is quite possible that the effect of the exchange rate depreciation on output is so strong that the exchange rate needs to depreciate by less than its steady-state depreciation to absorb the extra money, meaning that the interest rate rises. The problem at the end of the chapter explores the endogenous output case in more detail.

11.2.6 Testing the Dornbusch Model

The Dornbusch model may be neat and elegant, but of course the crucial question is whether it can successfully explain exchange rate behaviour and related phenomena. One would therefore like to test it, but it is not immediately obvious how one does so. One possibility is to derive some predictions from the model and see whether these predictions are satisfied. A prediction that might be made comes from looking at the implications of a downward sloping saddlepath for the relationship between the exchange rate and the interest rate. Specifically, we might observe that when e is high, the nominal interest rate i is low; also, when the real exchange rate $(e - p)$ is high, the real interest rate is low (not only is the nominal interest rate low but actual and expected inflation are high). It must be emphasised that these are relationships we would expect *if* we are on a downward sloping saddlepath. However, there is little empirical support for either of these predictions – see, e.g. Obstfeld and Rogoff (1996), pp. 621–6.

We might want to conclude that the Dornbusch model is hereby falsified, but might it alternatively be the case that a possible explanation is that we are not observing the economy on a *downward sloping saddlepath*? For example, it could be that the economy is moving in response to an anticipated increase in the money supply which has so far not occurred, as analysed above in subsection 11.2.4; in this case, we might have a depreciation associated with a higher, and not necessarily a lower, interest rate. Alternatively, perhaps the world is as described by the Dornbusch model with endogenous output and with an upward sloping saddlepath as analysed in subsection 11.2.5? In this case too, we would have a rather different relationship between interest rates and exchange rates than that predicted above. It might be concluded that these tests tell us absolutely nothing about the empirical relevance of the Dornbusch model.

A possibly more promising approach to testing the model might look at the predictions it makes about the effects of unanticipated monetary changes. More specifically, unanticipated monetary contraction (expansion) results in an immediate nominal and real appreciation (depreciation), followed by reversion to steady state. The main problem in doing this is to identify an *unanticipated* monetary change. It might be possible to identify a monetary change, but how does one know whether it was anticipated or unanticipated? A further point is that it is not enough just to identify an unanticipated monetary change, it is also necessary that the change must not be in response to a shift in the demand for money. To see the relevance of this point, suppose there is an unanticipated increase in the demand for money when the monetary authorities are targeting interest rates. Then what will happen is that the money supply increases to accommodate the increased demand for money at an unchanged interest rate. There should be no further ramifications of this for the economy – the interest rate does not change, so this prevents the monetary expansion having any effects on the real economy.

Eichenbaum and Evans (1995) develop a methodology for identifying unanticipated monetary changes, and find that monetary contraction does indeed lead to an appreciation, as well as an increase in interest rates, but there is a two-year lag before the effect of the contraction on the exchange rate peaks! So there is a violation of uncovered interest parity; one can presumably make money by shifting one's portfolio into the currency of the country that introduces the monetary contraction, since then one enjoys both a higher interest rate and expected appreciation.

Faust and Rogers (2003), consider the issue further. They find that the exchange rate response may be delayed or nearly immediate. They find large deviations from uncovered interest parity, and that monetary policy shocks may not account for a great deal of exchange rate variability.

So the prediction of the Dornbusch model that monetary contraction and expansion do lead to exchange rate appreciations and depreciations is confirmed, but the time path the exchange rate follows after the monetary change is not predicted at all. There does not seem to be any model that explains these results; why they occur seems to be very much a mystery.

An implication of the version of the model with endogenous or demand-determined output is that monetary contraction under flexible exchange rates has large effects on aggregate demand and output. There is some supporting evidence: see, for example, Obstfeld and Rogoff's discussion of the Great Depression (1996, pp. 626–30): they argue there was a divergence in economic performance between countries that abandoned the gold standard early and hence were able to pursue expansionary monetary policies, and those that clung to gold. It also makes sense of many actual episodes of monetary expansionary and contraction, such as the so called Volcker deflation in the United States in 1979 and the Thatcher disinflation in the United Kingdom from 1979–81. Both of these episodes involved large appreciations of the exchange rate and significant increases in interest rates, and were followed by considerable increases in unemployment and falls in output. Inflation also (eventually) fell; indeed, it was to combat inflation that the monetary contractions were introduced.

11.2.7 Assessment of the Dornbusch model

The Dornbusch model has been a key open macroeconomic model since it was introduced in 1976, in spite of the fact that it has not been very successful empirically. Perhaps its main strength is that it provides a coherent account of the relationship between current and future economic changes in an open economy context, taking explicit account of the ways in which the future and the present interact. For example, anticipated events affect the present because agents change their behaviour because of the anticipation, but changes in agents' current behaviour will have consequences for future economic events, and inasmuch as these are anticipated, there will be ramifications for the present, and so forth.

Nevertheless, at the theoretical level there are a number of limitations to the model of which the following are a few:

1. It assumes a world of certainty in which unanticipated events occur! This is not quite a contradiction – it is not contradictory to suppose that having experienced a completely unanticipated change, agents predict completely everything that is going to happen in the economy – it is just pretty unrealistic.
2. Asset holders are assumed to have foresight, but not other agents (e.g. consumers), who react just to current variables. In fact, agents' behaviour is not really modelled at all; instead, we are just given reduced-form expressions representing their behaviour. So demand for domestic goods depends on the real exchange rate; it might be thought that future values of the real exchange rate would affect agents' behaviour as well, but these effects are not captured in the model at all.
3. There is no role for current account or wealth effects. It seems that the country can borrow as much as it likes to finance any current account deficit it may have.
4. There is a complete absence of supply-side considerations; in a sense, it is even worse than the Mundell-Fleming model, where output is demand determined – the basic model assumes both sticky prices and exogenous output!

We would comment that it is not easy – in fact it is very difficult – to construct models that meet these criticisms yet preserve the existing desirable features of the model. In fact, it might be argued that many developments in theoretical open economy macroeconomics since 1976 can be interpreted as attempting to build models that do not have these deficiencies.

For example, the Obstfeld-Rogoff model, which we discuss in Section 11.4, might be regarded as a considerable advance. We would add that although there have undoubtedly been considerable advances in open economy macroeconomics since 1976, it seems that one area in which there has been a deficiency is that so far uncertainty has not been incorporated in a very satisfactory way.

11.3 The International Transmission of Monetary Policy Disturbances

What is the effect of monetary or fiscal expansion in one country on economic activity in another? This is the question of the international transmission of policy disturbances. We discuss this very briefly with the aid of a simple two country Mundell-Fleming model.

$$y = ae + fy^* + g, \tag{11-13}$$

$$y^* = -ae + fy + g^*, \tag{11-14}$$

$$m = -br + cy, \tag{11-15}$$

$$m^* = -br + cy^*, \tag{11-16}$$

where

  y (y^*) is domestic (foreign) income,
  m (m^*) is the domestic (foreign) money supply,
  e is the domestic exchange rate (domestic-currency price of foreign exchange),
  r is the world interest rate,
  g (g^*) is domestic (foreign) government spending,
  a, b, c and f (< 1) are positive constants.

Equations (11-13) and (11-14) are goods market equilibrium conditions for each country, and equations (11-15) and (11-16) are the money market equilibrium conditions. Each country's price level is constant and normalised to unity. With a flexible exchange rate, money supply equals money demand for each country separately, and each country's money supply is exogenous. So y, y^*, r and e are the endogenous variables, whereas m, m^*, g and g^* are policy instruments. Note the symmetry assumption – the countries are effectively the same, and are the same size (the small country assumption is relaxed). Also, with uncovered interest parity and zero expectations of exchange rate change, interest rates are equated internationally, so there is a common interest rate in both countries (which can hence be regarded as a world interest rate). Note the 'spillover terms' (denoted by fy^* and fy) in equations (11-13) and (11-14), indicating the effect of an increase in income in one country on income in the other for a given level of the exchange rate. The system of equations is easy to solve. First, by adding equations (11-13) and (11-14) we obtain:

$$y + y^* = \frac{g + g^*}{1 - f}. \tag{11-17}$$

By subtracting (11-16) from (11-15) we obtain

$$y - y^* = (m - m^*)/c. \tag{11-18}$$

So adding (11-17) and (11-18) we obtain the following expression for domestic income:

$$y = \frac{g + g^*}{2(1 - f)} + \frac{m - m^*}{2c}. \tag{11-19}$$

In this model, the world is ultra Keynesian – world income is determined by world government spending; since expenditure is not sensitive to the interest rate there is no crowding out of government expenditure via the money markets. However, domestic monetary policy is expansionary; here the mechanism is the exchange rate, not the interest rate. The really surprising result is that concerning foreign monetary policy, which is contractionary as far as the domestic economy is concerned. The explanation is that the foreign monetary expansion reduces foreign and world interest rates (remember we are no longer in a small country world – changes in each country's policies can have significant effects on world variables). Since the domestic interest rate has fallen, but there has been no change in the domestic money supply, the only way in which domestic money market equilibrium can be preserved is through a contraction of domestic income, which is brought about by an appreciation of the domestic exchange rate.

11.4 More recent literature – the Obstfeld-Rogoff 'Redux' model

There has been a huge amount of literature on open economy macroeconomics since the Dornbusch model appeared in 1976. Probably the most influential paper in this period has been Obstfeld and Rogoff (1995b), often referred to as the 'redux' paper. This combined three essential features:

1. Intertemporal optimisation. Consumers maximise an intertemporal utility function subject to an intertemporal budget constraint.
2. Imperfect competition.
3. Temporarily rigid prices. Together with imperfect competition, this means that output is demand determined in the short run. (Chapter 6, on nominal rigidities discussed this point; if price is above marginal costs and firms find it too costly to raise their prices, then it is optimal for them to increase output in response to an increase in demand.) A number of conclusions are derived in the paper:
   a. Monetary expansion results in a depreciation of the exchange rate and an increase in output in the short run.
   b. The exchange rate does not typically overshoot in response to a permanent unanticipated increase in the money supply.
   c. Monetary expansion is not neutral, even in the long run. This is because of the accumulation of assets in the transition to the new steady state; since the depreciation results in a current account surplus, in the new steady state wealth is higher because of

the accumulated extra stock of foreign bonds, and this wealth has real effects (on labour supply and output, for example). However, these long-run non-neutralities may not be very important quantitatively.

The main drawback with the redux model as it stands is that price adjustment is synchronised – prices are rigid in the first period, but adjust immediately to their new steady-state levels in the second and subsequent periods. More recent work has sought to rectify this deficiency, by postulating staggered price adjustment (i.e. not all prices are adjusted at once). Calvo and Taylor contracts (discussed briefly in Chapter 7) are the most popular types of price adjustment mechanisms assumed.

11.5 Conclusion

Monetary policy may work somewhat differently in an open economy than in a closed economy. Changes in the exchange rate are a crucial part of the open economy transmission mechanism. These changes may be a large and powerful way in which monetary disturbances are transmitted in an open economy.

How do these results change in a world of central banks which use the interest rate rather the money supply as their instrument? The answer is that unexpected changes in the interest rate would still be expected to produce movements in the exchange rate in the opposite direction, but that the dynamic time path of variables in response to this change may well differ. One important consideration is how persistent the change in interest rates is expected to be.

One reason the openness of the economy complicates monetary policy is that exchange rate changes will often feed through to prices, with consequences for the rate of inflation. It might seem that this gives an inflation targeting central bank another way of controlling inflation. However, changes in exchange rates affect prices with lags and in an uncertain fashion, and the changes in inflation they generate will be temporary. The exchange rate changes will have longer term effects on aggregate demand and inflation as well. Frequent changes in exchange rates may also be quite disruptive. So while it probably is a good idea for the central bank to pay attention to the exchange rate in its inflation targeting decisions, it probably is not a good idea to try to manipulate the exchange rate to achieve its inflation target.

Appendix to Chapter 11

Mathematical Analysis of the Dornbusch Model

Suppose we have the following dynamic system:

$$\begin{pmatrix} de/dt \\ dp/dt \end{pmatrix} = \begin{pmatrix} a_{11} & a_{12} \\ a_{21} & a_{22} \end{pmatrix} \begin{pmatrix} e(t) - \bar{e} \\ p(t) - \bar{p} \end{pmatrix} \tag{A11-1}$$

where $\bar{e}$ and $\bar{p}$ are the steady-state values of e and p. It is straightforward to write the Dornbusch model in this way. To solve, we conjecture that the solution has the form:

$$e(t) - \bar{e} = A_1 \exp\{\lambda t\},$$
$$p(t) - \bar{p} = A_2 \exp\{\lambda t\}. \qquad \text{(A11-2)}$$

Making the appropriate substitutions in (A11-2), we obtain:

$$\begin{pmatrix} \lambda - a_{11} & -a_{12} \\ -a_{21} & \lambda - a_{22} \end{pmatrix} \begin{pmatrix} A_1 \\ A_2 \end{pmatrix} = 0. \qquad \text{(A11-3)}$$

For (A11-3) to hold for nonzero A_1 and A_2, the determinant of the left-hand side matrix must equal zero, or hence

$$\lambda^2 - (a_{11} + a_{22})\lambda + a_{11}a_{22} - a_{12}a_{21} = 0. \qquad \text{(A11-4)}$$

This is known as the *characteristic equation* of the system. If we define A as the first matrix on the right-hand side of (A11-1), then we can write (A11-4) as

$$\lambda^2 - TR(A)\lambda + \Delta = 0, \qquad \text{(A11-5)}$$

where $TR(A)$ is the trace of the matrix, $a_{11} + a_{22}$, and Δ is its determinant, $a_{11}a_{22} - a_{12}a_{21}$. Solving, we obtain:

$$\lambda = \frac{TR(A) \pm \sqrt{\{TR(A)\}^2 - 4\Delta}}{2}. \qquad \text{(A11-6)}$$

Let the larger solution to (A11-6) be λ_1 and the smaller solution λ_2. Then the solution for the exchange rate can be written:

$$e(t) - \bar{e} = B_1 \exp\{\lambda_1 t\} + B_2 \exp\{\lambda_2 t\}. \qquad \text{(A11-7)}$$

B_1 and B_2 are constants, the values of which can be determined from initial (or possibly terminal) conditions. A similar expression can be derived for the price level. Then there are the following three possibilities:

1. $\lambda_1 > 0, \lambda_2 > 0$. In this case the dynamic system is globally unstable – it will diverge from the steady state regardless of initial conditions. The conditions for this to occur are that $TR(A) > 0$ and $\Delta > 0$.
2. $\lambda_1 > 0, \lambda_2 < 0$. Here the system will be unstable *except* when B_1 is zero, in which case the system is stable, in the sense that it converges to the steady state in the long run. The (necessary and sufficient) condition for this to occur is that Δ is negative. The condition can be interpreted as a condition on the relative slopes of the two loci. This is the saddlepath condition.
3. $\lambda_1 < 0, \lambda_2 < 0$. The system is now globally stable – it will converge to the steady state regardless of initial conditions. The conditions for this to occur are $TR(A) < 0$ and $\Delta > 0$.

Why Does the System Converge to the Steady State?

In other words, why, in the Dornbusch model does the system jump to the saddlepath following a once and for all unanticipated change in the money supply and not follow a divergent dynamic path with ever increasing or decreasing values of p and e? This is a question on which there has been a great deal of literature (see, e.g. Obstfeld and Rogoff, 1986). A way of excluding such bubbles is as follows: clearly, in the model as it stands, there is nothing to rule out a divergent dynamic path, so one needs to add something to exclude such a path. Suppose one added the condition that the exchange rate could not exceed a certain value (e_1, say) which may still be considerably in excess of its current value. Then if the bubble proceeds as previously specified, it will eventually hit e_1 and cannot depreciate any further. With p also having risen considerably, it should be clear from (11-7) that this would be incompatible with equilibrium – the only way in which such a price level would be compatible with equilibrium is if a massive rate of depreciation is anticipated, and this has been ruled out by the assumption that e cannot depreciate any further. Alternatively, suppose we consider the version of the Dornbusch model with endogenous output, then such a high value of p would be compatible with equilibrium in the money market, but only if there were a huge fall in income, which can only be brought about by a huge appreciation of the exchange rate. But an anticipated jump in the exchange rate cannot occur (the moment before the jump, agents would buy or sell the currency in question and the jump would occur then; but then the process repeats itself indefinitely). So it is impossible for the exchange rate to reach such a level; speculators would anticipate this, and not put the economy on this divergent dynamic path in the first place.

In models with maximising agents, the event that would eventually occur that would rule out the bubble can be derived from optimisation – it might be that agents holding the asset in question would be so wealthy that they would sell it and use the proceeds for consumption purposes. Anyway, the structure of the argument is clear – a divergent dynamic path means that something would eventually occur that would be incompatible with equilibrium; speculators with long-run perfect foresight realise this, so do not put the economy on such a path in the first place. Note that the argument does require there to be agents with long-run perfect foresight, whereas in deriving the equations of motion of the basic Dornbusch model nothing more is required than instantaneous perfect foresight.

PROBLEMS

1. Dornbusch Model with Endogenous Output.
   Consider the following version of the Dornbusch model:

$$dp/dt = \pi(y - y_n), \tag{P11-1}$$

$$y = \delta(e - p) + g, \tag{P11-2}$$

$$m = p + \varphi y - \lambda i, \tag{P11-3}$$

$$i = i^* + de/dt. \tag{P11-4}$$

Notation is standard, except for y_n, which can be interpreted as the 'natural rate of output' (and should be assumed constant). The endogenous variables are hence e, p, y and i. Equation (P11-1) is a Phillips curve, stating that inflation is proportional to the difference between actual output (which is now endogenous) and its natural rate. Note that equation (P11-2) simplifies the Dornbusch aggregate demand equation: there is no interest rate effect on aggregate demand, and no propensity to spend out of income. It also states that output is demand determined and hence endogenous in the short run – so the assumption of exogenous output of the original Dornbusch model is relaxed. You may assume that δ, π, ϕ, and λ are all positive.

a. Derive the expressions for the stationaries of the system. (That is, derive equations for $de/dt = 0$ and $dp/dt = 0$ in terms of e, p and the parameters. Note that since y is endogenous, it will be necessary to substitute for it.)

b. Derive expressions for the steady-state price level and exchange rate. Does the model possess long-run monetary neutrality?

c. Using the expression derived in (a), derive expressions for the slopes of the loci representing the stationaries in (e, p) space. (That is, derive expressions for dp/de for both stationaries.) What can be said about the signs of the expressions?

d. Depict the system diagrammatically.

e. Consider the effects of a permanent, yet unexpected increase in the money supply. Assume that e is a 'jump' variable, whereas p is a state variable and cannot jump (i.e. it is instantaneously sticky). Under what conditions will the exchange rate overshoot in response to the change? Illustrate diagrammatically. (You may assume that the system will converge to the steady state in the longer run.) Discuss your results.

2. Anticipated Money Supply Changes in the Dornbusch Model

Suppose there is an anticipated increase in money supply in the Dornbusch model (i.e. at time t_0 it becomes perfectly anticipated that the money supply will increase at time t_1). The economy is initially in the steady state and no other changes in exogenous variables are anticipated. Discuss the behaviour of the exchange rate, price level and interest rate on the adjustment path to the new steady state. Draw an appropriate diagram.

12

The Term Structure of Interest Rates

Often in macroeconomics we talk of 'the' interest rate, as though there is just one interest rate. In fact of course there are a huge number of different interest rates. Reasons why interest rates can differ include the tax treatment of the underlying asset, default risk, tax considerations and time to maturity. In this chapter we focus on issues relating to the 'time to maturity' – by which we mean the time until the bond is redeemed – and we abstract from other reasons why interest rates can differ. (In this chapter we will discuss the term structure of interest rates almost exclusively in terms of interest rates on bonds, whilst recognising of course that there are other assets for which the term structure of interest rates would be applicable.)

The topic of the term structure of interest rates may seem abstract and abstruse, but in fact it is relevant for many household decisions. For example, suppose a household anticipates a certain spending need in ten years' time – for example, suppose it envisages spending on university fees. Then it might save for such expenditure by buying a ten-year bond. But there are alternatives. For example, it could buy a short-term bond (say a six-month bond) and roll the proceeds over into another bond when each bond matures, until the ten years are up. Alternatively, it could buy a longer term bond – say a 30-year bond – intending to sell that after ten years. A household which is taking out a mortgage may be faced with a similar dilemma – should it take out a mortgage at a long-term fixed rate, or borrow using an adjustable rate mortgage, or some other possibility? It would seem clear that the relevant factors determining such a choice are probably expected return (or cost) and risk, but it may not be immediately obvious how these factors interact to determine the term structure of interest rates. Are short-term bonds riskier than longer-term bonds, or vice versa? It seems that we need some sort of theory to determine the relationship between interest rates on bonds of different maturities, and in this chapter we will review some of the theories that economists have developed in order to explain the relationship. In this chapter, Section 12.1 starts by considering the important topic of the definition of the term structure and Section 12.2 discusses why the term structure is of importance. Section 12.3 presents the hypothesis that is central to theories of the term structure, the expectations hypothesis, whereas Section 12.4 considers other theories. Section 12.5 tries to decide which hypothesis is correct and Section 12.6 draws some conclusions for the transmission mechanism of monetary policy.

12.1 Definition of the Term Structure

It is, first of all, necessary to define the term structure of interest rates. A 'strict' definition is as follows: suppose R_i is the yield to maturity of a pure discount bond with maturity i, and i ranges from 1 to T. Then the term structure of interest rates is given by

$$R_1, R_2, R_3, \ldots, R_T.$$

Note that the definition applies to pure discount bonds. A discount bond with a redemption value of £1 and a term of i periods promises to pay £1 i periods hence and its current price is $P_i = \pounds 1/(1 + R_i)^i$. Using the yield to maturity of a coupon bond would not really be appropriate, as a coupon bond is effectively an amalgam of discount bonds of different maturities. For example, a bond that pays £100 each year for ten years and then can be redeemed for £1000 can be thought of as comprising a combination of a one-year discount bond maturing for £100 in a year's time, a two-year discount bond maturing for £100 in two years time and so forth. Also, the bonds should be identical in all respects except for their maturities – they do not differ in risk of default, tax treatment, transactions costs, etc. A diagrammatic representation of the term structure of interest rates is the yield curve. An example is given in Figure 12.1.

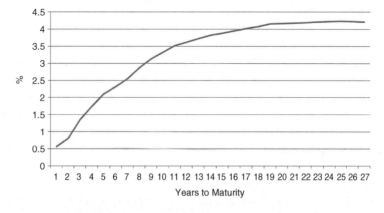

Figure 12.1 The Term Structure of Gilt Yields, 8th July 2011.
(*Source:* Bank of England website, 8/7/11)
Note: This is based on the yields to maturity of a number of gilt-edged securities, not discount bonds. Also, the curve has been drawn connecting a number of distinct points.

Sometimes the concept of *implicit forward rates* is introduced. If one can borrow and lend costlessly at the rates of interest given above, then one can borrow or lend for future time periods by issuing and investing in the appropriate mixture of bonds. For example, if I want to borrow a certain amount for a year in a year's time what I can do is issue a two-year bond and invest the proceeds in a one-year bond. After one year I will receive the maturity value of the one-period bond; in two years' time I will need to redeem the two-year bond, so essentially I am arranging to borrow a certain amount in a year's time, and repay it one year later. The rate at which I am contracting to borrow is given by the implicit forward rate, r_{12}, which is given by the formula $(1 + R_1)(1 + r_{12}) = (1 + R_2)^2$. Other forward rates are defined in an analogous fashion.

Although the strict definition of the term structure involves pure discount bonds, in practice the term structure is often represented by the yields to maturity of other bonds, such as government bonds. This is perhaps because discount bonds are often quite rare. The difference that measuring the term structure in this way makes may not be too important, provided the bulk of the payment associated with the bond is made at maturity.

12.2 Why does the Term Structure Matter?

There are several reasons why the term structure of interest rates is important for policy makers. First of all, and perhaps most significantly, if monetary policy affects the short-term interest rate, but investment depends on the long-term interest rate, understanding the term structure of interest rates is important in helping us understand the transmission mechanism of monetary policy. One would like to know precisely how changing short-term rates can and does affect longer term rates. Possibly, there are other actions the authorities can take to affect longer-term rates, but this depends, of course, on how such rates are determined. Secondly, the term structure may well be relevant for financing the government debt – if short-term interest rates are below long-term interest rates, might the government not reduce the cost of borrowing by borrowing short term? One needs to be careful with this argument. If the yield curve is upward sloping because of expected increases in future short rates, as would be predicted by the expectations hypothesis, for example, it may be impossible for such a policy to reduce the (expected) cost of servicing the national debt permanently, as the lower current cost of servicing the national debt would be offset by an expected increase in the future cost of servicing national debt. But if the expectations hypothesis fails to hold, then it may be possible to reduce the cost of servicing the national debt by issuing the right mixture of short-term and long-term bonds. Thirdly, it has sometimes been argued that the slope of the yield curve may be an indicator of future inflation – e.g. an upward sloping yield curve may mean that nominal interest rates are expected to rise, and this may be because of expectations of an increase in inflation. More generally, the term structure of interest rates may contain important information of relevance to policy makers.

12.3 The Implications of Risk Neutrality: The Expectations Hypothesis

The expectations hypothesis is perhaps the most basic theory of the term structure, stating that long-term rates are the average of the actual and expected future short-term rates over the period to maturity of the longer-term bond. It will hold if there are 'enough' risk neutral agents, who choose between bonds solely on the grounds of their expected returns. It follows that it does not matter, in terms of one's expected return, whether one invests in a sequence of short-term bonds, or just one long-term bond for the life time of one's investment, or any other combination of bonds of differing maturities. So, taking a simple two-period example, if one-period bonds pay 5%, and two-period bonds pay a return of 7% per period, it must be the case that in the second period, one-period bonds are expected to pay about 9%, so that a policy of buying the one-period bond and then, at the start of the second period, using the proceeds to buy another one-period bond will pay exactly the same (expected) return as buying the two-period bonds. The rationale behind the relationship is as follows: suppose this relationship were not to hold, then risk-neutral agents would buy the bond or combination of bonds which paid the higher return, selling those that offer the lower return, and in doing this they would cause expected returns from the different strategies to be equated. Suppose that in the above example, short-term interest rates were expected to remain at 5% in a year's time, then speculators might be expected to buy two-year bonds, financing their purchase by issuing one-year bonds and, in a year's time, issuing more one-year bonds in order to pay off the initial borrowing. They will do this until the expected returns are equated. So we can state the theory as follows, using R_{ij} to denote the interest rate on a bond issued at time i to be redeemed at time j:

$$(1 + R_{02})^2 = (1 + R_{01})(1 + E[R_{12}]). \tag{12-1}$$

Taking logs, and using the approximation that $log(1 + x)$ equals x for small x, we derive

$$R_{02} = \{R_{01} + E[R_{12}]\}/2. \tag{12-2}$$

This states that the two-period interest rate equals the average of the current one-period interest rate plus the one-period interest rate expected to obtain in one period's time. More complicated, but analogous, expressions can be derived for more than two periods. The essential result is that the long rate of interest equals the average of the short rates expected to prevail over the period of the loan. It follows that the yield curve is upward sloping if and only if short-term rates are expected to rise. The hypothesis has seemingly clear-cut implications for the transmission mechanism of monetary policy. The main way in which a cut in short-term rates will affect longer term rates is through changing expectations of future short rates. If a cut in the short-term interest rate does not change expectations, then there will be some reduction in the long-term interest rate, but it will be fairly small. For example, a 1% cut in a six-month interest rate will reduce the ten-year interest rate by about 0.05% under the expectations hypothesis if it does not change expectations of future interest rates. However, if a lower short-term interest rate generates expectations that short rates will be lower in the future, then there will be a greater impact on the long-term interest rate (and hence a greater impact on spending, and so forth); for example, if the change is expected to be permanent, it will translate into an equivalent (i.e. 1%) decline in the longer-term interest rate. Another way consistent with the expectations hypothesis whereby the monetary authorities might seek to change longer term interest rates is through changing expectations about future short rates in other ways, perhaps by making suitable announcements. A point that needs to be borne in mind is that presumably expectations about future short-term interest rates determined by the central bank are influenced by beliefs about how the central bank will behave in the future, which in turn may be affected by observations of how the central bank has behaved in the past. So the central bank needs to take into account, when setting interest rates, the effects of these actions on expectations of its future actions and hence on its ability to affect expectations in the future.

So far, we have not distinguished between real and nominal interest rates; indeed, the theories we discuss in this chapter are models of the nominal term structure, whereas it is generally agreed that it is real interest rates that are relevant for expenditure decisions. However, if there is a fair amount of inertia in inflation, changes in nominal interest rates should translate into (approximately) equivalent changes in real interest rates; if inflation does not exhibit such persistence, then a nominal interest rate increase that signals a tighter monetary policy and hence lowers expectations of future inflation should have a greater effect on future real than on nominal interest rates and hence be more powerful than looking just at nominal rates would suggest.

What are the implications of the expectations hypothesis for the government's financing of the national debt? The answer is that the maturity structure of debt is irrelevant if the government seeks to minimise the expected cost of servicing its debt – if short rates are below long rates, any interest saving in borrowing short will be offset (in expected terms) by higher future short rates.

12.4 The Implications of Risk Aversion: Other Hypotheses of the Term Structure

The expectations hypothesis will hold if 'enough' agents are risk-neutral, so if the hypothesis is to fail, it must be because most agents are risk averse. It is not immediately obvious how risk aversion affects the term structure of interest rates; in fact, there is a plethora of theories. For example, Table 1 on p. 496 of Cuthbertson and Nitzsche (2004) lists six different hypotheses of the term structure. Apart from the pure expectations hypothesis (which is equivalent to what we have called the expectations hypothesis above), there is the constant term premium hypothesis, the liquidity preference hypothesis, the time-varying risk hypothesis, the market segmentation hypothesis and the preferred habitat theory. We will focus our discussion on the preferred habitat theory and the liquidity preference hypothesis, which can be attributed to Hicks.

12.4.1 The Preferred Habitat Theory

The expectations hypothesis assumes that bonds of different maturities are perfect substitutes, so agents will always pick the assets generating the highest expected returns over the period in question. It therefore assumes risk-neutral behaviour by 'enough' agents. The polar opposite assumption, that of extreme risk aversion, underlies the 'preferred habitat' theory, according to which the return on bonds of a given maturity is determined by the supply of, and demand for, bonds of that maturity (which is, of course, always true), and that under no circumstances will agents shift between bonds of different maturities in response to changes in relative expected yields (which is extremely implausible). The yield curve could hence have any shape. (However, the 'preferred habitat' theory does have the implication that an increase in the supply of bonds of any particular maturity should raise the yield to maturity of such bonds.) We would argue in criticism of this theory, that although some agents might display the extreme risk-aversion required for the hypothesis to hold, it is extremely implausible that all, or most agents so behave. Surely there will be some agents who will be willing to shift to holding or issuing bonds of different maturities if expected returns change sufficiently? Also, many agents may have some flexibility in the timing of their future consumption – for example, a couple might be intending to take a cruise after their retirement – and might adjust the timing of their consumption in response to changes in the expected cost of undertaking it. Households who wish to replace furniture, appliances, or cars might likewise have some flexibility in when they do so, and in how much they spend when they do make the purchases. So it seems that the idea that expected rates of return have no effect on the term structure is extremely implausible.

12.4.2 Hicks's Theory

Hicks propounded a theory whereby the long rate will usually exceed the short rate by a 'risk premium'. He argued that borrowers usually want to borrow long, whereas lenders typically want to lend short, so market equilibrium requires the return on long-term lending to exceed that on short-term lending by enough to encourage a sufficient number of lenders to switch from lending short to lending long (see Hicks, 1946, pp. 146–7). The long rate therefore equals the average of expected future short rates plus the term premium, so that instead of (12-2) we have

$$R_{02} = \{\rho + R_{01} + E[R_{12}]\}/2, \qquad (12\text{-}3)$$

where ρ is the 'risk' or 'term' premium. The theory can explain why the yield curve is usually upward sloping. If short-term interest rates are expected to stay constant, then long-term rates will exceed short-term rates because of the term premium. Only if short-term interest rates are expected to decline can the yield curve be downward sloping.

If there is a constant term premium (or at least a term premium the central bank cannot influence), then the hypothesis has exactly the same implications for monetary policy as the expectations hypothesis; however, it does mean the government can reduce the expected cost of its borrowing by issuing short-term, rather than long-term, debt.

Hicks's assumption that borrowers typically prefer to borrow long and lenders prefer to lend short has been questioned. Consider the distinction between 'capital risk' and 'income risk'. If one's main concern is a steady stream of income (e.g. widows and orphans may have this concern), one may prefer to lend long. On the other hand, concern about the value of one's capital may induce one to hold short-term bonds. So it is not necessarily the case that risk aversion implies a premium on long-term bonds.

The above discussion does not take into account price-level uncertainty due to inflation. A long-term bond may guarantee one's income in nominal terms for a long time. However, it certainly does not guarantee its real value. Simple calculations suggest that this may be extremely susceptible to small changes in the rate of inflation. Suppose one is expecting to receive £100 in nominal terms in interest on a bond in 30 years time. Then if inflation is going to average 2% over the next 30 years, the real value of this sum in 30 years time will be £55.21. Inflation of 3% will reduce the real value to £41.20, whereas 10% inflation means that the real value is eroded to just £5.73. Moreover, historically, such rates of inflation are by no means unprecedented. So the *real* income risk on long-term bonds may be considerable.

A further point is that changes in inflation may magnify the capital risk on long-term bonds. Suppose an increase in actual and expected inflation raises nominal interest rates; there is considerable evidence that this happens. Then there is a nominal capital loss on long-term bonds when inflation rises, and over time inflation erodes the real value of the bonds still further.

So price level (and inflation) uncertainty may magnify both the income and capital risk on long-term bonds, and hence imply that, if such bonds are to be held, they need to offer a 'premium'. If changes in short-term interest rates (roughly) reflect changes in the rate of inflation then there is (arguably) much less income and capital risk (in real terms) from holding short-term bonds. This would seem to restore Hicks's theory. However, it can also be questioned whether his hypothesis that risk-averse borrowers prefer to borrow long is correct. Consider a household taking out a mortgage on a property. It may have a choice between a fixed rate mortgage and a variable-rate mortgage. On the former, it pays a fixed-rate rate for the term of the mortgage. On the latter, the interest rate is adjusted periodically according to some formula by the lender. It might seem that the fixed-rate mortgage exposes him to lower risk, but this is not necessarily the case. Suppose shorter-term interest rates vary with the rate of inflation, as postulated by the Fisher hypothesis, and also with the rate of house price inflation. Then by borrowing using the adjustable mortgage, the household hedges against house price inflation risk – if house price inflation is higher than expected, interest payments over the course of the term of the mortgage will be higher as well, but they will be lower if house price inflation is lower, and a risk-averse household might prefer this option. It does not therefore seem possible to say whether there is a positive term premium based solely on these a priori arguments based on risk aversion.

12.5 Which Hypothesis is Correct?

There has been a massive amount of empirical work on the term structure of interest rates, which we do not intend to review here – useful summaries are Shiller (1990) and Cuthbertson and Nitzsche (2004).[1] A major difficulty in testing the theories is, of course, that of measuring expectations. Not only does one need to measure expected future short-term interest rates, but one needs to measure the expectations of those agents whose behaviour is crucial for market equilibrium – i.e. the marginal agents. It seems a fair assessment of the empirical work on the topic to say that it is inconclusive.

However, the expectations hypothesis seems implausible – for example, it seems difficult to explain why the yield curve is usually upward sloping if it holds. If the hypothesis were to hold, then with no clear time trends in interest rates and rational expectations, the yield curve would be as likely to be upward sloping as downward sloping. But it seems equally implausible to suggest that expectations of future short rates have no effect on long rates.

Nevertheless, the following would seem to be a reasonable opinion to take about the term structure of interest rates: something like Hicks's hypothesis is correct, with long rates equal to expected future short rates over the relevant period plus a term premium, which is usually, but not always positive. The term premium depends, in part, on the quantity of bonds of that particular maturity outstanding – if the stock of such bonds increases, their expected return needs to increase to induce enough agents who otherwise would not hold such bonds (in sufficient quantities) to switch to holding such bonds. It seems there is very little evidence on whether increases in the stock of bonds of a particular maturity do affect their yield (relative to other assets).[2] It may be difficult to gather much evidence, since changes in the stock of such bonds may be fairly slow, until more recently, when large budget deficits and quantitative easing have produced large changes in the stock of government bonds held by the public.

12.6 Conclusion

If monetary policy decisions are unexpected but once they have occurred are expected to have some degree of permanence – for example, the central bank raises its policy rate when it was

---

[1]Campbell (1995) is another useful reference.
[2]One study is Gowland and Goodhart (1978), which tried and failed to find supply-side effects of debt management operations on UK long-term yields. Some of the evidence on the effects of quantitative easing is discussed in Chapter 21.

not expected to do so, and where the interpretation of the bank's actions is that it has shifted to a more contractionary monetary policy – then we would expect changes in short-term rates to be reflected in significant changes in long-term rates, with a corresponding impact on spending. Changes in inflationary expectations should mean that the change in real interest rates is greater than the change in nominal interest rates. However, a temporary change in the policy rate (e.g. an interest rate increase takes place one month before it was expected to, without giving rise to changed expectations about interest rates at other future time periods) might not be expected to have much impact on long-term rates, nor will the implementation of a change which had been previously anticipated.

It seems, then, that we would expect changes in short-run interest rates to be effective in affecting economic activity provided they are unexpected and if they are also expected to have some degree of permanence once they have occurred.

PROBLEMS AND DISCUSSION QUESTIONS

1. Suppose that the current and all expected future short-term interest rates are currently 5%; the expectations hypothesis holds so all longer-term interest rates are also 5%. Suppose now that the current interest rate rises to 6%. The interest rate is expected to revert back gradually to a level of 5% as follows:

$$i_j = 0.05 + 0.9(i_{j-1} - 0.05) \qquad \text{(P12-1)}$$

   How does the term structure of interest rates change?

2. If the expectations hypothesis is correct, does quantitative easing (i.e. the purchasing of assets such as long-term government bonds by the central bank) make any sense at all?

3. Suppose there is a term premium on longer-term government bonds which depends, inter alia, on the outstanding quantity of such bonds. What implications does this have for government debt management policy?

13

The Stock Market

O ne of the main ways in which monetary policy affects aggregate demand and hence output is through changing a variety of asset prices, and these changes affect spending in several ways. There are many different assets that might be considered. We would emphasise four: bonds, shares, foreign exchange and property. Changes in bond prices are essentially changes in interest rates and we have discussed how these change consumption spending and investment in Chapters 3 and 4. Changes in bond prices may also have balance sheet effects and impact on investment that way, as discussed in Chapter 10. Effects via the exchange rate were discussed in Chapter 11. In this chapter we concentrate on effects via the stock market. The housing market is considered in the next chapter. There are a number of other assets that might be thought relevant, such as gold and other commodities. However, the prices of such assets are determined in the international market, and as the UK is a fairly small economy there is little that monetary policy can do to affect world prices. Instead, an expansionary monetary policy may raise the domestic currency price of commodities through depreciating the exchange rate and such effects might be described as an 'exchange rate effect'. However, for share prices it is somewhat different. Monetary policy can, we intend to show in this chapter, significantly affect domestic share prices. Given that domestic shares are held mainly by domestic residents, this will raise domestic wealth and hence spending.[1] Foreign share prices might be outside the influence of the Monetary Policy Committee, but inasmuch as domestic residents hold foreign shares, an increase in foreign share prices as well will raise

---

[1]Economists have found it difficult to explain why most equity is held by domestic residents; indeed this is the so-called 'home-bias' puzzle, the literature on which was started by French and Poterba (1991).

domestic wealth and spending, and a depreciation of the exchange rate will raise the domestic value of wealth even more. One could imagine a rather different world – completely different from the one in which we live – in which domestic agents were fully diversified and held mainly foreign shares, in which case a rise in the domestic share price index would have a minimal effect on domestic wealth, although an exchange-rate depreciation would now have a considerable effect on wealth as valued in domestic currency terms.

We start in Section 13.1 by outlining a theory of share price determination, which should shed some light on how monetary policy affects share prices, considered in Section 13.2. Section 13.3 considers the question how share prices affect economic activity and in Section 13.4 we discuss the question whether (and if so how) monetary policy should take share price changes into account. Section 13.5 draws some conclusions.

13.1 The Determination of Share Prices: Efficient Markets, Rational Agents and Bubbles

A useful starting point for explaining the determination of share prices is the standard 'arbitrage' equation:

$$P_t = E_t[P_{t+1} + D_{t+1}]/(1 + r). \tag{13-1}$$

This states that the price of a share at time t equals the discounted present value of the sum of its expected price next period (P_{t+1}) and the dividend expected to be paid to a holder of the share at time $t + 1$, D_{t+1}. We assume that at time t, the dividend has just been paid so it does not enter into the equation. By 'dividend' is meant any payment or benefit the holder derives from holding the share at the time in question. So for shares, the 'dividend' would include the dividend, but in addition if a company returns money to shareholders in any other way (such as a share buyback) or offers shareholders benefits in kind, the monetary value of these would enter into the dividend term as well. The expected price plus dividend is discounted back by the relevant interest rate to obtain the present value.

Why should this equation hold? Let us suppose that agents require an expected return of r to hold the asset. This may well include an allowance for risk. Perhaps they have an alternative to holding the asset and r is the return which if expected on the share would just induce them to hold the share rather than the alternative asset. If the share is expected to produce a return greater than r – that is, if $E_t[P_{t+1} + D_{t+1}] > P_t(1 + r)$ – then they will buy the share and bid the price up, whereas if the inequality is reversed, they will sell it and bid the price down. This process will continue until Equation (13-1) holds and there is no expected excess return from holding the asset. For this to happen there must be some agents with rational expectations, but it is not necessary that all agents have rational expectations – it is sufficient that 'enough' agents have such expectations. Irrational agents[2] might, in the absence of rational agents, cause the price to deviate from its 'efficient' level (i.e. the level given in 13-1) but then rational agents might be expected to perceive the money making opportunity, jump in to make the relevant purchases or sales and hence return the asset price to that given by Equation (13-1).

The equation gives the price of an asset at time t as dependent on, inter alia, its expected price at time $t+1$. We might suppose that this price, in turn, is determined by a formula similar to (13-1), giving the price of the asset at time $t+1$ as the present value (as of time $t+1$) of the expected price plus dividend at time $t+2$, and this might in turn be expected to depend on the expected price plus dividend at time $t+3$, and so on indefinitely. Algebraically, applying (13-1) for the next period and substituting back into (13-1) we get:

$$P_t = E_t \left(\frac{E_{t+1}[P_{t+2} + D_{t+2}]}{(1+r)^2} + \frac{D_{t+1}}{1+r} \right). \tag{13-2}$$

Substituting in turn for $t+2$, $t+3$ and so forth, we obtain

$$P_t = \frac{E_t P_{t+n}}{(1+r)^n} + \sum_{i=1}^{n} \frac{E_{t+i} D_{t+i}}{(1+r)^i}. \tag{13-3}$$

In deriving this equation, we use the so-called 'law of iterated expectations', namely that the expectation of an expectation is just the expectation, or, for example, $E_t[E_{t+1}[x_{t+2}]] = E_t[x_{t+2}]$. If we let n in Equation (13-3) tend to infinity, and suppose we define the fundamental value (F_t) of the share by

$$F_t = E_t \sum_{i=1}^{\infty} \frac{D_{t+i}}{(1+r)^i} \tag{13-4}$$

and its 'bubble' component by

$$B_t = (\lim n \to \infty) \frac{E_t P_{t+n}}{(1+r)^n}, \tag{13-5}$$

then the price of the share is given by

$$P_t = B_t + V_t. \tag{13-6}$$

So the price of a share equals the bubble component plus its fundamental value. If we assume that the bubble term is zero, then we have the Efficient Market Hypothesis (EMH), which states that the price of an asset equals the present value of its expected future stream of

---

[2] By 'irrational' agents we mean all those agents who do not make their decisions as fully rational informed, maximising agents, basing their expectations of the future price of a share on all available relevant information. There are many different ways in which agents may be irrational; noise traders and boundedly rational agents have featured extensively in the literature, but we do not intend to discuss this literature at any length in this chapter.

dividends:

$$P_t = \sum_{i=1}^{n} \frac{E_{t+i} D_{t+i}}{(1 + r_i)^i}.$$

(13-7)

We have written the formula to incorporate the possibility that the discount rate might be time-dependent, so that r_i is the relevant (per-period) discount rate i periods hence. The hypothesis has a number of implications; for example, an asset price changes if and only if its fundamental value changes, which in turn implies that it changes only if either the expected future stream of dividends changes or the discount rate changes. So, according to this approach, asset prices change if and only if there is news, so asset prices are unpredictable ('news' by definition, is unpredictable). Also, large changes in share prices would seem to require large changes in fundamentals.

However, the truth of the EMH depends (in part) on the bubble term being zero, or, equivalently, the present value of the expected price of the asset must go to zero.[3] Why might this be the case? Again, there has been a considerable amount of literature on this, and there seems to be a consensus that, at least in a wide range of economies, there cannot be bubbles with rational agents. The basic idea behind these arguments is that, if there were an asset the value of which grows faster than the discount rate permanently, then the wealth of agents who hold it will also grow indefinitely, and they will eventually want to sell the asset and consume – no agent will want to hold the asset indefinitely. But if it is anticipated that the price of the asset will fall in the far distant future for such a reason, then agents in the not quite so distant future will, anticipating the price fall, also sell the asset and this will lead to an asset price decline at that moment in time. Agents who make their decisions slightly earlier than this will also sell the asset, and so on until we reach the present. The whole process unravels and a bubble does not start in the first place.[4]

It might be noted that this argument against bubbles presupposes there are rational agents whose decisions determine the price of the asset in *all* future time periods. It also requires that agents making their decisions today anticipate the behaviour of agents into the indefinite future. These are demanding requirements. Suppose, instead, that it is anticipated that because of some irrationality agents will bid the price of the share above its efficient level k periods hence. Then the argument against the existence of a bubble collapses – rational agents will bid the price of the asset above its efficient price *now*. So it would seem possible to have bubbles if some agents are irrational. It might also be worth noting that if there is a bubble, it is not irrational to participate in the bubble. Empirical support for this is provided in a remarkable article by Peter Temin and Hans-Joachim Voth (see Temin and Voth, 2004),

---

[3]We would also note that, since share prices cannot be negative, there cannot be a negative bubble, so although share prices may exceed their fundamental values because of bubbles, they cannot fall short of them.

[4]See, for example, Santos and Woodford (1997) for discussion of the conditions under which asset price bubbles are possible.

who obtained records on the behaviour of a bank that participated actively in the South Sea bubble of 1720.

There is a massive amount of literature on the efficient markets hypothesis, which we do not intend to review here. Instead, we would argue, first of all, that the Efficient Markets Hypothesis, interpreted as stating that share prices *always* equal their fundamental values, is clearly wrong (and this statement implies that share prices *sometimes* do not equal their fundamental values, not that they never do). There are many reasons for this conclusion, including the following:

1. There are periods when shares seem massively overvalued compared with their efficient values. An example is the internet price boom that ended in March 2000. Several studies argued persuasively that the share prices of some internet companies were considerably greater than anything that could be reasonably justified on the basis of the present discounted values of their future dividends.[5]

2. Work by Shiller (1981) showed that stock prices moved too much to be justified by subsequent movements in dividends; the relevance of this point is that one can use the EMH to derive predictions about the variability of dividends and of share prices, and these predictions seem to have been falsified. Shiller's work has proved quite controversial and there are a number of technical issues involved. However, it seems that his basic conclusions survive.

3. At the theoretical level, Sanford Grossman and Joseph Stiglitz have proved the impossibility of informationally efficient markets (see Grossman and Stiglitz, 1980). The basic argument is quite simple: suppose the stock market were informationally efficient, and stock prices followed a random walk. Then there would be no incentive for any agent to gather information about the stock market, and hence no information would be gathered. But the EMH does require there to be agents who both acquire and use information; these agents identify 'mispricings' (i.e. deviations of share prices from fundamental levels) and buy or sell the relevant shares as might be appropriate to make an above average return, but in doing so they bring the market back to its fundamental level.

4. Crashes (i.e. large falls in share prices) occur from time to time, for example on Monday 19 October 1987 when the Dow Jones Industrials index fell by 22.6%. Crashes arc not incompatible with the EMH, but the only way they are compatible is if there is a large deterioration in fundamentals (i.e. in the present value of dividends). There did not seem to be any such culprit in this case, and there are examples of other crashes that seem unaccompanied by any such large deterioration in fundamentals.

5. Researchers have unearthed a whole series of 'anomalies' – i.e. movements in share prices that seem to violate the EMH. An example is the well-known January effect, but there are a whole large number of other such anomalies. (See, for example, Siegel, 2002, chapter 12).

6. A number of studies have documented the effects of changes that should not affect share prices according to the EMH but do. An example is a share's inclusion in, or exclusion

---

[5]One reference is Ofek and Richardson (2002).

from, a particular share index, such as the FTSE 100 index in the UK. This index includes the most highly capitalised companies in the UK (i.e. those with the highest stock market capitalisation), and every quarter some companies are removed from the index (because they are taken over or disappear for some other reason or because their market capitalisation falls) and other companies are added to replace them (these will generally be companies whose market capitalisations have risen). The exclusion or inclusion of a company from the index should not affect its share price according to the EMH as it should not affect the present value of its expected stream of dividends. Nevertheless, studies of the shares of companies that are added to or removed from various stock market indices (e.g. Shleifer, 1986) have shown that there is a share price reaction. The reason is that the inclusion of a share within the index means that so-called index funds, which do not actively trade shares but hold portfolios of shares that attempt to replicate the index, need to buy the share. If the EMH is correct, such purchases when a share is included within the index, which can be considerable given the prevalence of index funds, would be offset fully by sales by other investors, but this does not seem to happen.

This is not an exhaustive list of all the deficiencies of the EMH. One should also note some of the strengths of the EMH. There are many share price movements, such as those which happen when a company makes an earnings announcement, that are quite compatible with the EMH. Also, one of the central predictions of the EMH, that one cannot systematically beat the market, seems to be confirmed – for example, studies of the returns earned by so-called investment professionals show that on average they do not beat the market. So what is one to conclude? I believe the following conclusions are warranted:

1. The EMH is correct, at least roughly, much of the time.
2. However, bubbles do occur from time to time; sometimes there can be massive deviations of share prices from their fundamental values for this reason.
3. Bubbles invariably burst. When they do so, share prices may remain overvalued for a period of time until they return to 'fundamentals'.

A few comments are warranted. The statement that the EMH is correct 'roughly' means that there can be departures from strict efficiency because of transactions costs and perhaps some other costs, such as calculation costs, the costs of ascertaining whether a company's shares are undervalued, and if so, by how much. One might imagine that potential investors can freely obtain some information on a company, and this might provide prima facie evidence that the shares might be undervalued, but much further work is required to show whether this is actually the case. In such circumstances the departures from efficiency, and hence the opportunities to make excess profits, have to be great enough to compensate investors for such costs. What these costs do is create a 'band' within which share prices can fluctuate without generating opportunities for excess profits; within these bands, share prices are determined by the interaction of the supply of, and demand for, shares of agents who are trading shares for reasons other than their expectation of their return. This gives the opportunity for various market anomalies to arise – it might be that certain agents have to sell or buy shares for reasons unrelated to their expected return (such as their being included in or excluded from an index), and such actions lead to movement in the share price within the band, without their being any opportunity to make excess expected profits.

Although bubbles can occur from time to time, we do not understand why and how they start and why or how they end. Bubbles do generally seem to start when there is some invention or innovation (such as railways in the 1840s in Great Britain and the internet in the late 1990s), which would under the EMH cause a rise in share prices. However, although the initial rise in prices may be perfectly compatible with the EMH, some agents expect higher returns than is warranted rationally, and bid prices higher; other agents may take advantage of such expected price rises and buy more shares, hence accelerating the process and so forth. Bubble dynamics which would seem to be the result of the behaviour of both rational and irrational agents, can get quite complicated with, in particular, rational agents trying to anticipate the behaviour of irrational agents. However, we do not have adequate theories along these lines. Similarly, we might expect that a bubble collapses when 'enough' agents decide a share is overvalued and sell; the bubble may halt temporarily, and other agents who previously were in the market merely because of their expectations of future capital gains also sell, and this precipitates a collapse, but again making this precise is not at all easy.

Note that we have suggested that after the collapse of a bubble share prices can remain above their 'efficient' levels for some period of time. We might describe this as a 'bear' market, characterised by the following condition:

$$P_t > E_t[P_{t+1} + D_{t+1}]/(1 + r). \tag{13-8}$$

No rational agent will hold the share in these circumstances, so shares are held exclusively by irrational agents. However, it must also be the case that rational agents cannot exploit this market inefficiency to make money by selling the shares short. But there are several reasons why short selling may be expensive, risky and, in some circumstances impossible because of legal and institutional constraints. In short, there may be short-selling constraints.[6]

The above theory of the stock market is compatible with the impossibility of systematically making excess returns on the stock market.

13.2 Monetary Policy and Share Prices

We now consider how monetary policy might affect share prices. Suppose, firstly, that the EMH holds, so (13-7) shows how share prices are determined. There are hence two, and only

---

[6]See, for example, Jones and Lamont (2002).

two, ways in which monetary policy might affect share prices. Specifically, it might work by affecting either the discount rate or expected dividends.

The discount rate in turn as the sum of the relevant risk-free rate plus a risk premium, so we can write the relevant discount term for dividends to be received i periods in the future is $R_i + \Delta_i$, where R_i is the i-period interest rate and Δ_i is the relevant risk premium. If we consider that monetary policy is implemented through changing the short-run interest rate, then the extent to which it affects the ith period discount rate depends on the extent to which it is perceived to be permanent. (Our discussion of the term structure of interest rate in Chapter 12 is relevant here.) So if monetary policy moves just the short-run interest rate, it will change asset prices only through its effect on the present value of short-term dividends, which is unlikely to be very large. Also, there is a possibility that it might affect the risk premium. As far as expected dividends are concerned, there might well be an effect; suppose monetary policy stimulates the economy, then this is likely to raise spending; many firms may experience an increase in their profits and hence be expected to pay higher dividends. So we might conclude that monetary policy raises share prices inasmuch as it reduces both longer term and shorter term interest rates, and inasmuch as it stimulates economic activity and spending (and therefore expected dividends).

What happens now if we admit the possibility of share price bubbles? Monetary policy might affect the bubble term, although how it might do this is not entirely clear, since we do not have a workable theory of bubbles which would enable us to assess such effects. One might conjecture that an abundance of cheap credit might create a bubble if other preconditions are met, and restrictions of credit in a bubble that has lasted some time might well cause a collapse, but more than this it is difficult to say. So an expansionary monetary policy may raise share prices either by raising the fundamental value of shares or by creating or strengthening a bubble, or both. If it does both, the effect could well be sizeable.

On the other hand, what happens if share prices are above their fundamental levels, as suggested as a possibility above? This might occur in the aftermath of a bubble collapse, with shares held exclusively by irrational agents and rational agents are unable to exploit the overvaluation because of short-selling constraints. It might be that in these circumstances monetary policy has no effect on share prices – the effect depends solely on how the expectations of irrational investors are affected, and it is almost impossible to say how these will change.

An expansionary monetary policy need not always raise share prices. Suppose it is expected to lead merely to higher inflation with associated negative real effects, then it might well cause a fall in share prices. So whether an expansionary monetary policy does or does not raise share prices is an extremely complicated question – it may depend on whether agents believe that the monetary policy is correct or a mistake.

Given the complexity of the relationship between monetary policy and share prices it is not at all surprising that empirical work attempting to uncover such a link has not been too successful.

13.3 The Effects of Share Price Changes

There are perhaps two main ways in which an increase in share prices might affect spending in the economy. Firstly, it might increase investment spending, since firms will find it cheaper to raise equity capital. Secondly, it raises the wealth of shareholders, and hence might be expected to raise their spending. In fact, as pointed out by Poterba (2000), it follows from the household's intertemporal budget constraint that an increase in wealth must lead to an increase in consumption sometime over its lifespan, with the implausible exception of a household that bequeaths the entire amount of the increase in wealth to the next generation. The effect of an increase in share prices on consumption is basically an empirical question. Poterba surveys the evidence, and it seems that a marginal propensity to consume out of wealth of about 0.03 is a rough consensus estimate for the effect of stock market gains on consumption. However, Case, Quigley and Shiller (2005) find a minimal effect of stock market changes on consumption.

13.4 Should the Monetary Authorities Attempt to Stabilise Share Prices?

Bubbles may be harmful for a number of reasons. They may distort resource allocation, as more resources are sucked into the sectors experiencing the bubble than would be efficient. Their collapse (which is inevitable since bubbles always collapse) may cause significant redistribution of wealth and in some cases give rise to a financial crisis. They may also complicate the task of macroeconomic management, given that the effects of a share price collapse on aggregate demand may be highly uncertain. But how should they be tamed, if not eliminated? Should monetary policy be used for this purpose, or are there other ways of tackling them? It might also be noted that share prices might fluctuate considerably because of fluctuations in their fundamental value, and since monetary policy can (as argued above) affect the fundamental value of shares, so we might ask whether we should try to stabilise the level of share prices even if such fluctuations are due to fluctuations in fundamental values.

It has often been suggested that central banks should seek to stabilise asset price bubbles. One might ask first of all whether an inflation targeting central bank should do this as part of its inflation mandate or whether this is something it should do in addition, providing it is meeting its inflation target. One might also ask whether it should try to stabilise share prices about their fundamental levels (i.e. to try to eliminate, or at least mitigate, departures from efficiency such as bubbles and crashes) or whether it is fluctuations about some particular reference level of the stock market that the bank should be concerned about. If the former, then there is the non-trivial problem of determining what the efficient level of stock market prices actually is.

An inflation targeting central bank should, as part of its mandate, take into account stock market behaviour at least to some extent in assessing its policy since a stock market boom may lead to higher spending and higher inflation, hence requiring a tighter monetary policy, and its actions by-product to meet its inflation target will also have consequences for share prices. But suppose it is meeting its inflation mandate with room to spare, and has some discretion as to what to do with interest rates. It could raise them slightly if it wanted to curtail a bubble or decrease them slightly if share prices were unusually depressed but why should it do this? The answer would have to be that there may be benefits from stabilising share prices over and above those of meeting its inflation target. As there probably are some benefits from stabilising share prices in addition to those of meeting the inflation target (as argued above), it would not be unreasonable to argue that while the primary focus of the central bank must be on meeting its inflation target, it should in addition, and if it can without prejudice to meeting the inflation target, put at least some weight on reducing share price fluctuations in its decisions.

13.5 Conclusion

Unfortunately we do not have a very satisfactory understanding of how share prices are determined, and in particular how and why bubbles start and collapse. Nevertheless, there should be little doubt about the direction of monetary policy changes on share prices, at least within a credible inflation targeting regime – i.e. interest rate reductions should boost share prices – and inasmuch as such changes affect spending decisions, this is one of the many ways in which monetary policy decisions may impact on the real economy.[7] So we feel justified in concluding that monetary policy should certainly take share price movements into account in making its decisions, and perhaps seek to reduce excessive fluctuations in their prices if it can do so without prejudicing its other goals.

DISCUSSION QUESTIONS

1. Is there such a thing as a 'rational' bubble?
2. Does the existence of Warren Buffett disprove the Efficient Markets Hypothesis?
3. Should policy seek to eliminate bubbles in share prices, or seek to reduce fluctuations in share prices even if these are due to changes in fundamentals?

---

[7]If we do not have a credible inflation targeting regime, things may be different – an expansionary monetary policy may be expected to lead to higher inflation and the stock market may fall as a consequence.

14

The Housing Market

T he housing market, in particular, is often believed to be important in the transmission of monetary policy, yet this market is hardly discussed at all in most monetary policy textbooks. There are a number of reasons why the housing market is of interest; for example, there have been large changes in both nominal and real house prices in the United Kingdom in the post-war period. Figure 14.1 shows real house prices (i.e. house prices divided by the retail price index) from 1975 to 2010; between 1977 and 2007 they approximately tripled.

The role of housing in the 2007–2009 credit crunch and recession is also something that needs to be considered. House price increases may stimulate spending and hence raise output, but expectations of rising incomes may raise house prices, so there may well be relationships in both directions between economic activity and house prices. In this chapter we discuss some of the ways in which the housing market may play a role in the transmission mechanism of monetary policy and consider some related policy issues. There are a number of ways in which the housing market may affect spending in the economy, and it is important to distinguish between these different mechanisms. It should be emphasised that when analysing the impact of housing on the economy, we should consider both direct and indirect effects. Housing investment (the building of houses together with repair, refurbishment and maintenance spending) enters directly into GDP. However, there may be indirect effects as well, if, for example, non-housing consumption spending is affected by an increase in house prices. In fact, we discuss no fewer than six possible ways in which house price changes may affect economic activity.

Figure 14.1 Real House Prices in the UK.
(*Source:* Nationwide Building Society and Office for National Statistics)

14.1 The (non?) Wealth Effect of Higher House Prices

Sometimes the following argument is presented: 'Housing prices are an important component of wealth which . . . affects consumption spending. Hence expansionary monetary policy . . . which raises housing prices . . . also raises household wealth . . . which raises consumption spending . . . and aggregate demand . . . ' (Mishkin, 2007, p. 62). However, we need to be careful with this argument. Consider a household that does not intend to move house. Then a rise in house prices, holding other variables constant, will not affect the household's intertemporal budget constraint at all and hence should not affect its behaviour. What is wrong, then, with the Mishkin argument? The basic point would be that although a rise in house prices does, obviously, raise the value of an asset the household owns and thus increases its wealth, this does not change its consumption (of non-housing items) as the price of consuming housing services rises and this absorbs the increase in wealth. So the rise in house prices may increase the household's overall level of consumption, but the increase consists entirely of the increased value of its consumption of its own-housing services; it does not increase spending on non-housing items and hence aggregate demand is unchanged.[1]

---

[1] For further discussion of this argument, see Buiter (2010).

For households who do not intend to consume the same level of housing for the rest of their lives, there can be positive or negative wealth effects. The following very simple framework may shed some light on this question. Suppose there are two goods that a household consumes: housing (h) and general consumption goods (C). The relative price of housing (the ratio of the price of housing to that of general consumption goods) is q. Suppose the household has an initial endowment of $\bar{h}$ units of housing and y units of the consumption good. Then its budget constraint can be written:

$$y + q\bar{h} = C + qh. \tag{14-1}$$

Let us suppose, further, that it has a utility function $U(C, h)$ and also, to isolate the wealth effects of a change in house prices, that the utility function is Leontief, so that the household consumes the goods in fixed proportions. Let us assume that it consumes them in equal proportions, or $C = h$. This can be interpreted as a normalisation. Then carrying out the appropriate maximisation of utility subject to the budget constraint we obtain:

$$h = C = \frac{(y + q\bar{h})}{(1 + q)}. \tag{14-2}$$

For the effect of a change in the real price of housing on (non-housing) consumption[2] (which can be described as the wealth effect of the increase in the real price of housing), we can derive:

$$\frac{\partial C}{\partial q} = \frac{\bar{h} - y}{(1 + q)^2}. \tag{14-3}$$

What this equation tells us is that the effect will be positive if the household's initial endowment of housing is greater than its endowment of income, which means that in this case the household will want to 'trade down' and consume less housing than its endowment. If the household wants to do the opposite, then the effect will be negative. But since, on average, households can neither trade up nor trade down, this implies that the aggregate net wealth effect is zero.

Consider an example. Suppose there are two households, each of whom is currently living in a house valued at £200 000. But suppose the first household (perhaps a couple about to retire) intends to downsize, and exchange their property for one worth half the price. The second household (expecting a significant increase in their income in the next few years) intends to move to a property worth 50% more. Then after having made their respective property transactions, the first household realises £100 000 which presumably it can use to increase its consumption over its lifespan whereas the second household has to reduce its lifetime spending by the same amount. Suppose that house prices double. Each household now owns a house worth £400 000. Abstracting from moving costs and other transactions costs, the first household will now realise £200 000 (instead of £100 000) which will be available for

---

[2]We shall henceforth in this chapter use the word 'consumption' to mean 'non-housing consumption'.

consumption when it trades down and buys a house for £200 000; the second has to find an extra £200 000 (instead of £100 000) when it moves from a house worth £400 000 to one costing £600 000. So it can be seen that the effects in aggregate cancel.

It seems then the contention that there cannot be an 'aggregate' wealth effect from a rise in house prices is basically correct. However, there still may be a net wealth effect if the marginal propensity to spend on consumption goods differs between households – for example, those who lose may contract their spending more (because of credit constraints) than those who benefit.

14.2 The Substitution (or Relative Price) Effect of Higher House Prices

When the price of housing rises relative to other goods and services, we would expect households to substitute away from housing towards the consumption of other goods and services. For example, a household approaching retirement might 'trade down' to a cheaper house and use the remaining money derived from selling the house for consumption purposes. A household which is contemplating buying a house might react to an increase in house prices in several ways. It might decide not to buy a house after all, but continue renting, and hence consume more. It might, on the other hand, postpone the purchase of a house and/or buy a cheaper property, hence attenuating the affect on consumption. Note that for a household trading down, a rise in house prices unambiguously raises consumption, with both the wealth effect and the relative price effect causing expenditure to switch from housing to non-housing goods. However, for a household intending to trade up, (and this of course includes those who do not currently own a house) the overall effect is ambiguous.

The following simple framework, which extends that presented in the previous section, may shed some light on this issue. Let us suppose that the household's utility function, instead of being Leontief, is Cobb-Douglas:

$$U = h^{\alpha} C^{1-\alpha}. \tag{14-4}$$

The maximisation subject to the budget constraint gives the following equations for demand for housing services and for consumption:

$$qh = \alpha[y + q\bar{h}]. \tag{14-5}$$

$$C = (1 - \alpha)[y + q\bar{h}]. \tag{14-6}$$

Here, an increase in house prices increases consumption and will reduce demand for housing services, except for a household that initially holds no housing at all. So it seems that Mishkin's argument can be made sound if 'raises household wealth' is replaced by 'raises the relative price of housing'. In fact, equation (14-5) is a simplified version of the relationship one might estimate if one believed that wealth effects were important in housing and one might interpret the coefficient estimated as the 'wealth elasticity of the demand for housing'.

We should point out that the above framework is static; applying it to an intertemporal context, we would interpret C as lifetime consumption, so that a permanent increase in house prices might be expected to raise the intertemporal time profile of consumption by a fraction of the increase. A temporary change in house prices might be expected to have a much smaller effect.

14.3 A Simple Model of the Housing Market

In order to help us think about the effect of monetary policy on housing, it is helpful, as often is the case, to use a model. Here we describe a model due to Peter Sinclair (see Sinclair, 2005, pp. 35–9) that enables us to analyse the dynamics of house prices.

We start off with what is essentially a supply curve of housing:

$$\delta H + \dot{H} = f(q). \tag{14-7}$$

The right-hand side is the supply of houses – essentially how many are built in a given time period. This depends simply on the real price of housing, q, the price of houses divided by some overall price index. So $f(q)$ is the supply function of housing; we would expect it to be increasing in q but do not impose any further restrictions. It could be that factors such as planning restrictions make supply fairly inelastic with respect to price. The left-hand side of (14-7) tells us that the houses supplied either offset the depreciation of the housing stock, or add to the net stock of housing. (H is the stock of housing and δ the rate at which the housing stock depreciates.) Equation (14-7) is depicted in Figure 14.2.

The curve labelled $\dot{H} = 0$ shows the combinations of values of q and H for which the stock of housing is constant. A greater stock of housing means that the total depreciation of the housing stock is greater and more houses need to be built to keep the housing stock constant. Therefore an increase in H needs to be accompanied by a rise in q to keep H constant.

A second equation gives the demand for housing. Let us suppose (a very simple assumption), that households allocate a constant fraction of their incomes to housing:

$$QH = kY. \tag{14-8}$$

Q is the rental price of housing, or the cost of consuming housing services over a period of time. Its definition is discussed in the Appendix to this chapter, where it is shown that it takes the form:

$$Q \equiv q(r + \delta - \dot{q}/q). \tag{14-9}$$

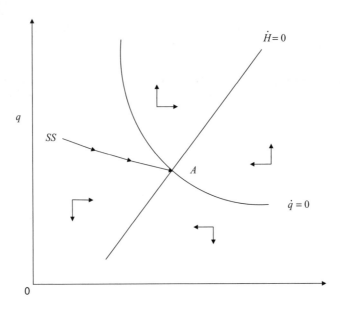

Figure 14.2   The Sinclair Model of the Housing Market.

Here r is the real rate of interest. So the rental price of housing depends positively on the real interest rate and on depreciation, but negatively on the expected change in real house prices.

Combining Equations (14-8) and (14-9) and rearranging them, we obtain the following dynamic equation for the real price of housing:

$$\dot{q} = q(r + \delta) - kY/H. \tag{14-10}$$

Equations (14-7) and (14-10) constitute a two-equation dynamic system in q and H, and can be analysed using phase diagrams. Consider Figure 14.2. The $\dot{H} = 0$ locus, derived from (14-7), shows the combinations of q and H which are compatible with zero net investment in housing (a constant housing stock). To the right of the locus, H is falling and vice versa to the left. This is shown by the horizontal arrows in the diagram. The $\dot{q} = 0$ locus shows the combinations of q and H which are compatible with no change in the real price of housing, q. From (14-10) this is easily seen to be a rectangular hyperbola. To the right of the locus, $\dot{q}$ is positive, so q is increasing; this appears to be a destabilising force. Looking at the diagram, it is apparent that the system has a saddlepath, but other dynamic paths are divergent. The saddlepath is labelled SS and we shall assume that the system follows the saddlepath to the steady state. Reasons for assuming that the system does converge to the steady state were discussed in our earlier chapter on the Dornbusch model (Chapter 11) and we shall make such an assumption here. An assumption of long-run perfect foresight is perhaps sufficient for such a conclusion. But we would point out that were such an assumption not made, we could follow a divergent dynamic path for a period until speculators realised that the path was divergent; in this way we could have a bubble which would in due course collapse.

We can use this framework in the standard way to analyse the effects of various shocks. Consider, for example, the effects of a permanent, unanticipated, fall in the real interest rate (r). Suppose the system is initially in a steady state, with just replacement house building taking place. Then the interest rate change shifts the $\dot{q} = 0$ locus rightwards; there is no reason for the $\dot{H} = 0$ locus to shift. The saddlepath associated with the new dynamic system lies above the initial steady state and if the system is to converge to its new steady state it must move to this saddlepath instantaneously. How is it to do so? We suppose that q is a 'jump' variable but H is instantaneously sticky, and this means there must be a vertical movement in q. After the price has jumped up, it then follows the new saddlepath, with real house prices falling and the stock of houses rising, until the steady state is reached. The amount of house building is given by the supply curve which in turn depends on the real price of housing. It follows that the impact of the change on house building and hence on aggregate demand is greatest instantaneously and gradually wears off. It should be pointed out, however, that even in the new steady state, house building is higher than in the old steady state. This is because the new steady state has a higher stock of houses than the original steady state and hence replacement housebuilding needs to be greater as well.

Other (positive) shocks to the demand for housing would have similar effects, with an instantaneous jump in house prices followed by a gradual reversion to the new steady state. Of course, shocks are unlikely to be permanent. It is straightforward to analyse the effects of a temporary shift in demand in this framework.

The framework captures a number of important features of the housing market, in particular emphasising that the adjustment path to a shock may be complex and take some time to work itself out. However, it does not explicitly incorporate several other important aspects of the housing market, in particular transactions costs and liquidity constraints. In the following sections, we will consider the implications of introducing such features.

14.4 Transactions Costs and Housing

When people buy property, they often pay solicitors' and surveyors' fees, employ moving firms and spend money on household goods such as carpets, furniture and curtains after they move in. In the United Kingdom, there is a tax (stamp duty) payable by purchasers on the price of the property purchased. The costs of looking for, finding and contracting to buy a property are not at all trivial, and the whole process is time consuming and stressful. Sellers also incur certain costs, such as their estate agent's fees (if they are employed). All these costs can be regarded as the transactions costs of buying and selling property.

Inasmuch as these costs involve purchasing goods and services, they contribute to aggregate demand. These costs are related to the turnover of the housing stock, but there are reasons to believe that when the housing market is more buoyant, turnover is higher. One reason for this is that in order to buy a house, one typically has to make a down payment, and the higher a household's house is valued, then the more they will be able to use as a down payment when they move. The reverse phenomenon, of households entering into 'negative equity' (the value of their house is less than the value of the mortgage used to buy the house) so they may be essentially 'locked in' and unable to move, is familiar to many households in the UK. (A model with these properties is described in Stein, 1995.) So given that there is a positive relationship between house prices and turnover, another way in which higher house prices may contribute to raising aggregate demand is through increased spending on these transactions costs as the volume of property transactions increases.

Transactions costs also mean that the housing market is unlikely to be efficient (in the technical sense of efficiency discussed in Chapter 13); they also mean that the decision to buy a house is generally a long-term decision, so it is longer term changes in housing prices that are likely to have significant effects on consumption behaviour, of the type we have considered in Section 14.2 above.

14.5 Collateral Effects of Increased Housing Wealth

If the value of a household's main asset rises, it has more collateral and is able to borrow more; moreover any credit constraint to which it might be subject is relaxed. So we might expect a rise in house prices to raise consumption for this reason. However, it might be emphasised, given the household's intertemporal budget constraint, that if it does raise expenditure in the short term, that expenditure will need to be lower in the longer term if households are to balance their books. Also, when house prices rise, banks may be more confident about the value of their mortgages secured on such assets, so may increase their lending for this reason. Again, these effects are likely to be temporary, and be reversed in the longer term, as the loans are repaid. Although these effects may be temporary, they can still be quite large.

Things may be slightly different when we consider the effects of falls in house prices. Consider a household that, because of a temporary fall in its income, cannot keep up with its mortgage payments and its property is repossessed by the mortgage lender. Then if the lender cannot recoup the amount it is owed by selling the house, then it can (in the UK) pursue the household for the remainder of its debt, and this may impose a permanent, negative wealth effect on this household and hence its lifetime consumption falls. So there may be an asymmetry between increases and decreases in house prices on consumption, with the latter having a greater effect. Note that for this effect to operate, lenders have to be able to pursue borrowers for debt remaining after the property has been sold and the proceeds used to pay off the loan. Technically, lenders have 'recourse' and this is usually the case in the UK. In contrast, in the US, mortgage debt is often 'non-recourse', meaning that the lender cannot pursue the borrower for anything more than the amount the collateral (the house) realises when sold (although this may not apply in all states).

14.6 Empirical Evidence on the Causes and Effects of House Price Changes

There is, as might be expected, such a huge amount of empirical work on housing that we cannot even begin to review it in any depth. Instead, we shall just mention and discuss briefly a number of relevant studies. Case *et al.* (2005) study a panel of 14 countries and of US states and conclude that there is a 'statistically significant and rather large effect of housing wealth upon household consumption' (abstract). In the international study, the elasticity of consumption with respect to housing wealth is between 0.11 and 0.17. Campbell and Cocco (2007) use household level data and find that older homeowners have an elasticity of consumption to house prices increases as high as 1.7, whereas younger renters have an elasticity insignificantly different from zero. (These are the largest and smallest elasticities uncovered.) Goodhart and Hoffman (2008) carry out a fixed-effects panel VAR for 17 countries for the period 1970–2006. They find a significant multidirectional link between house prices, broad money, private credit and the macroeconomy. Moreover, the linkages are greater in the 1985–2006 subperiod than the earlier one, which they interpret as reflecting the effects of financial liberalisation. And also 'the effects of shocks to money and credit on house prices are stronger when houses prices are booming than otherwise' (Goodhart and Hoffman, 2008, p. 202). It is not clear how to interpret this result. Aron *et al.* (2010) estimate consumption functions for UK, US and Japanese households, and emphasise the difference between Japan, where there has been little household credit liberalisation since the 1970s, and the UK and the US, where there has been massive credit liberalisation over this period. Higher house prices seemed to boost consumption spending in the UK and US, but not in Japan, suggesting that it is the collateral effects of higher house prices that are important in explaining their impact on consumption.

14.7 Should Policy Seek to Reduce or Stabilise House Prices and if so How?

It can be argued that it would be a good idea if house prices could be stabilised, or at least if bubble/bust cycles in house prices could be avoided, and also if house prices could, on average, be lower in real terms. There are several reasons for this:

1. Volatility and large changes in house prices might (almost certainly will) result in arbitrary and unfair redistribution of wealth. For example, the massive increase in real house prices in the UK in the last few decades has meant a considerable transfer of wealth towards those who purchased houses early in this period or already were home-owners at the beginning of the period and away from those who purchased houses late in the period, or who have yet to purchase property. Some who might otherwise have bought property may decide not to do so, and to rent permanently; such individuals still suffer if their rents are higher because of the property price increase. Also, those households who lose their

houses because they are unable to pay their mortgages suffer. House price increases may also mean a considerable intergenerational redistribution of resources.

2. A bubble in an asset price will result in a misallocation of resources; there will be excessive investment in a (reproducible) asset if its price is above its 'equilibrium level'. In the case of housing, there may also be a distortion in the choice households might face between owner-occupation and renting. The choice between these two types of tenure may be quite complicated – a number of factors that should influence the choice, and reasons why the choice might not be socially optimal, are given in Appendix B.

3. House price volatility has contributed significantly to many financial crises. If the bubble in an asset price is financed (largely) by borrowing, a collapse in the asset price may cause severe financial difficulties for many lenders, with possibly severe spillover effects on the rest of the economy.

4. The contribution of house price changes to aggregate demand is uncertain but may be quite strong; if house price fluctuations could be reduced this might well make the task of demand management much easier.

It is not clear whether it would be desirable to stabilise the price of an asset about a constant level or about its efficient level, if, indeed, it is desirable to stabilise it at all. If its efficient level changes, it might be thought desirable if the actual price follows the efficient price – this will avoid the misallocation of resources referred to in (ii). We will take it that the desirable policy is to stabilise the price about its efficient level, to prevent bubbles and crashes taking place, but this then of course raises the question how one identifies changes in the efficient price. In practice, the most that can or should be done is probably to reduce large and obvious overvaluations and undervaluations, and to prevent and mitigate rapid increases or falls in house prices. But if this is the case, how should this be done? We have already discussed how monetary policy should be used to stabilise stock prices in the previous chapter, and much of that discussion is relevant here. There are several suggestions which might more specifically be relevant for the housing market:

1. Changing the cost of property transactions

Sometimes a tax has been suggested as a way of curbing speculative activity on asset sales or purchases: the most notable example is that of a 'Tobin tax', intended to combat speculative activity in the foreign exchange market. At the moment there is a tax on the purchase of houses in the UK, Stamp Duty. Might this be increased as a way of improving the behaviour of the housing market? The answer to this question must be an emphatic 'no'. It is not clear whether such a tax would be stabilising or destabilising. Indeed, Friedman long ago produced an argument that one would expect speculation to be stabilising, arguing that rational speculators would buy when the price is low and sell when the price is high, and this would tend to be stabilising (see Friedman, 1953, p. 175). However, this argument is not necessarily correct – rational speculators should buy when they expect the price to rise, and sell when they expect the price to fall, which is not exactly the same as 'buy cheap and sell dear'. In an important contribution, Hart and Kreps (1986) produce an example where speculation can be price destabilising with rational expectations and perfect competition. However, all this shows is that rational speculation may be price destabilising, not that it must be. Whether speculation is in fact stabilising or destabilising is an empirical question, but this seems to be something on which there is no definitive evidence.

However, on other grounds, increasing the costs of buying and selling houses must be considered undesirable. Such costs reduce labour mobility, and in doing so may raise unemployment. It may also impede labour re-allocation, hence reducing long-run growth. So we would conclude that there is no case at all for increasing the cost of transacting in the housing market; in fact, it would seem appropriate to reduce these costs so as to improve the workings of the labour market.

2. A Property Tax

There is a property tax in the United Kingdom used to finance local government called council tax; it is based on 1991 property values, and properties are allocated to one of eight different bands, depending on their 1991 value. Local authorities determine their own rates of property tax, but the ratios between the amounts paid on properties in the different bands are determined by central government. For example, the amount charged on properties in the highest band (Band H) is exactly double that charged in one of the intermediate bands, Band D; the lowest amount that can be charged is on Band A properties, and this is two-thirds the amount that is charged on Band D properties.

It might be preferable to introduce a revised system of council tax, where the tax is based on an estimate of market value, with the tax rate a percentage of this value. The question arises as to how these valuations will be arrived at. Actual sales prices could be used where possible, with valuations updated using figures for house price changes for regions and for types of property. The basic point is that such a scheme would be stabilising as far as house prices are concerned. (The scheme would have a number of other merits, which we do not go into here.) Suppose the rate of tax is 1%, and someone is contemplating increasing the offer he makes on a house by £1000. Then if he does this, and the offer is accepted, then he will have to pay an extra £10 a year for as long as he lives in the house (and this amount would be increased as the valuation is increased in line with any formula that is used to uprate property prices.) So this should reduce the extra amount he will be willing to offer for the house, and hence have a stabilising effect on house prices.

However, it is not clear how stabilising such a tax would be; one would guess that it would have some stabilising effect, but not a large effect, and it could be used in combination with other measures also designed to stabilise property prices.

3. A Maximum Loan to Value (LTV) Ratio

The way this would operate is as follows: mortgages would be restricted to a certain percentage of the value of the property, say 80%, so if a property is bought for £100 000, the largest mortgage a buyer would be allowed to take out to help finance the purchase would be £80 000. This should lead to a lower level of house prices; it might also reduce the magnitude of house prices booms which are typically accompanied by increases in actual LTV ratios, and this would not happen, or at least would be limited, under this scheme. It might be possible also to alter the maximum LTV ratio to offset housing booms and busts, raising the ratio in a housing bust and lowering it in a boom.

Even if a maximum LTV ratio does not reduce the variability of house prices, it should mean that any given fall in house prices should be less costly for the banking sector, and hence less likely to cause some of the financial sector problems we have witnessed in the 2007–2009 financial crisis and its aftermath. With an LTV ratio of 80% in force, house prices would have to fall by at least 20% from their previous peak before banks would even start to be adversely affected by defaults on mortgages. In practice, they would have to fall much more before they seriously threatened a bank's solvency. Since almost certainly not all of a bank's mortgages will have been issued when house prices were at their previous peak, and since many borrowers will have paid back some of what they initially borrowed, most mortgages should be well under 80% of the previous peak value of the house in question, so house prices would have to fall by a considerable amount before they had any significant effect on banks' solvency.

Although a maximum LTV ratio would almost certainly reduce house prices, it is not clear that it would benefit new house buyers, who would need to put up higher deposits. But they may still benefit. For example, a new buyer might be able to buy a house for £100 000 with a maximum LTV of 80% in force, so she would need to put down a deposit of £20 000 as well as take out a mortgage of £80 000 to purchase the property. With no such scheme in force, the house might cost £120 000, but the purchaser might be able to borrow 90% of the cost, so would need to take out a mortgage of £108 000 as well as put down a deposit of £12 000. So with the LTV scheme in place, the household does need to save an extra £8000 for a deposit, but would need to borrow £28 000 less. A household would have to have a very high discount rate not to prefer this. It can be argued (see Ortalo-Magné and Rady, 2006) that the amount of down payments households can put down can have a very significant effect on house prices.

4. Increasing the Supply of Housing

The supply of housing in the United Kingdom is heavily constrained by planning restrictions. This is not the place for an extensive discussion of whether and how such restrictions should be eased.[3] We would point out that increasing the supply of housing (by which we mean shifting the supply curve of housing, by making more housing available at any given real price of housing) may have a considerable effect on the price of housing. For example Muellbauer and Murphy (1997) estimate a (long-run) price elasticity of demand for housing of -0.52 implying that a 10% increase in the housing stock would reduce the real price of housing by 19%. However, it is very difficult to do much to change the stock of housing in the short term – given the longevity of the stock of housing, the amount of housing built in any one year is trivial compared with the total stock. Nevertheless, over a period of several years, it might be possible to increase the stock by (say) 5%, reducing the real price of housing by nearly 10%, so it should be possible to use supply side policies to stabilise house price fluctuations at least to some extent. There is the additional point that inasmuch as such policies are anticipated and expected to reduce house prices (and house price growth) they should reduce current house prices – it is straightforward to use the Sinclair model presented in Section 14.3 to show this.

---

[3]The question has been addressed in the Barker Reports of 2004 and 2006. See Barker (2008) for discussion and references.

14.8 Conclusion

We would conclude that housing and house prices do play an important role in the macro-economy and in the transmission of monetary policy. An expansionary monetary policy might be expected to raise house prices and this should raise economic activity in a number of different ways. There might be a permanent (relative price) effect on consumption, but only if the increase in relative house prices is expected to be fairly long lasting. There may be effects in the shorter term as more houses are built and turnover in the housing market increases. There may also be effects as households are able to borrow more and banks are willing to lend more with the higher value of collateral that higher house prices provide, but because of household budget constraints, extra spending initially will be offset by lower spending later.

Undoubtedly monetary policy makers need to, and will, take house price fluctuations more into account when making their decisions. However, there are reasons other than facilitating the achievement of inflation targets for stabilising and reducing house prices. For such a purpose the main tools should perhaps be a maximum LTV ratio (acting on demand) and measures to increase both the supply and supply elasticity of housing (clearly a supply side measure), supplemented by a suitable property tax.

If the supply elasticity of housing is increased, this should increase the power of monetary policy to raise economic activity by stimulating house building, as any given rightward shift in the demand curve for housing will generate more housebuilding. However, since an increase in the supply elasticity of housing means that house prices increase less when an expansionary monetary policy is implemented, some of the other effects mentioned above (e.g. those involving collateral) may be weakened, so overall it is not clear what effect raising the supply elasticity of housing will have on the efficacy of monetary policy although it would still be a desirable change. However, a maximum LTV ratio, which policy makers will be able to raise to stimulate the economy in a slump, hence mitigating the 'zero lower bound' constraint, would be a powerful addition to their tool kit.

Appendix A

Calculating the Rental Cost of Housing

Suppose I buy a house for P_{h0} at time 0 and sell it for P_{H1} at time 1. I borrow to pay for the house; the nominal interest rate on the loan is R. This is payable when I sell the house at time 1, but it is calculated in terms of the money initially invested in the house. So, at time 0 I pay P_{h0} for the house but this is entirely borrowed, so there is no cost in terms of forgone consumption at time 0; at time 1 I receive (in money terms) P_{H1} from selling the house but need to pay $(1 + R)P_{H0}$ to the lender. The cost is hence $(1 + R)P_{H0} - P_{H1}$ in money received at time 1; divide this by the price of consumption goods at time 1 to obtain the cost in terms of goods received at time 1 and also divide the resultant expression by the relevant discount term to obtain the cost in terms of time 0 goods. In terms of period 0 consumption, the relevant cost is hence

$$Q = \frac{(1+R)P_{H0} - P_{H1}}{(1+\rho)P_1},$$

(A14-1)

where ρ is the *real* discount rate for consumption. To obtain (14-9), re-write (A14-1) as

$$\frac{(1+R_H)P_{H0}}{(1+\rho)P_1} - \frac{P_{H1}}{(1+\rho)P_1} = \frac{(1+R_H)P_{H0}P_0}{(1+\rho)P_0P_1} - \frac{P_{H1}}{(1+\rho)P_1}.$$

(A14-2)

Since $P_{Hi}/P_i = q_i$ for $i = 0, 1$ and $P_1/P_0 = 1 + \pi$, where π is the rate of inflation, we can write (A14-2) as

$$\frac{1}{1+\rho}\left[\frac{(1+R)q_0}{1+\pi} - q_1\right] = \frac{q_0}{1+\rho}\left[\frac{1+R}{1+\pi} - 1 + 1 - \frac{q_1}{q_0}\right] = \frac{q_0}{1+\rho}\left[\left\{\frac{R-\pi}{1+\pi}\right\} - \left\{\frac{q_1-q_0}{q_0}\right\}\right]$$

(A14-3)

The first term in braces in the expression in square brackets on the right-hand side of this equation can be defined as the real interest rate (r); the numerator of the second term in braces in the limit as the time period between period 0 and period 1 converges to zero can be written as $\dot{q}_0$, the instantaneous rate of change of q. This almost takes us to (14-9). (A14-3) contains a term multiplying the whole expression by $1/(1+\rho)$, but this can be incorporated in the constant term (k) in (14-8). The analysis in this Appendix has not included the depreciation rate, but it is straightforward to do this and obtain an expression such as (14-9).

Note: the real interest rate is here defined as $r \equiv (R - \pi)/(1 + \pi)$ instead of just $R - \pi$ as is common in macroeconomics. To realise that the former is the correct definition, consider the following. Suppose someone invests £X at a nominal interest rate R. At the end of the year, he has £$X(1+R)$ returned to him as interest and principal, but since prices have risen, his real return is $X[(1 + R)/(1 + \pi) - 1]$, which is equivalent to the former definition of the real interest rate. (However, the two definitions may not differ very much if inflation is low.) Another point is that the real interest rate is usually defined with respect to expected inflation, but since the actual and expected inflation rates are equivalent in the model in this chapter, this is not a problem.

Appendix B

The Choice between Renting and Owner-Occupation

There are the following advantages (both private and social) of owner-occupation over renting:

1. Owner-occupiers hedge a flow of future housing services. The alternative, that of using the income generated by the asset(s) that otherwise would have been used for the purchase of property to pay the rent exposes a household to two risks – that the income stream might

change and that rents might change – that can be avoided by purchasing a property (see Sinai and Souleles, 2005, for further discussion of this effect).

2. Owner-occupiers have a greater incentive to look after, maintain and decorate etc. the property they live in than renters; there is an agency 'problem' between landlords and tenants, as landlords cannot specify everything that needs to be done to maintain the property optimally in the contract.

3. Owner-occupiers have a greater stake in the neighbourhood in which they live than renters; they are more likely to support measures to increase the value of property in their neighbourhoods, such as taking part in neighbourhood watch schemes, opposing damaging development and so forth.

On the other hand, renting has the following advantages over owner-occupation:

1. Owner-occupation, particularly if financed by a mortgage, exposes the household to a high degree of risk if it experiences a shock which means it cannot continue to pay the mortgage or needs to sell on disadvantageous terms.

2. Because of the costs of buying and selling property, owner-occupiers are less mobile than renters. This reduces labour mobility, making the labour market less flexible; this may raise unemployment and, by impeding structural adjustment, reduce longer term growth.

3. Depending on the nature of credit markets, house purchase may distort a household's intertemporal consumption, as they may need to save for the down payment and in the early years of the mortgage they may need to devote considerable resources to paying interest and repaying principal on the loan – there may be frontloading effects, discussed in the chapter on the costs of inflation (Chapter 9).

Assessing whether, on balance, there is too much or too little home-ownership is not easy. Some of the costs and benefits are private, but some have spillovers on to the rest of the economy. There may be a bias in the tax system toward owner-occupation, but credit market imperfections may offset this. The high return to investment in housing in the UK until 2007 and general government encouragement of owner-occupation may mean that owner occupation is too high.

DISCUSSION QUESTIONS

1. Are there any reasons why, and is there any evidence that, countries that have experienced lower fluctuations in house prices have more stable economies?

2. Suppose we are initially in the steady state in the Sinclair model of the housing market, and there is a sudden permanent decline in the real interest rate. Describe the short-run and long-run effects of the price of housing. How would a temporary rise in the price of housing differ?

3. Would it be a good idea for the government to cut stamp duty on house purchases in a recession and raise it in a boom?

15

Fiscal Policy

B y fiscal policy is meant decisions taken by the government about the level or composition of its expenditure and its taxation. Both fiscal policy and monetary policy might be thought of as ways in which the overall level of spending in the economy might be changed, and hence used to influence inflation and unemployment, yet currently it seems that monetary policy is used exclusively for controlling inflation. Why is this? We shall start by discussing two opposing views of fiscal policy (the Keynesian and Ricardian) in Sections 15.1 and 15.2, respectively. In Section 15.3 we consider some of the empirical evidence on fiscal policy. Section 15.4 assesses the role fiscal policy has in stabilisation policy and Section 15.5 sums up.

15.1 The Keynesian Approach to Fiscal Policy

We have already discussed briefly the Keynesian view of fiscal policy in Chapter 2. According to the simplest 'Keynesian cross' model, the following equation determines national income:

$$Y = \frac{a + I + G - bT}{1 - b},$$ (15-1)

where b is the marginal propensity to consume. The simple Keynesian government expenditure multiplier is hence the reciprocal of the marginal propensity to save, so that if this is 0.1, the multiplier is 10. Obviously this is far larger than anyone thinks plausible; one should further modify the expression by introducing the marginal propensity to tax and the marginal propensity to spend on imports, but the resulting multiplier will still be quite large. The size of the multiplier will, in addition, depend on how monetary policy operates. If it is assumed that monetary policy targets the interest rate, then these multipliers are unaltered. However, if the monetary authority targets the money supply (more strictly, does not adjust it when government spending changes), the government expenditure multiplier will be lower.

A possibly surprising result is that the balanced-budget multiplier – the effect of an increase in government spending when the government raises taxes so that its budget stays balanced – is unity, not zero. This can easily be seen from Equation (15-1) by equating G and T. One way of interpreting this result is that changes in government spending are more powerful than equivalent changes in taxation. If the government increases its expenditure by £1bn, that contributes directly to GDP. The recipients of the £1bn will spend it in accordance with their marginal propensities to consume, but one would expect that the effect of this on demand would be exactly the same as if they had received the £1bn as a tax cut. Putting the point another way, a balanced budget increase in expenditure means that the increase in expenditure itself counts as an equivalent increase in GDP, but further effects from its raising disposable income are neutralised by the increase in taxation, and just the 'first round' effect of the increase in government spending remains.

Turning to tax changes, it seems that the relevant multiplier (again from (15-1)) is $b/(1-b)$, lower than the government expenditure multiplier, but still arguably of reasonable magnitude in contemporary economies.

15.2 Ricardian Equivalence

That tax changes have any effect on aggregate consumption would be denied by proponents of Ricardian equivalence, which asserts that changes in the time path of taxation to finance a given stream of government expenditure have no effect on consumption. The basic idea can be illustrated very simply. Suppose a representative consumer who lives for two periods has the following budget constraint:

$$C_1 + C_2/(1+r) = Y_1 - T_1 + (Y_2 - T_2)/(1+r). \tag{15-2}$$

C_i, Y_i and T_i represent consumption, income and taxation, respectively in period i (where i can equal 1 or 2) and r is the interest rate at which the consumer can freely lend or borrow. We suppose that the government is subject to a similar budget constraint:

$$G_1 + G_2/(1+r) = T_1 + T_2/(1+r). \tag{15-3}$$

G_i is government spending in period i. The equation states that the present value of government spending equals the present value of taxes. It follows, as can be seen easily by substituting Equation (15-3) into (15-2), that for given government expenditures in the two periods, changing the time pattern of taxation has no effect at all on consumption in either period. To illustrate the point in another way, suppose a consumer receives a £100 tax rebate; he realises that this means that his taxes will be higher by an amount £100$(1+r)$ in the future, and that these effects exactly cancel out. His intertemporal budget constraint is unchanged; he can consume exactly the same, intertemporally, as before the tax increase, so he should (rationally) choose exactly the same time path of consumption.

The Ricardian view implies that budget deficits (given the time path of government expenditures) have no effect on aggregate demand, and it is not surprising that this has given rise to considerable controversy. It has been pointed out that the result is based on some extremely strong assumptions, which are discussed below. The crucial question, though, is how relaxing these assumptions in the direction of reality will change the conclusions.[1] These assumptions include:

1. Perfect capital markets

Clearly Ricardian equivalence requires agents to be able to borrow and lend as much as they like (subject to their budget constraints). If they cannot do this because they are subject to credit rationing (discussed at greater length in Chapter 10), then a tax cut that boosts the after-tax incomes of credit-constrained households should raise their consumption. Effectively, the government is acting as a financial intermediary. Suppose I would like to spend an extra £1000 now and would be perfectly happy to borrow this amount and repay £1050 next year, but cannot find a lender to make the loan. Then a government tax cut may effectively provide this loan; in giving me £1000 in lower taxes now, and levying £1050 next year in higher taxes, the government is doing what financial intermediaries perhaps should be doing, but are not. So a fiscal policy of this kind can be very effective when credit markets seize up, as in the worldwide credit crunch of 2007–2009.

It has sometimes been argued though, that when credit constraints are endogenised, Ricardian equivalence re-emerges, even with imperfect credit markets (see, e.g. Yotsuzuka, 1987). Consider the example above, where I receive a tax cut of £1000 but expect an increased tax bill of £1050 next year. Then a lender might consider that since my net income next year will be lower, I will be less able to repay what he has lent me, and therefore he will cut my credit limit by £1000, making me no better off than previously. It is not clear that such arguments, though, which are based on particular examples of how credit constraints may operate, show that in general credit constraints invalidate Ricardian equivalence. The theoretical argument is by no means robust. For example, suppose that an individual's credit constraint is so tight that he cannot borrow anything, then the lender will be unable to tighten the credit constraint any further, so we would expect a tax cut directed to this individual to increase his consumption.

2. Rational, fully informed agents

Ricardian equivalence requires agents to be fully informed and rational, in the sense that they realise that the tax cut they are receiving implies future tax increases of equal present value. Many agents may not be rational, and not realise that the tax cut they are currently receiving will be offset by a tax increase in the future of equivalent present value. Clearly, they

---

[1] For further discussion of the assumptions underlying Ricardian equivalence, see Barro (1989) or Elmendorf and Mankiw (1999), section 4.2.

might regard this as an increase in their lifetime resources, and consume more. This issue clearly needs to be explored in a model with both rational and uninformed agents; one question is whether the presence of uninformed agents means that rational agents react more to a tax cut or increase than they otherwise would.

3. No uncertainty

The standard argument for Ricardian equivalence assumes an absence of uncertainty; the question that arises is whether introducing uncertainty changes the basic result significantly. Uncertainty can be introduced into the framework in a number of ways. It could be that an individual who receives a tax cut does not know whether he is going to be taxed more in the future. For example, it could be that the government will raise taxes sometime in the future to pay off the debt incurred through this tax cut, but it is uncertain who will incur the incidence of the tax will be. Then the uncertainty of future disposable income increases, and it may well be the case that consumers react by *reducing* current consumption, which means a negative effect of the tax cut on consumption. Alternatively, a tax cut now could be financed by a higher income tax in the future; if people are uncertain about their future incomes, this will reduce their uncertainty about their future net of tax incomes, and under certain assumptions this will raise current consumption. (Chan, 1983, develops arguments of this type.) It seems then, that the relevance of uncertainty for Ricardian equivalence is quite complicated and the effects could go in either direction.

4. Lump-sum taxes

Clearly, taxes in practice are not lump sum. If income tax is cut today, but increased sometime in the future, then we might expect some agents to work more today and work less when the tax is increased in the future. So there might be an expansion of economic activity when taxes are lower.

5. Infinitely Lived Consumers[2]

In a celebrated article which revived interest in Ricardian equivalence, Barro (1974) showed that Ricardian equivalence held even if an agent had finite lives, but households were connected to future households by means of operative intertemporal transfers. The basic idea is that if a household receives a tax cut of £1000, to be financed by a tax increase of equivalent present value on one of their descendents, then the household will bequeath a correspondingly higher amount to its descendents, keeping their consumption unaltered. The assumptions underlying this conclusion are incredibly strong and unlikely to be satisfied in practice; Bernheim and Bagwell (1988) in an ingenious article show that under essentially the same assumptions, everything is neutral – i.e. increases in proportional income taxes are neutral. This can be regarded as a reductio of the approach.

Nevertheless, it is not clear how important finitely-lived consumers who do not behave as postulated by Barro are in the failure of Ricardian equivalence to hold in practice. It has been pointed out that in practice much of the repayment of the debt that is incurred by tax

---

[2]In our 'demonstration' of Ricardian equivalence above, we did not assume infinitely-lived households. However, the government was finite lived in this example. It is usually assumed that governments are infinitely-lived and it is when this assumption is made that one usually needs an assumption of infinitely lived households as well to generate Ricardian equivalence.

cuts does in fact fall on the same generation of tax payers. Also, introducing finitely-lived consumers into a model that retains the other assumptions underlying Ricardian equivalence is a plausible way of obtaining a model with non Ricardian properties, as was done by Blanchard (1985).

In summary then, it seems that the assumptions underlying Ricardian equivalence do not hold, but it is not clear what a plausible alternative framework is. To some extent, the issue is empirical, but although there has been a huge amount of empirical work on the topic, the evidence seems inconclusive.

15.3 Empirical Evidence

There is, of course, an extensive empirical literature on the effects of fiscal policy and of budget deficits which we cannot even begin to review satisfactorily. Here, we just mention and discuss briefly a few relevant papers.

There was considerable literature produced in the 1980s on the effects of budget deficits. Interest in the topic was kindled by the Reagan budget deficits of that era. Evans (1985) is a good example of this literature. This paper failed to find any relationship between budget deficits and interest rates over a long period of American history, which the author interpreted as evidence in favour of Ricardian equivalence. There are other possible interpretations of such evidence, though. Bernheim (1987) provides a fairly thorough review of both theory and empirical evidence, and concludes that although the evidence is mixed and inconclusive, 'there is a significant likelihood that deficits have large effects on current consumption, and there is good reason to believe that this would drive up interest rates.' (Bernheim, 1987, p. 264).

Perotti (1999) explores the intriguing idea that fiscal policy may differ between 'good' times and 'bad' times; more specifically, in good times (i.e. when government debt is low) government expenditure increases have standard Keynesian effects, whereas in bad times (when debt is high), they may have the opposite effects, so that fiscal consolidations in countries with high government debt may be expansionary. Mertens and Ravn (2011) and Romer and Romer (2010) provide more recent evidence on fiscal policy. The former provides evidence that anticipated tax cuts are contractionary prior to implementation, whereas implemented tax cuts have persistent expansionary effects. The latter paper employs the so-called 'narrative' approach to identifying fiscal policy shocks, and shows that fiscal shocks can be extremely powerful – for example, 'that a tax increase of 1 percent of GDP reduces output over the next three years by nearly three percent', (Romer and Romer, 2010, p. 764). It seems, though, that both these papers only consider the effects of fiscal policy in 'good times' (i.e. when the debt-GDP ratio is not too high) and do not consider the possibility that these effects may be very different when the debt-GDP ratio is high.

15.4 The Role of Fiscal Policy in Stabilisation

It is clear that fiscal policy can affect aggregate demand and expenditures in a number of different ways. This is of course of particular relevance to the credit crunch of 2007–2009. Fiscal policy, in particular, might work in the following ways:

1. We might expect deficit-financed tax cuts to be effective in stimulating spending in an economy hit by shocks to the financial sector – as already argued, the government can use fiscal policy to substitute for financial intermediaries that for some reason have become incapable or reluctant, at least for some time, of fulfilling their intermediation role adequately.

2. We would also expect government spending to be effective in raising output even in a Ricardian world where price rigidities mean that changes in aggregate demand can affect output and employment. This is because of the balanced budget multiplier effect of government spending we discussed earlier. In fact, Christiano, Eichenbaum and Rebelo, (2011) argue that the government expenditure multiplier may be quite large in an economy where the interest rate is constant. In one version of their model, the government expenditure multiplier is 3.7. The explanation is that government spending increases raise output in the standard way, but this leads to a rise in expected inflation, driving down the real interest rate, boosting demand still further and so forth.

3. Temporary changes in some taxes might in particular be effective. Examples are the temporary reduction in VAT rate introduced in late 2008 (see, in particular, Crossley, Low and Wakefield, 2009, Barrell and Weale, 2009 and Blundell, 2009) and the car scrappage schemes introduced in a number of European countries in the aftermath of the credit crisis (see Crossley, Leicester and Levell, 2010). In the latter scheme, owners of older, less fuel efficient cars were given a financial incentive to trade their cars in for newer more fuel-efficient vehicles. Temporary tax changes (and subsidies) of this kind might be particularly effective in encouraging consumers to change the timing of certain expenditure decisions; car purchase, in particular, is a good example of a major purchase decision that can often be brought forward or postponed. A temporary scheme financing investment might also be particularly effective. However, other types of temporary tax change might have much less impact. A temporary reduction in income tax may (even in a non-Ricardian world) have little effect on consumption because consumers may base their consumption on their permanent or life-cycle income, and temporary tax changes may have little effect on this. Another qualification that needs to be made is that if such temporary changes in taxes are made frequently for stabilisation purposes, they may come to be anticipated, and this may be counterproductive. Suppose, for example, that a recession seems imminent and it is believed that the government will soon cut taxes on certain consumption goods. Then before they do so, consumers may reduce their spending on such goods, intending to purchase them after the tax cut, but in the mean time making the recession worse.

However, there is another important qualification that needs to be made at least as far as using deficit-financed fiscal policy is concerned. Suppose it is the case that budget deficits are expansionary, at least under certain circumstances. Does it follow that if we are in a recession, or at least if we consider the level of aggregate demand to be too low, we can continue to raise expenditure and the budget deficit without limit until we reach a satisfactory level of output? This might seem implausible. The reason is, of course, that this might lead to a massive increase in the stock of government debt; this, as suggested in the chapter on the term structure of interest rates (Chapter 12), might be expected to raise long-term interest rates; it might also increase expectations of default on the government debt, and both these effects might be expected to be contractionary. We hence have the following hypothesis about fiscal policy: it is quite expansionary for low levels of government debt, but as government debt rises, the fiscal policy multiplier falls and eventually turns negative. Modelling this, and providing relevant empirical evidence, would seem to be an important priority for future research. Evidence that increases in projected US budget deficits and government debt raise interest rates is presented by Laubach (2009).

So fiscal policy can affect aggregate demand and output, but should it be employed for stabilisation purposes? It might be that there are other, superior, policy tools. We might distinguish two cases – normal times and crisis times.

By 'normal times' we mean a situation where the lower floor to interest rates is not binding. Monetary policy can therefore be used to either stimulate or contract the economy, as might be appropriate. We argue elsewhere in this book that monetary policy might well be quite effective in such circumstances. But is there any role for fiscal policy in addition? A powerful case can be made against fiscal policy being used for stabilisation purposes in circumstances where monetary policy might be expected to be effective; in other words, monetary policy almost certainly has a comparative advantage in stabilising the economy.

If one is considering changing government spending for stabilisation purposes – and this, as exemplified by the balanced budget multiplier theorem should be more powerful than changing taxation – one should realise that the implementation lag may be quite long. Expenditure changes are usually announced some time in advance of their implementation; one reason for this is that it may take time to actually start the expenditure after the decision to make the expenditure has been made. For example, suppose one decides to build a new hospital, then a considerable length of time might elapse before any expenditure is actually incurred – one may need to draw up plans and obtain planning permission, line up contractors and so forth. Seasonal factors may be relevant as well, for certain types of expenditure. On the other hand, monetary policy decisions can be implemented immediately, and monetary policy is quite flexible. The MPC makes monetary decisions every month and the amount of stimulus can be large or small. It may be that monetary policy actions take some time to have any impact on output and employment, but this is also the case with changing taxes, and the implementation lag is definitely longer for fiscal policy.

However, in a crisis, when interest rates have been reduced as much as they can, fiscal policy may be relevant. The government may want to run a larger budget deficit, and implement temporary tax reductions. However, this leaves the very tricky question of when the fiscal stimulus should be reversed.

So if fiscal policy should not be used for stabilisation, how should it be conducted? Barro (1979) has argued that optimal fiscal policy involves keeping tax rates and the debt constant – one does not want tax rates to be changing continually, as this will mean that individuals will be shifting their behaviour constantly in response to these changes, and such changes are probably not desirable, the problem being exacerbated if the changes come to be anticipated. So a policy of keeping the debt-GDP ratio constant (possibly adjusting for cyclical factors) has much to commend it. However, it might be argued that there is a critical level of the debt-GDP ratio above which the risk of default grows significantly. The consequences of exceeding such a ratio may be extremely unpleasant, as has been confirmed by the experience of a number of countries in the eurozone in the aftermath of the worldwide credit crunch. Then the closer one is to the critical level, the more constrained one is from using fiscal policy in an expansionary direction if one wants to, and the greater the risk that unforeseen events might push the economy too close to the critical level. Accordingly, the lower the debt, the better from this point of view, so as it takes time to reduce debt, the best policy might therefore be one of gradually reducing the debt-GDP ratio over time. See the discussion in Wren-Lewis (2010), who concludes that 'a policy that results in the government debt-to-GDP ratio declining (albeit gradually and erratically) in normal times seems appropriate.' (p. 85)

One innovation in the UK was the establishment in May 2010 by the incoming coalition government of the independent Office of Budget Responsibility, the main responsibility of which is to produce the fiscal and economic forecasts that the Chancellor uses in his budget. There is a growing worldwide trend towards using such bodies, sometimes called fiscal councils. Their use may have been inspired by the perceived success of central bank independence throughout the world; many policy makers may have had a desire to do for fiscal policy what central bank independence has done for monetary policy. Nevertheless, there are important differences; independent central banks are actually responsible for implementing monetary policy whereas fiscal councils do little more than forecast and produce analysis, fiscal policy decisions remaining with the government.[3]

15.5 Conclusion

Although fiscal policy may usefully complement monetary policy in a time of crisis, it is generally appropriate that monetary policy is the main tool to use for stabilisation purposes. Fiscal policy may be quite powerful in certain circumstances but not in others; but precisely what these circumstances are is not well understood.

---

[3] A website maintained by Simon Wren-Lewis of Oxford University contains some extremely useful information on fiscal councils: http://www.economics.ox.ac.uk/members/simon.wren-lewis/fc/fiscal_councils.htm

DISCUSSION QUESTIONS

1. Would a requirement that governments balanced their budgets be a good idea?
2. Are there any circumstances under which a fiscal contraction can be expansionary?
3. It has sometimes been suggested that excessive government budget deficits might lead to inflation. Under what circumstances would this occur?

CHAPTER 16

Evidence on the Effectiveness of Monetary Policy

Nowadays, economists tend to believe that expansionary monetary policy increases in output and employment in the short run (six months to two years?) and in the longer run causes higher prices/inflation. What is the evidence for these effects of monetary policy?

It would be easy to identify the effects of monetary policy on economic activity if we could identify unanticipated monetary shocks that are exogenous, in the sense that they are unrelated to contemporary, past or anticipated changes in economic activity. We would then need just to see whether such shocks were followed by systematic changes in output or employment. But how do we identify such shocks? We cannot take two identical economies and increase the money supply in one, while leaving it unchanged in the other, and see what the effects are. There is uncertainty over which variable is the best measure of monetary policy – is it a narrow monetary aggregate, a broad monetary aggregate, or an interest rate, such as the federal funds rate (in the US) or what? If we do decide on which measure of money to use, then how do we identify unanticipated changes in it? If it is unanticipated, it might be (say) a response to an unanticipated money demand shock, which is accommodated if the central bank is targeting a short-term interest rate, and which would therefore not be expected to have any effect on economic activity.

In this chapter we very briefly discuss some of the literature on this issue. Evidence can be divided into 'reduced form' and 'structural'. Reduced-form evidence, discussed in Section 16.1 looks at the relationship between changes in money and (say) output, without exploring the mechanism whereby monetary changes might have this effect. Structural evidence, considered in Section 16.2, is where a model is built and estimated (say a sophisticated IS-LM model), and conclusions about the effects of monetary changes are drawn by examining what the model predicts about the effects of monetary changes. So in the IS-LM context, an increase in the money supply will reduce the interest rate according to the elasticity of demand for money, the interest rate reduction will increase investment spending according to the relevant interest elasticity, and this will raise income according to the multiplier. If one has estimates of these elasticities and the multiplier, one can work out the effects of an increase in the money supply on income.

16.1 Reduced-Form Evidence

16.1.1 The Narrative Approach

As pioneered by Friedman and Schwartz (1963) this involves studying the historical record to explore the link between monetary changes and changes in economic activity.[1] They applied the National Bureau of Economic Research business cycle methodology to this issue; this involves using various techniques to identify turning points in statistical series, so that for example, turning points in monetary growth might be identified as well as in various series representing economic activity. Their conclusion is that 'Changes in the behavior of the money stock have been closely associated with changes in economic activity, money income and prices.' (Friedman and Schwartz, 1963, p. 676). So they produce evidence of a *correlation* between monetary changes and economic activity. However, what evidence is there that causation runs from money to economic activity? (Inferring causality from correlation may be described as an example of 'post hoc, ergo propter hoc' reasoning.) One alternative explanation is that of reverse causation – i.e. an increase in money income causes the increase in the money supply in some way. This could happen if the monetary authorities are attempting to stabilise interest rates. An increase in income (due to some nonmonetary change) will tend to raise the demand for money and hence interest rates; the monetary authorities may thus expand the money supply to bring interest rates back to their targeted levels and in this way a correlation between money supply and income changes may be observed without there being a causal link from money to income. Alternatively, there could be a third factor related to both money and income. For example, a budget deficit may be the driving force behind changes in both income and the money supply.[2]

Friedman and Schwartz give three reasons for thinking that the relationship between money and income they uncover should be interpreted as due primarily to changes in money being

---

[1] Those who do not wish to read the full 700 pages of Friedman and Schwartz are recommended instead to read just the final chapter ('A Summing Up') which provides a succinct statement of their findings.
[2] Tobin (1970) produces an argument of this kind.

causally responsible for changes in income: (i) The changes in money tend to precede changes in income. (ii) The institutional mechanism whereby the money supply is determined changed considerably in the period considered (1867–1960) with, for example, the demise of the gold standard and the founding of the Federal Reserve in 1913. Had the causal link been from income to money, the different institutional arrangements would have meant different correlations would have been observed between money and income, contrary to what happened. (iii) Detailed analysis of specific episodes of monetary changes show (they claim) that many of these changes could not plausibly be regarded as due to contemporaneous or subsequent changes in economic activity. For example, as the US was recovering from the Great Depression, the Federal Reserve more than doubled reserve requirements in three stages in 1936 and early 1937. As predicted by the money multiplier model, there was a contraction of the money stock, and the result was a severe contraction in 1937–38. Friedman and Schwartz argue that the increase in reserve requirements could in no way be explained by the subsequent fall in economic activity (it would seem bizarre in the extreme for policy makers to raise reserve requirements if they anticipate a recession) and that the most plausible interpretation of the evidence is that the monetary contraction was an exogenous shock that caused the decline in economic activity.

Romer and Romer (1989) update Friedman and Schwartz. One possible problem with the narrative approach is that there may be unconscious bias in the choice of monetary shocks. They consider as shocks only those episodes when the Federal Reserve attempted to 'actively shift the aggregate demand curve back in response to what it perceived to be "excessive" inflation' (Romer and Romer, 1989, p. 134). Six episodes of monetary contraction were identified on the basis of a scrutiny of the contemporaneous records of the Federal Reserve System. They conclude that 'the negative monetary shocks we have identified are followed by marked downturns in real economic activity that cannot be predicted from the past behavior of the economy' (Romer and Romer, 1989, p. 149).

16.1.2 Statistical/Econometric Evidence

Such evidence involves using a variety of econometric techniques to identify money supply shocks, and then relates these to subsequent movements in relevant economic variables such as output and employment. Christiano, Eichenbaum and Evans (1999) provide a thorough discussion of work of this genre. Typically, a monetary policy shock is identified with the disturbance term in a regression of the instrument of monetary policy (perhaps the federal funds rate) on some information set. In other words, the shock is the change in the monetary policy instrument that cannot be explained by the relevant information used by the econometrician. There are a number of questions that might be raised by this procedure; one might want to know whether the econometrician has included all relevant information in the regression, and how one would choose the correct functional form, and so forth. Anyway, having identified monetary policy shocks, the next task is to relate these shocks to the relevant variables of interest. Christiano *et al.* (1999) conclude that 'after a contractionary monetary policy shock, short term interest rates rise, aggregate output, employment, profits and various monetary aggregates fall, the aggregate price level responds very slowly, and various measures of wages fall, albeit by very modest amounts', (Christiano, Eichenbaum and Evans, 1999, p. 69).

16.2 Structural Evidence

Structural macroeconometric models were much used in the 1960s and 1970s. However, they fell foul of Lucas's (1976) powerful critique. The basic point is that to use such models for policy analysis, one needs to assume that the estimated parameters do not change when the money supply rule is changed. This assumption may well not be satisfied. For example, suppose that unanticipated movements in the money supply cause changes in output, as the Lucas surprise supply function would suggest. Then the result may be an equation positively relating money and output. Now suppose that policy makers try to exploit this relationship, introducing a systematic monetary policy rule to stabilise output. Then as soon as economic agents realise what is going on, they will anticipate the monetary changes implied by the rule, but these will mean that the monetary changes are no longer unanticipated, in which case they will have no effect on output.

We would also mention that there has been a vast amount of work on building dynamic general equilibrium models. Such models typically comprise households who optimise intertemporally, maximising firms and a variety of different distortions and market imperfections. Such models are typically not estimated but 'calibrated' – that is, reasonable values of the relevant parameters of the model are imposed and the predictions of the model derived, and compared with what is considered reasonable, or with the stylised facts. One example of such a model is Christiano *et al.* (2005), who present such a model with staggered wage contracts that 'accounts for the observed inertia in inflation and persistence in output' (p. 1).

Finally in this section we should mention that much work has appeared applying vector autoregression (VAR) methods to measuring the effects of monetary policy. Such models are a type of dynamic multivariate model that explicitly recognises the interdependence of all economic variables. They were introduced by Sims (1980). In analysing monetary policy, a crucial question is that of the identification of monetary policy shocks; an important recent contribution to the literature is Bernanke, Boivin and Elaisz (2005) who present what they call a factor augmented vector autoregressive (FAVAR) approach.

16.3 Conclusion

It is reasonable to conclude on the basis of the available evidence that monetary policy shocks do have a considerable effect on output, employment and inflation. However, there may indeed be long and variable lags between monetary policy changes and their effects on output, employment and inflation. Also the relationship may change, often in unpredictable ways.

DISCUSSION QUESTIONS

1. Are there any reasons why money supply changes might precede changes in income in the same direction, yet the money supply changes do not cause the changes in income?
2. Describe the 'narrative approach' to evaluating the effects of monetary policy disturbances. How much faith should we put in the conclusions emanating from this approach?
3. What is the difference between 'structural' and 'reduced form' evidence? Does either have claim to superiority over the other?

CHAPTER 17

The Targets and Instruments of Monetary Policy

Central banks are often given a target of some sort to achieve. Governments may, if they are of the benevolent type, be thought of as maximisers of social welfare and if they are not benevolent, in a democracy the electoral system may induce them to behave as though they are. However, telling a central bank to maximise social welfare is too vague – how does one know whether the central bank is achieving it or not? It is often the case that the central bank is given some sort of more specific target – currently, in the UK and many other countries, it is given a particular rate of inflation as its target. It is quite easy to ascertain whether the central bank is meeting such a target, and it is judged and rewarded or penalised on how well or badly it meets such a target.[1]

Recent years have seen the growth of the so-called 'target culture'. Many organisations, and individuals within organisations, are given targets to achieve and are rewarded or penalised appropriately. Presumably there are reasons (probably relating to incentives and information) why it might be appropriate to operate in this way; we do not discuss the literature or join the debate on this issue; instead we will just assume that it is appropriate to base policy on some

---

[1] In the UK, the only explicit 'penalty' for failing to meet the inflation target is that the Governor of the Bank of England is required to write a letter to the Chancellor of the Exchequer, explaining why the target has been missed and what the Bank is doing to remedy the situation. More specifically, he is obliged to do this every three months when the target is missed by more than one percentage point in either direction, so inflation rates of more than 3% or less than 1% should generate a letter. Apart from that, there is little else the government can do, although it can fail to re-appoint the Governor when his term expires and he is eligible for re-appointment.

sort of target, and discuss the various issues that relate to this – e.g. which target should central banks be given, and how should they be rewarded and/or punished for hitting or missing their targets?

One, older, tradition in economics (due to Tinbergen) asserts that a policy maker needs as many instruments as targets. An instrument is a tool the policy maker has control over that he uses to try to achieve his target; it is 'a policy-controlled variable that can be set exactly for all practical purposes' (Poole, 1970, p. 198). However, sometimes the policy maker will have a choice between instruments; he may be able to choose either the monetary base or an interest rate as an instrument but not both. In the former case, interest rates will be determined by the market, whereas in the latter, the monetary base is determined endogenously.[2]

In this chapter we start by presenting in Section 17.1 Poole's analysis of the choice of monetary policy instrument; Section 17.2 considers the use of the nominal interest rate as an instrument and Section 17.3 focuses on monetary targeting. Inflation targeting has now by and large replaced monetary targeting, and this is discussed in Section 17.4. The question whether central banks should target output as well as inflation is considered in Section 17.5, while Section 17.6 analyses an alternative to inflation targeting that has sometimes been suggested, that of nominal income targeting. Section 17.7 turns to the topical question of the transparency of monetary policy decisions and the final section presents concluding thoughts.

17.1 The Choice between Instruments: Poole's Analysis

Poole (1970) presented an influential analysis of the choice between the interest rate and the money supply as instruments in a closed economy. Suppose that, in the context of an IS-LM model, where the authorities wish to stabilise output, a choice has to be made whether to use the interest rate or the money supply as their instruments. The choice has to be made before it is known what shocks are going to impact the economy; that is, a particular value of either the interest rate or money supply is chosen, and then a shock hits the economy; moreover, it is supposed, quite unrealistically in the case of the money supply, that they control each variable exactly.

The basic result is that, with shocks to money demand, it is preferable to use the interest rate as an instrument whereas with shocks to expenditure, the money supply should be chosen. The results can be illustrated diagrammatically in an IS-LM framework.

Figure 17.1 shows the effects of shocks to the demand for money. Such shocks mean that the LM curve shifts – the combination of interest rate and income compatible with money

---

[2]For an excellent review of some of the issues discussed in this chapter, see Clarida, Galí and Gertler (1999).

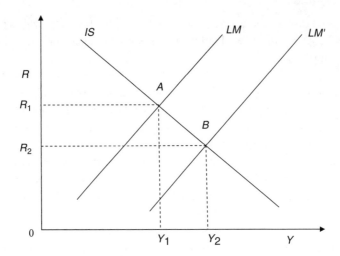

Figure 17.1   The Poole Model, Monetary Shocks.

market equilibrium for any given money supply changes. Specifically, suppose the LM curve shifts between LM and LM', because of changes in the amount of money demanded at any given interest rate. Then if the authorities keep the money supply constant in response to the shock and let the interest rate adjust, the economy moves between A and B and income between Y_1 and Y_2. However, if the authorities instead keep the interest rate constant there is no change in income. Shocks to the demand for money change income through changing the interest rate, so keeping the interest rate constant prevents this from happening – an increase in money demand is accommodated through an increase in the money supply with no change in interest rates and hence there is no impact on the real economy. The effect of expenditure shocks is shown in Figure 17.2. Suppose the IS curve shifts between IS and IS', then if the money supply is held constant the economy fluctuates between income levels Y_1 and Y_2.

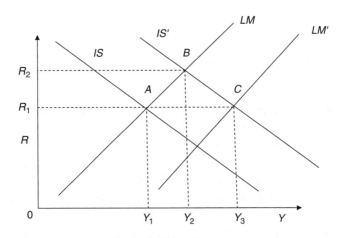

Figure 17.2   The Poole Model, Real Shocks.

If the interest rate is held constant, though, the fluctuations are greater, between income levels Y_2 and Y_3. The basic idea is that with shocks to the IS curve, holding the money supply constant means that the interest rate tends to adjust in a stabilising manner, rising when expenditure rises and so forth, whereas keeping the interest rate constant prevents it from having this stabilising role.

To evaluate Poole's argument, remember it is made in the context of a static, closed economy IS-LM framework. The government's only objective is to stabilise output; stabilising interest rates, for example, or inflation, does not enter into its objective function. In spite of these limitations, the central message of the Poole analysis, that the government's choice of which instrument to use may well depend on the type of shock to which the economy is subject, should certainly hold in more complex models.

However, using the money supply as an instrument, is not feasible – it is not something the policy maker can control with any precision at all, as we have seen. It may be able to control the monetary base, but given the tenuous relationship between this and the money supply, it is not clear that this would be superior to using the interest rate as an instrument even in the face of real shocks. A further complication is that it is not clear which measure of the money supply is the best measure to try to control.

Instead of the money supply being regarded as an instrument, it is sometimes regarded as an *intermediate target*, that is, not something which is an ultimate objective of policy, but something which it is thought desirable to target as it is related to some of the desirable objectives of policy in a predictable way. We discuss monetary targeting in Section 17.3.

Applied to an open economy, Poole-type analysis suggests that it is the exchange rate that should be held constant in the face of monetary shocks, whereas expenditure shocks imply that it is the money supply that should be used as an instrument (see Niehans, 1984, Chapter 13). This is relevant to the choice of exchange rate regime, but not something we will consider further in this book.

17.2 The Nominal Interest Rate as an Instrument

Poole's analysis suggests using the interest rate as an instrument in the face of monetary shocks. However, keeping the interest rate constant in the face of shocks does generate a risk of instability. Suppose the nominal interest rate is held too low – i.e. given inflationary expectations, the resulting real interest rate generates excess demand and inflation. The rise in inflation tends to raise the nominal interest rate via the Fisher effect; if the central bank increases the money supply and brings nominal interest rates back to their previous level, then the real interest falls, raising aggregate demand still further, and so on. However, this danger can be avoided by adopting an appropriate feedback rule, whereby the interest rate is changed by more than the change in expected inflation (see below).

Why use the nominal, and not the real interest rate as an instrument? One important reason is that it may be extremely difficult to measure the real interest rate. The real interest rate is usually defined as the nominal interest rate minus expected inflation, but it is not at all obvious how to measure the expected inflation rate, especially since inflationary expectations may vary widely over the population. If inflationary expectations are given in the short run, changes in the nominal interest rate translate into an equivalent change in the real interest rate. However, an unexpected reduction in nominal interest rates might be expected to raise inflationary expectations, if anything, so such effects magnify the effect of nominal interest rate changes on the real interest rate.

It also has to be decided which nominal interest rate should be used as an instrument. At the moment in the UK, the MPC decides on the rate of interest paid on bank reserves. This is called 'Bank Rate' and is regarded as its instrument. Some other interest rates are linked, either explicitly or implicitly, to this (for example, some flexible rate mortgages have an interest rate of Bank Rate plus 0.99%). The Bank intervenes in money markets, to ensure that other short-term interest rates approximate this rate. Generally it succeeds in doing this, but there are times, such as in the aftermath of the financial crisis of 2007–2009, when some short-term rates diverged quite markedly from Bank Rate. In the US, the instrument is the federal funds rate, the rate of interest at which banks lend to each other; however, it is not clear that this is under the direct control of the Federal Reserve, so perhaps it is better described as an intermediate target.

17.3 Monetary Targeting

Policy makers have often targeted monetary aggregates. 'Targeting' is a better term to use than 'instrument', as policy makers have in practice often missed such targets by a considerable amount; they may be able to control the monetary base fairly precisely, but as we have seen the link between this and the money supply is often pretty tenuous. In the United Kingdom, monetary targeting started under a Labour administration with Denis Healey as Chancellor in 1976, and continued under the Conservative government that was elected in May 1979. However, in the monetary targeting episodes of the 1970s and 1980s the targets were usually missed (generally exceeded), although it is possible to argue that the policy was successful in that it achieved its objective (namely a reduction in inflation) even though the targets were often missed. This argument may have some plausibility, but it is not too satisfactory to have a target that is generally missed. Instability in the demand for money might be argued to be the main culprit behind these target misses. Some relevant points relating to monetary targeting are as follows:

1. It is difficult to reconcile the lender-of-last resort function of the central bank with strict monetary targeting. For example, suppose that monetary growth is above target but the banking sector is experiencing a liquidity crisis which requires the central bank to act as lender-of-last-resort, then one may not want the central bank to curtail its lender of last resort lending merely because monetary growth is excessive.

2. It is not at all clear which monetary aggregate is relevant for targeting purposes. Indeed, monetary aggregates are constantly being redefined, so perhaps the targeted monetary aggregate needs to be redefined periodically. There is of course the complication due to Goodhart's law, according to which any variable that comes to be used as a target loses its significance by so doing or 'any observed statistical regularity will tend to collapse once pressure is placed on it for control purposes' (Goodhart, 1989, p. 377, fn.1). Although it is applicable in a number of contexts, it was developed in the context of monetary targeting.[3]

3. Information on monetary aggregates is available only with a lag and is subject to revision – this complicates the problem of targeting the money supply, as opposed to targeting the interest rate, information about which is available instantaneously.

4. Monetary targeting, if pursued rigorously, may also mean considerable volatility of interest rates (and/or exchange rates). This may not be desirable – for example, financial institutions may find it difficult to cope with volatile interest rates, which may also be politically unpopular.

The main reasons for the abandonment of monetary targeting were almost certainly the failures to hit the targets when targeting was practised, and the realisation that setting interest rates in order to meet an inflation target was a superior way of proceeding. Under interest rate targeting, money demand shocks have no effect on interest rates, as indeed is appropriate with an inflation target, but – provided a correct interest rate adjustment policy is followed (real interest rates need to rise when there is a positive shock to inflation, for example) – generate appropriate policy responses to real and inflationary shocks.

17.4 Inflation Targeting

Since about 1990, inflation targeting has spread around the world. New Zealand was the first country to implement an explicit inflation target with the passage of the Reserve Bank Act of 1989. By 2010, 29 countries had formally adopted inflation targeting.[4] There are a number of issues that might be discussed relating to inflation targeting:

1. Inflation targeting should be distinguished from price level targeting. The main difference concerns what happens if the target is missed. An inflation target of 3% might be thought equivalent to a price level target of 103 where today's price level is 100. However, suppose the actual inflation rate is 4%; then should next year's target be an inflation rate of 3% again or a price level target of (about) 106, which translates into an inflation target of about 2%? (Putting the point in another way, are overshoots or undershoots corrected?) Perhaps an inflation target is to be preferred for this reason as it should mean a less volatile rate of inflation. However, Eggertsson and Woodford (2003) argue for a price level target as

---

[3]As an obvious example of the law, consider the American political consultant who observes that the presidential candidate whose party wins the state of X always wins the presidency, and therefore advises the candidate to put all his resources into winning the state of X.

[4]See Table 1 on p. 1245 of Svensson (2011) for a list of countries and dates of adoption.

a way of combating a liquidity trap. We are not aware, however, of any central bank that is subject to a price-level, as opposed to an inflation, target. Possibly price level targeting may be superior from a stabilisation perspective; however, it might be inferior from a welfare perspective as the rate of inflation diverged more frequently from, and by more from, its optimal rate. It might be, for example, of considerable concern if a central bank embarked on a programme of considerable deflation in order to achieve a price level target that had been missed because of a period of excessive inflation.

2. It needs to be decided which inflation rate should be targeted – in other words, how should the rate of inflation for targeting be measured?

3. Over what time period should the inflation target be hit? That is, the inflation target that is given to the central bank today should be to achieve a certain rate of inflation but over what time period? In the UK, the target is supposed to be for all time periods, but in practice is perhaps a medium term target – say for between one and two years. A rationale for this is that attempting to hit an inflation target for shorter time periods would not be too easy, and if it is done, it might be done in a way which does more harm than good (e.g. by producing large fluctuations in exchange rates). But also, it would prejudice the hitting of the inflation target over a longer period, so even from the inflation targeting perspective a focus of trying to hit the inflation target precisely over short time periods may not be advisable.

4. In looking at the macroeconomic consequences of inflation targeting, it might be noted that it produces appropriate reactions to aggregate demand disturbances – for example, a negative aggregate demand shock tends to reduce both prices (inflation) and output. Reducing interest rates should boost aggregate demand, and this should raise both inflation and output, which may be the desired outcome.

5. However inflation targeting might be thought problematic in the face of (severe) aggregate supply shocks. Suppose the economy is at a satisfactory level of both output and inflation and is hit by a severe negative aggregate supply shock, which both reduces output and raises inflation. Then inflation targeting may dictate a contractionary monetary policy, which might be expected to amplify the negative effect of the policy on output and employment, which may not be desirable. However, there are the following points that might be made about this argument:

    a. It is not clear what the best policy is in the face of a negative supply shock.

    b. It is possible to exclude commodity prices etc. from the price index used for targeting purposes.

    c. It is possible for the target to be changed.

    d. There is a 'band' around the target which may give the central bank some leeway in responding to aggregate supply shocks. In the UK, there is effectively a band of 1 percentage point about the target. It might be advisable for the central bank in 'normal' times to try to keep inflation as near to its target as possible, to allow at least some room for fluctuations of this kind.

    e. Given the time lag between monetary policy changes and inflation, it is impossible for the central bank to hit the inflation target at all times, and if inflation is high because of temporary commodity price increases then there may be nothing it can do to hit the inflation target in the near term. So it is appropriate that temporary commodity price fluctuations be accommodated without a change in monetary policy, whereas longer term commodity price fluctuations probably should induce some response in monetary policy, and this is what such a framework induces.

17.5 Should Central Banks Target Output as well as Inflation?

It might be argued that governments (and the central banks they controlled) in the United Kingdom and in many other countries effectively followed a full employment target in the three decades or so after the Second World War but this led to accelerating inflation. It seems that giving the central bank an unemployment (or real output) target is not a good way to proceed, even if unemployment is of major concern. If the unemployment target is below the natural rate of unemployment, then it seems that accelerating inflation is inevitable. It is often extremely difficult to know what the natural rate of unemployment is, and also it may well change. It is now clear that monetary policy has a central role to play in causing inflation, so it is probably essential to give a central bank an inflationary target of some sort. Indeed, it could be argued that an inflation target is a better way of achieving an unemployment target than targeting unemployment itself. If inflation starts decelerating, this is evidence that (in certain circumstances) unemployment is above the natural rate, so we would expect the monetary authorities to pursue more expansionary monetary policies, hence pushing unemployment back toward the natural rate, and they can do this without knowing what the natural rate of unemployment actually is. (This can be described as an example of 'obliquity' – the idea that the best way to achieve a goal is to pursue some other goal rather than the goal itself.)

However, it is unreasonable to suppose that central banks do not or should not take output and employment into account when making decisions. For example, it has been suggested that the behaviour of many central banks can be described by a so-called Taylor Rule:

$$i_t = a + b(\pi_t - \pi^*) + c(y_t - y^*). \tag{17-1}$$

Here y^* is the output target and π^* is the inflation target. Sometimes, it is formulated in terms of expected inflation rather than actual inflation. Also, if central banks do not have accurate information about the current level of income when making their decision, y_t in the equation would be replaced by the central bank's best estimate of income using its available information. b and c are nonnegative coefficients, showing how policy reacts to divergences of inflation and output from their targets respectively. The case of 'pure' inflation targeting is captured by $c = 0$. One important question is whether b is greater or less than unity. If $b > 1$, the central bank raises the real interest rate in response to a rise in inflation, so the rule is stabilising. On the other hand if $b < 1$, the central bank does not raise nominal interest rates by the full amount of the increase in inflation when inflation rises, hence reducing the real interest rate, giving rise to the possibility of an explosion in inflation. Since the rule was propounded by Taylor (1993), a huge amount of effort has gone into estimating Taylor rules for various economies and such a rule is a staple feature of many macroeconomic models. Clarida, Galí and Gertler (2000) estimate a Taylor rule for the United States, finding that there was a significant change in monetary policy in 1979, when Paul Volcker was appointed Chairman of the Board of Governors of the Federal Reserve System. They find that policy was accommodative before Volcker, letting short-term interest rates decline as inflation rose, whereas Volcker (and Alan Greenspan, who succeeded him in 1987) pursued a much more aggressive policy, raising real interest rates in response to higher expected inflation. One persistent problem in estimating Taylor rules has turned out to be that the information which policy makers were using to make their decisions at the time may have been highly inaccurate, so that estimation using more accurate information may not be appropriate.

17.6 Nominal Income as a Target

The suggestion is that the target should be set in terms of nominal GDP growth, equal to the sum of inflation and real income growth. So a nominal income target of 5% could be satisfied with inflation of 5% and real growth of zero, or zero inflation and 5% real growth, and so on. Although advocated by a number of economists and commentators it seems it has never in fact been practised by a central bank. It would seem to have substantial merits. It would probably induce the same response to aggregate demand disturbances as an inflation target – if there is a negative demand shock, reducing both inflation and output, both an inflation targeting central bank and a nominal income targeting central bank will respond in an expansionary fashion. As far as a negative supply shock is concerned, in the case of an inflation targeting central bank, the response will be to increase interest rates in order to reduce inflation, which may not be the appropriate response. In the case of a GDP targeting central bank it is not clear what it should do, as the effect on nominal GDP could go in either direction. However, it is difficult to see how a prolonged slump could emerge, as would be a distinct possibility under inflation targeting, so GDP targeting may be better in response to supply shocks, but this is something that really needs further analysis. As with price level targeting, as far as we are aware, there is no country that has adopted, or is considering adopting, such a policy.

17.7 The Role of Transparency and Central Bank Independence

The issue of central bank independence has already been discussed. A related issue is that of transparency. This is the idea that central banks should reveal information about their procedures and intentions (by, for example, being required to publish minutes of their meetings and/or the governor being required to testify before congress or parliamentary committees, etc.) A review article of the literature on transparency (Geraats, 2002) distinguishes five types of transparency: political, economic, procedural, policy and operational. Also, transparency is defined as the presence of symmetric information between the central bank and the public. It seems that transparency is generally desirable, although there are exceptions. There may be a link with central bank independence. If the central bank is not independent, opacity (the opposite of transparency) may be a way of shielding the central bank from undesirable political pressure. However, there are some reasons why total transparency may not be desirable. For example, whilst the minutes of MPC meetings may summarise discussion in the meetings, they do not reveal which specific members of the committee said what. A reason for this is that when minutes of such a committee do report what specific members of the committee actually say, they tend to become much more circumspect in what they say, which may not be desirable. Also at a more theoretical level, reasons can be given why complete transparency may not always be desirable (see, e.g. Amato, Morris and Shin, 2008). One recent survey article is Blinder *et al.* (2008).

17.8 Conclusion

As far as the UK is concerned, it seems that the debate over what the central bank should target has been settled. In 1997, it was decided that it should target the inflation rate, and that this is the target for all time periods. Generally it seems to have worked well (the experience of the credit crunch and recession of 2007–2009 is discussed elsewhere in this book). There seems to be no demand to change what is targeted at all. The most plausible alternatives – those of a price level target and a nominal GDP target seem to have their merits, but have so far not been tried by any central bank and are not advocated by any serious commentators. Other proposals for reform include changing the index the central bank targets and changing the inflation target itself. The main plausible change that has been suggested for the inflation target has been to include asset prices (particularly house prices) in the index; however, we have argued elsewhere in this book that this would not be a good idea, and that central banks may well react appropriately in response to asset bubbles within their inflation remit – for example, a stock market boom may presage higher inflation, so a more contractionary monetary policy may be implemented because the central bank is seeking to achieve its inflation target. There is no need to add share prices, for example, into the index the central bank targets. Changing the inflation target has also been discussed elsewhere; it has been argued that this would almost certainly not be a good idea.

DISCUSSION QUESTIONS

1. Should the remit of the Bank of England be changed so that it is expected to put at least some weight on unemployment in monetary policy decisions?
2. Discuss the pros and cons of real interest rate targeting.
3. Should the exchange rate be taken into account at all in monetary policy decisions? If so, how?

CHAPTER 18

The Transmission Mechanism: How does the Central Bank Influence the Behaviour of the Economy?

In this chapter we summarise much of the discussion of earlier chapters and seek to present an account of how monetary policy works in an advanced economy such as the United Kingdom. Section 18.1 presents a step-by-step account of how the monetary policy currently operates in the UK. Section 18.2 brings together and summarises much of the discussion in earlier chapters, presenting a long but possibly not comprehensive list of the various ways in which monetary policy can impact upon the economy. Section 18.3 considers the issue of whether monetary policy is symmetrical – i.e. do increases and reductions in interest rates have the effects on aggregate demand of the same absolute value? Section 18.4 concludes.

18.1 How the Bank of England Attempts to Meet its Inflation Target

1. The Bank of England, which was granted operational independence by the incoming Labour government in 1997, has been given a target rate of inflation by the government. Since 2003 the target rate of inflation is 2%, defined in terms of the Consumer Price Index.

2. The inflation target is (supposedly) a target for all time periods. The Bank of England is expected to meet the target in the coming month, in the next six months, in a year, in five years' time and fifty years' hence and so forth.

    Commentary: the target can more realistically be thought of as a medium-term target – perhaps a time period of six months to two-years is relevant. It is well known that monetary policy acts with a lag, so it is unreasonable to expect policy measures to have much effect on inflation in less than six months. Similarly, most policy measures will have much of their effect within a period of two years. Perhaps the only way in which monetary policy could bring about a sharp change in inflation in less than six months is via the exchange rate – a sudden appreciation of the exchange rate, due to a large unanticipated rise in interest rates, would reduce the prices of many imported items and feed through to the CPI, although this effect would be subject to lags. However, the extra volatility this would imply for both the exchange rate and interest rates could be extremely disruptive and the exchange rate appreciation would need to be reversed sometime in the future. Furthermore, generating a slump now in response to a temporary surge in inflation might well reduce inflation in one to two years' time, when it might be at or below its target, so even from an inflation-targeting perspective such a policy would not be desirable. For an exploration of some of the problems of fine tuning the inflation rate, see Saborowski (2010).

3. The Monetary Policy Committee (MPC) of the Bank of England is responsible for making monetary policy decisions to meet the inflation target. The MPC has nine members. Four are external members, chosen by the Treasury. The five internal members of the committee are the Governor, two Deputy Governors and two other Bank employees chosen by the Bank. The committee usually meets on the Wednesday and Thursday after the first Monday of each month, announcing its decision at 12 noon on the Thursday. There can be exceptions if, for example, there is a General Election on the Thursday, as there was in May 2010.

4. The Bank of England's main and usual policy tool for controlling inflation is a short-term interest rate (the rate of interest on reserves held at the Bank of England by banks) although there are some circumstances under which it may use other policy tools (see below).

5. The main determinants of the underlying rate of inflation are inflationary expectations and the pressure of demand on resources, both actual and anticipated. There are several temporary factors which might affect inflation (indirect tax changes, weather conditions, exchange rate movements, commodity price changes, etc.). Generally it is believed, as discussed above, that it is not appropriate to try to offset the effects of these factors on inflation provided they are temporary; however, if they become permanent, then perhaps they should be offset. Basically, if the committee believes that inflation is threatening to rise above its target, it needs to take action to reduce actual or future demand, which hence means an increase in current interest rates, or (increased) expectations that interest rates will be raised sometime in the future.

6. As well as deciding upon the interest rate each month, the MPC releases various other information – it publishes the minutes of its meeting, and the voting record of its

members – but after a time lag, so it comes to be known, for example, whether all its members voted for the decision or, if not, what alternative(s) some of its members might have voted for. The publication date of its minutes is the Wednesday of the second week after the meeting takes place. The MPC is also responsible for producing a quarterly *Inflation Report*, which is followed by a news conference.

7. The extent to which an interest rate decision by the MPC changes demand depends (inter alia) on the extent to which it is unexpected. If a quarter-point increase in interest rates is anticipated, and this is what the committee delivers, then this should not cause any change in aggregate demand. So to have an impact, the committee needs to deliver a surprise. But what is relevant is not just the current interest rate, but also the expected future time path of interest rates and whether this changes. It might be, for example, that the public is expecting an increase in the short-term interest the following month, so if the interest rate unexpectedly increases this month, there is a change only in the interest rate expected for this month. On the other hand, some increases in interest rates could be expected to be permanent. In deciding whether an increase is temporary or permanent, members of the public may take into account the statement that typically accompanies the interest rate decisions, and information revealed by the minutes of meetings and the voting record of MPC members. If it is revealed that several members of the MPC voted to raise interest rates at a meeting without being successful this may well increase expectations of future increases in interest rates.

   We have noted that expectations of future interest rates are important determinants of current interest rates, especially longer term interest rates. Everything members of the MPC do which can affect expectations of their future interest rate decisions can affect current longer term interest rates and hence demand, output and inflation. Speeches of MPC members can hence be extremely important.

8. So by its actions the MPC can change present and expected Bank Rates. These may translate into changes in both short and longer term interest rates, depending on how the term structure of interest rates is determined (see our discussion in Chapter 12 above). But there also may be lags before changes in the policy rate change interest rates faced by borrowers and lenders. There is evidence that the reaction of such interest rates may often be delayed and incomplete, and that there is considerable heterogeneity in how financial institutions adjust interest rates. Evidence on this is provided by Fuertes and Heffernan (2009). And this was before the financial crisis! There is evidence that UK banks' marginal long-term funding costs, crucial for many of their interest rate decisions, and which formerly used to track the Bank of England's policy rate quite closely, have sometimes moved in a different direction, particularly during the financial crisis when they shot up. (See Bank of England, 2011, p. 14, Chart 1.9). These funding costs, by the second half of 2011, have come down considerably, but are still significantly above Bank Rate.

9. The interest rate chosen by the MPC is the interest rate paid on reserves. This may well affect other interest rates in the economy as many other interest rates are tied, either formally or informally, to this interest rate. The Bank also intervenes to ensure that short-term money market rates are approximately the same as the rate chosen by the

Bank of England. It does not always succeed in doing this, as was evidenced in the recent financial crisis.

10. As we know from economic theory, the relevant interest rate for agents is the real interest rate, not the nominal interest rate. Generally, however, because of inflation inertia, changes in nominal interest rates will generally translate into changes in real interest rates in the same direction. Also, if an increase in interest rates is believed to be disinflationary, it will cause some fall in expected inflation, and hence mean a greater increase in real interest rates. On the other hand, it is possible that an unexpected increase in interest rates is taken to mean that the MPC expects inflation to be higher, and this in turn leads to an increase in inflationary expectations. It is not clear that this could ever lead to an increase in nominal interest rates reducing real interest rates – it would mean, for example, a surprise $\frac{1}{2}$% increase in the interest rate increasing expectations of inflation by more than $\frac{1}{2}$%, and this does not seem at all plausible.

11. By 'quantitative easing', discussed more thoroughly in Chapter 21, the MPC may be able to reduce long-term interest rates, for given expectations of future short rates. By reducing the net supply of longer term bonds held by the public, it raises their price and hence reduces the interest rate on these bonds. Expectations of future quantitative easing or contraction, and also of the government debt, may also be important factors affecting longer term interest rates, over and above expectations of future short rates.

12. By reducing (actual and expected) short-term and long-term interest rates, the Bank affects spending in a large number of different ways, which are discussed below.

13. By changing demand and expectations, the MPC is able to influence, although not control precisely, the rate of inflation.

Monetary policy making is not easy, because the effects of monetary policy changes are both uncertain and work with a lag. If there were uncertainty but no lags, there would not be a problem as policy could be adjusted immediately in response to an unexpected development. On the other hand, lags without uncertainty would not create a problem – policy makers would just set the policy instruments so they have their desired effects after the relevant length of time.

It should also be stressed that the economy is continuously being buffeted by many other shocks which are impossible to predict. Those who criticise economic policy makers should contemplate the problem of driving a car with a 5 second delay before changes in the accelerator have any effect, where these effects are uncertain and where the car is continually being hit by random shocks.

18.2 How Changes in Interest Rates Affect Economic Activity

We have discussed extensively ways in which monetary policy may affect aggregate expenditure in this book. Here, we bring together the possible mechanisms. We consider an expansionary monetary policy that produces a fall in both short-term and long-term interest rates; then there are the following ways in which this may affect at least one of the components of aggregate expenditure:

1. **Direct Effects on Consumption**
    i. There is the standard intertemporal substitution effect raising consumption as individuals, both borrowers and lenders, substitute current for future consumption.
    ii. Income effects are positive for borrowers, negative for lenders. Possibly these cancel out in aggregate; at the very least, we would not expect the net effect to be particularly large.
    iii. Credit-constrained individuals may consume more when interest rates fall.

2. **Direct Effect on Investment**
    i. There is the standard 'direct' effect of lower interest rates on investment; the DPV of investment projects rises, so some which were previously not worth undertaking now become profitable. Longer-term investment may react more than shorter or medium-term investment projects, but short-term interest rates may be relevant for inventory decisions.
    Lower long-term rates may also raise asset prices, and this may affect spending in a number of different ways.

3. **Effects of Higher Share Prices**
    i. Consumption might rise because of the wealth effect of higher share prices.
    ii. Investment might rise through a 'Tobin's q' effect.

4. **Effects of Higher House Prices**
    (See our discussion in Chapter 12 for elaboration of these ideas.)
    i. There has been controversy over whether there is a positive wealth effect of higher house prices on consumption.
    ii. A higher relative price of housing tends to increase consumption of non-housing items.
    iii. Higher house prices imply an increase in house building via a Tobin's q type mechanism.
    iv. Higher house prices imply an increase in expenditure related to house-moving, assuming that higher house prices mean more turnover in the property market.
    v. Higher house prices may raise consumption via a collateral effect on borrowers.
    vi. Higher house prices may raise consumption via a collateral effect on banks.

5. **Effects of Higher Bond Prices**
    i. There may be a wealth effect of higher bond prices on consumption.
    ii. A rise in bond prices may increase the net worth of firms and hence investment (the balance sheet channel).

6. **Effects of a Depreciated Currency**
    i. An exchange rate depreciation (a higher price of foreign exchange) may mean (as discussed in Chapter 11) a rise in exports and a fall in imports, switching demand away from foreign goods towards domestic goods.
    ii. The domestic currency value of foreign assets rises because of a currency depreciation, and this may generate more domestic spending. To the extent that domestic agents have foreign currency debts, the effect may be in the opposite direction.

7. Effects via Expectations

    i. If output and income are expected to be higher in the future because of the other effects mentioned above, then that may raise output and expenditures today. If inflation is expected to be higher in the future, it may stimulate more spending now, or possibly do the reverse. In fact, there are a myriad of possible ways in which current spending may be affected.

So, we have identified 17 different channels of monetary policy transmission! It might be possible to dismiss some of them, perhaps the wealth effect of house price changes. But the list might not be exhaustive and with a little ingenuity it might be possible to come up with additional channels.

18.3 Is Monetary Policy Symmetrical?

By this is meant the question whether increases and decreases in the relevant monetary policy instrument have effects of exactly the same magnitude on output and inflation; that is, if an increase in interest rates of 1% reduces output by 2%, can we conclude that a decrease in interest rates of 1% raises output by 2%? The answer to this question is (almost certainly) 'no'; we might expect a contractionary monetary policy to be more powerful than an expansionary monetary policy. The reason has to do with bankruptcies. When a firm goes bankrupt, it typically stops spending and producing. There is a sudden negative effect on aggregate demand as it stops buying intermediate inputs from other firms and as its workers who lose their jobs reduce their consumption spending. If some firms go bankrupt, other firms and consumers may anticipate the possibility that there may be more bankruptcies, and hence reduce their spending for that reason. Increases in interest rate may cause bankruptcies, but there is no offsetting effect in the opposite direction when interest rates fall – firms do not suddenly come into existence and start producing. Lower interest rates and a more favourable business environment may encourage the setting up of new firms, but this will typically take time.

Far more serious than this may be bankruptcies of banks, such as happened in the Great Depression in the United States, where, without deposit insurance, banks failed and depositors in those banks lost their deposits. Effectively this meant that their deposits were wiped out and not surprisingly this led to a large contraction of aggregate demand. One might compare the effects of a reduction in the money supply by £1000 if caused by a bank defaulting or by an open market operation. The former might well lead to an immediate fall in spending of £1000 if the depositor is credit constrained. In the latter case, the household swaps one asset for another and this might have negligible effects on its spending. So the effect of a change in the money supply almost certainly depends significantly on how it is brought about.

18.4 Conclusion

Monetary policy works by affecting a large number of rates of return and asset prices. There may well be considerable lags between monetary policy decisions and their impact on output, unemployment and inflation. The power of monetary policy may depend on factors that may change over time; for example, the effects of interest-rate reductions on consumption could depend significantly on how indebted consumers are and the state of the banking system. Monetary policy making in such an environment is far from easy.

DISCUSSION QUESTIONS

1. Of the various channels of monetary transmission discussed in Section 18.2 above, which do you consider to be the most important? Are there any that can be ignored?
2. Why might the strength of the monetary policy transmission mechanism change over time?
3. Why might it matter whether monetary policy is symmetrical?

19

Monetary Policy in Practice

I n this chapter we consider monetary policy in practice. Section 19.1 presents a very brief history of monetary policy in the UK since 1971 whereas Section 19.2 describes the monetary policy decision making institutions in the USA and eurozone. However, because of space constraints, we do not discuss the history of monetary policy in these countries. Section 19.3 considers some additional issues and Section 19.4 concludes.

19.1 Monetary Policy in the UK

In 1971 the Bretton Woods system broke down. The next few years saw an acceleration of inflation as (arguably) a full employment target was pursued without much concern for other goals. This resulted in the adoption of monetary targets by the Labour government of 1974–79 which seemed to have some success in reducing inflation. The Thatcher government continued with monetary targets, adopting the so-called Medium Term Financial Strategy that involved targets for both the budget deficit and the money supply. Monetary targeting was effectively abandoned towards the end of the 1980s, which saw the so-called Lawson boom. In response to rapidly rising inflation, the government responded with a contractionary monetary policy, reinforced by entry into the Exchange Rate Mechanism (ERM) in 1990. The Bundesbank's contractionary monetary policy, in response to the severe shock of German reunification, constituted a severe deflationary shock to the UK economy. Britain's forced exit from the ERM in September 1992 was followed by the rapid adoption of inflation targets. The economy recovered and inflation remained subdued. In May 1997, the incoming Labour Government gave the Bank of England operational independence, and required the Bank to pursue an inflation target. A nine-person Monetary Policy Committee was set up to decide upon monetary policy (essentially the short-term interest rate). The Bank of England is expected to follow the precise terms of its remit, which are as follows: it is expected 'to maintain price stability' and 'subject to that, to support the economic policy of Her Majesty's Government, including its objectives for growth and employment'.

The Bank of England Act, which was passed in 1998 and contains the relevant legislation, requires the Chancellor to specify what price stability consists of and also the Government policy objectives. If the actual inflation rate deviates from the target by more than one percentage point, the Governor of the Bank of England is obliged to send an open letter to the Chancellor explaining why inflation has missed the target, outlining the policy action taken to deal with it, and setting out the period within which inflation is expected to return to the target and how the approach meets the government's monetary policy objectives. Initially, the target was 2.5% in terms of the RPIX (the retail price index excluding mortgage rates), but this was changed in December 2003 to 2% in terms of the CPI.

The Bank of England's operating procedures have changed considerably over the period of its existence (i.e. from 1694). However, it has always set a particular interest rate which has changed its name a fair number of times: until 1972 it was the Bank Rate; it was then the Minimum Lending Rate until 1981, when it became the Minimum Band 1 Dealing Rate. In 1997, it became the Repo Rate and, finally, in 2006, it became the official Bank Rate. Figure 19.1 shows the level at which it has been set since 1975.

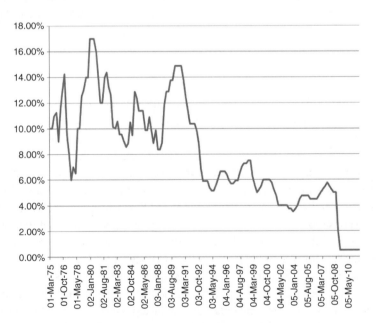

Figure 19.1 End of Quarter Bank of England Policy Rates since 1975.
(*Source:* Bank of England Statistics)

19.2 Other Central Banks

The United States central bank, the Federal Reserve System, has a seven-member Board of Governors. Members of the Board are appointed to 14-year non-renewable terms;[1] they are appointed by the president and subject to ratification by Congress. At the moment, two of the positions are unfilled as Congress has not approved the President's nominations. The governor, currently Ben Bernanke, is chosen from amongst its members; he or she is appointed for a four-year term which can be renewed. Its monetary policy decisions are made by the 12-member Federal Open Markets Committee, consisting of the seven governors of the Federal Reserve System and five of the heads of the 12 regional Federal Reserve boards.

The Federal Reserve is not subject to a formal inflation target. Instead it is obliged by the Federal Reserve Act to seek maximum employment and stable prices. This is sometimes referred to as a 'dual mandate'. However, it is emphasised that these are long-run goals, and the Federal Reserve is granted independence from political interference in achieving these goals. As already mentioned, it has a target range for the federal funds rate (currently 0 – 0.25%). Announcing the target range, and taking action to ensure that the rate stays within the bands is the main way in which it has undertaken monetary policy. It pays interest on reserves at 0.25%, and can lend to financial institutions via its discount window facility. There are several different rates it may charge on this; the interest rate on what is called 'primary credit' is 0.75%. (The figures given for the current values of various interest rates in this section are their values as of July 2011.)

The European Central Bank, which came into existence in 1999 to manage the newly instituted single European currency, has a six-person Executive Board, appointed by the European Council. Monetary policy decisions are taken by its 23-member Governing Council, which consists of the Executive Board plus the governors of the central banks of the 17 countries that are members of the eurozone. It meets twice a month; at the first meeting of the month it takes its monetary policy decision and at the second meeting it discusses other issues. It does not publish its minutes although it does hold a news conference after its policy making decision. There are three interest rates it makes decisions on: the interest rate on its deposit facility (currently $^{3}/_{4}$%), that on its main refinancing operations (currently 1.5%) and that on its marginal lending facility (currently 2.25%). It is mandated to pursue price stability within the eurozone; the Governing Council has defined price stability as an increase in the HICP (Harmonised Index of Consumer Prices) of not more than 2% per annum. Note that since the word 'increase' is used, rather than 'change', it seems to be ruling out price deflation as inconsistent with price stability.

---

[1] However, a member can be appointed to fill the unexpired portion of a term vacated by another member who does not serve his or her full term, in which case he can serve for this unexpired portion plus a full 14-year term.

19.3 Further Issues

19.3.1 Interest-Rate Smoothing

Suppose the MPC sets the interest rate that is best suited to meet the inflation target, then presumably it might be expected to change this interest rate only when it receives news – and as news is as likely to be positive as negative, this means it is as likely to change interest rates in an upwards as in a downwards direction. So under this scenario, interest rates, or at least the Bank Rate, should follow a random walk. However, there is considerable evidence of interest rate smoothing (i.e. movements of the interest rate in one direction are more likely to be followed by further movements in the interest rate in the same direction). There are a number of possible explanations for this. One is that interest rate volatility is costly. Suppose there is a shock that means the optimal interest rate jumps by 1% above its current level, but there is a 30% chance that half of this will be reversed next period. Then instead of increasing the interest rate by 1% today and then reducing it by 0.5% next month with a 30% probability, it might instead raise the interest rate by 0.5% today and only if the shock which might have caused such an interest rate also to be optimal next period does not occur, will it raise it by 0.5% again next month. Such a policy considerably reduces both the size and number of interest rate adjustments. A somewhat different justification of interest-rate smoothing is provided by Woodford (2003b).

19.3.2 Analysis of MPC Behaviour

A number of studies have looked at the voting record of the MPC and various issues stemming therefrom. For example, do external members vote in a different way from internal members? Other issues include the frequency of meetings and the number of members (both internal and external). One paper is Hansen and McMahon (2010), which presents evidence that not only do external members of the MPC have information not available to internal members, but they may exaggerate their expertise to obtain reappointment. Harris, Levine and Spencer (2011) seek to explain the dissent voting behaviour of MPC members.

19.4 Conclusion

The main instrument of monetary policy in the UK is the rate of interest paid on reserves (Official Bank Rate) which is determined by the Bank of England's MPC. Changes in this, and expectations of future changes in it, affect a whole range of other interest rates in the economy; asset prices may change as well and as a consequence expenditure decisions are influenced. There are a large number of ways in which demand may be affected; moreover, there are a fair number of factors which determine how powerful or weak these linkages may be (for example, the overall level of debt may affect how powerful an effect interest rate changes have on consumption).

DISCUSSION QUESTIONS

1. Should house prices be included in the price index that an inflation targeting central bank targets?

2. How should an inflation targeting central bank react to (a) a temporary increase in commodity prices, due to an earthquake in commodity producing countries; (b) a permanent increase in commodity prices, due to regime change in important commodity producing countries; (c) evidence that the underlying rate of productivity growth is faster than anticipated; (d) evidence that the amount of spare capacity in the economy is lower than previously thought?

3. For each of the shocks mentioned in Question 2, discuss how a central bank with (a) a price level target and with (b) a nominal GDP target would react. What conclusions, if any, do you draw about the desirability or otherwise of these alternative targets for monetary policy?

CHAPTER 20

The Worldwide Credit Crunch and Recession of 2007–2009

'So someday, no one can tell when, there will be another speculative climax and crash. There is no chance that, as the market moves to the brink, those involved will see the nature of their illusion and so protect themselves and the system.'

(Galbraith, 1961, p. xxii)

'*The This-Time-is-Different Syndrome*: . . . financial crises are things that happen to other people in other countries at other times: crises do not happen to us, here and now. We are doing things better, we are smarter, we have learned from past mistakes. The old rules of valuation no longer apply. The current boom, unlike the many booms that preceded catastrophic collapses (even in our country), is built on sound fundamentals, structural reforms, technological innovation, and good policy . . . '

(Reinhart and Rogoff, 2009, p. 15.)

Why was the financial crisis which reached its climax in 2008 such a surprise? Why did so many intelligent and knowledgeable people get it so totally wrong? And what are the lessons for monetary policy? This chapter obviously cannot do more than touch on some of the many issues raised by the worldwide credit crunch and recession. We begin in Section 20.1 by presenting a brief history of the crisis. Section 20.2 considers the much asked question why the crisis was such a surprise, and does attempt to answer the question. Section 20.3 covers the policy response to the crisis, including reforms to minimise the chances of such a crisis happening again. Section 20.4 discusses the question of the implications of the crisis for the discipline of economics, and Section 20.5 concludes.

20.1 A Brief History of the Crisis and Recession

Here, we will present only the briefest of sketches of what happened. There are ample accounts elsewhere.[1]

It is well known that the crisis had its roots in the developments in the US subprime market in the first half of the first decade of the new millennium. There had been a massive expansion of lending to many households who previously would have been unable to take out mortgages. Many of these households had no income, no job, no assets (so they were sometimes referred to as NINJA households), and the mortgages were often for a very high percentage of the price of the property. For example, the median combined loan-to-value ratio for subprime loans was 90% in 2003 and rose to 100% in 2005 (see Mayer, Pence and Sherlund, 2009, p. 31). It seems clear that expectations of continual increases in property prices must have underpinned such lending. However, the first hint of trouble in the subprime mortgage market came in the middle of 2005 and things rapidly deteriorated. The boom in house prices ended in 2005 and house prices fell at an annual rate of 10% from mid 2006 to 2008 (Mayer *et al.*, 2009, p. 45). Defaults and foreclosures surged. In February 2007, several large subprime mortgage lenders started to report losses. In August 2007, BNP Paribas stopped redemptions from some of its funds because it was unable to value the assets in these funds backed by US subprime mortgage debt. The LIBOR (London Interbank Offered Rate) shot up; this is a benchmark used for pricing much interbank lending and borrowing. Institutions heavily reliant on wholesale funding experienced difficulties, including Northern Rock, a former Building Society which went public in 1997 and which in September 2007 was subject to the first bank run in the United Kingdom for over 140 years. (The previous run had been in 1866, and the victim was Overend and Gurney, a London discount bank.) There were continual tensions in the money markets. In March 2008 Bear Stearns was taken over by J P Morgan and in September 2008 the crisis climaxed with the bankruptcy of Lehmann Brothers, which gave rise to an unprecedented global panic in the world money markets. A number of large banks worldwide were rescued; in the UK HBOS was taken over by Lloyds and the Royal Bank of Scotland had to be rescued; and there was the failure of three Icelandic banks in October 2008. Governments and central banks responded in a number of ways, supplying liquidity, guaranteeing deposits, injecting a huge amount of capital and doing all they could to prevent a wide-scale financial meltdown which would have had catastrophic consequences.[2] Such a

---

[1] One gripping, blow by blow account is Sorkin (2009). For an examination of the causes of the crisis see Bean (2010).

[2] If, in particular, the payments system had broken down, then effects would have been far more serious than they actually were, as would have been the case had there been many more bank runs and if more financial institutions had been allowed to fail.

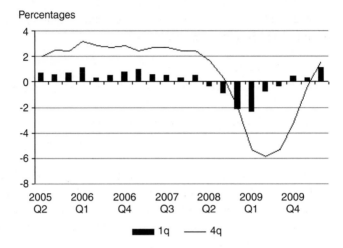

Figure 20.1 UK GDP Growth 2005–9.
(*Source:* Office for National Statistics)

catastrophe was averted, but at considerable cost. The immediate result was a sharp reduction in credit availability and a consequent fall in aggregate demand, causing a worldwide recession. Stock markets fell. Governments (and central banks) responded by cutting interest rates significantly and using various fiscal policy measures to boost demand. A recession still ensued but did not last; a year later most of the world's economies had emerged from recession.[3]

As of the time of writing (July 2011) a gradual worldwide recovery seems to be continuing. The main problem facing many governments now is that of large budget deficits or debts, and it may be several years before it is clear how well they deal with these; there is also the possibility that the recovery might stagnate.

20.2 Why was the Crisis such a Surprise?

There are a fair number of possible explanations, of which we discuss and review a few:

1. Many commentators expressed concern at the large rise in property prices in the period leading up to the crisis in the USA, UK and many other countries and some also commented on the large associated build up in debt, but this was not thought (by many) to be dangerous: some doubted whether there was in fact a bubble; others thought that if property prices did fall, their adverse macroeconomic effects could be offset by expansionary monetary policy, as had happened after the collapse of the dot-com bubble in March 2000.
2. Few understood the new financial instruments that were being developed; by conventional measures of risk the financial system did not look particularly vulnerable in 2007.

---

[3] See Figure 20.1 for output growth in the UK between 2005 and 2009.

3. The collapse of the US subprime market in 2007 was not deemed an earth-shattering event – the sums involved ('just' $50bn) were minimal compared with the size of the global financial system.

4. The success of inflation targeting, adopted and practised by many central banks in the 1990s and 2000s perhaps contributed to the 'This Time is Different' (TTID) Syndrome.

5. The East Asia financial crisis of 1997–1998 – a pretty big event that was also largely unanticipated – was attributed to factors irrelevant to the developed world: inadequate regulation, corruption, excessive speed in capital market deregulation, imperfectly credible fixed exchange rate schemes, etc., again contributing to the TTID syndrome.

6. In the UK, the reforms whereby the Financial Services Authority (FSA) became the sole regulator of financial services may have had a role to play: the FSA concentrated more on the 'micro' task of protecting consumers, the Bank of England focused on its inflation targeting, meaning that there was no one who could take an overall view of the stability of the financial system.

Sometimes the crisis is attributed to 'unrestrained greed'. However, it is not clear why unrestrained greed should have produced a crisis in 2007–8; presumably human beings have always been greedy, so why should it have produced a crisis then and not at other times? But rather than greed, it may have been the case that collective self-delusion was a much more relevant factor.

20.3 The Policy Response

We should distinguish between the measures that were taken more or less immediately to shore up the banking system, shorter-run policy (to combat the effect of the crisis on aggregate demand, output and employment) and longer-run policy (to offset the longer-run consequences, in particular the massive increase in public sector debt such crises usually entail).

20.3.1 Monetary Policy

Short term-interest rates in many countries were reduced quickly to near zero. In the UK the Bank of England reduced its policy rate from 5% to 0.5% over a period of months. In the chapter on the term structure of interest rates (Chapter 12), we argued that it is reasonable to suppose that long-term rates are the average of expected future short rates plus a term premium, which inter alia depends on the stock of longer-term bonds. Since expectations of future short-term interest rates almost certainly fell as well, this tended to reduce longer-term interest rates. Quantitative easing (purchases, mainly of longer term government bonds, by the central bank) which can be thought of as a way of reducing the term premium and hence also reducing longer-term interest rates, was introduced in March 2009. So both short-term and long-term interest rates fell considerably. However, there are some necessary qualifications. The first is that it was some time before interest rates in the important interbank market fell; these are the rates at which banks can lend to each other and would incorporate a risk premium, which shot up at the time of the crisis. The interest rate over which the central bank has control is a safe interest rate, whereas interest rates more relevant for economic decisions may incorporate a risk premium and move in a different direction. A second point is that although nominal interest rates fell considerably, it is not clear that real interest rates also fell, as inflationary expectations presumably fell also with the onset of the crisis.

Monetary policy has two functions (at least) in a crisis – contributing to saving the banking system and offsetting the recessionary effect of the crisis on aggregate demand. In the panic following Lehman Brothers' bankruptcy, there was a major worldwide collapse of confidence in the financial system, and the immediate task was to save the financial system. Had the financial system collapsed, the consequences would have been dire in the extreme, and something comparable to the Great Depression of the 1930s could have ensued. However, such a catastrophe was averted; there was, however, a collapse of lending by the banks, which, when combined with the effects of the crisis on the spending decisions of many individuals and companies, was severely deflationary.

The deflationary factors in the aftermath of the crisis were the fall in lending by the banks, the effects of asset price declines on spending, the rise in certain interest rates incorporating a risk premium, expectations of lower, possibly negative inflation (tending to raise real interest rates) and the collapse of confidence. An expansionary monetary policy can offset all of these deflationary forces to some extent, although sometimes it may take some time, and in the aftermath of the crisis the effects of the collapse of both of confidence and of bank lending were so great that they dwarfed anything monetary policy could do to offset these effects. A more expansionary monetary policy, by enabling banks to borrow more cheaply, should enable them to lend more. If safe interest rates fall, then with a given risk premium, risky interest rates should fall as well, and inasmuch as the policy tends to reduce risk and increase confidence, the risk premium should decline as well. The fall in safe interest rates should raise asset prices, as discussed elsewhere in the book. By making it clear, by both their announcements and their actions, that they will continue to pursue their inflation targets, central banks can allay fears of disinflation and, by helping prevent a collapse in the banking system, they should allay the fall in confidence.

20.3.2 Fiscal Policy

The crisis saw a large increase in government spending and fall in tax revenue, as massive amounts of money were poured into the banking system and the recession caused both corporate and individual tax receipts to plummet. Governments responded to the crisis by spending more and cutting taxes. In the UK, for example, the government announced a temporary cut in VAT and various other fiscal measures designed to stimulate the economy.

In combating a financial crisis, an increase in the deficit may be entirely appropriate: the credit crunch means that some individuals and companies cannot borrow to finance spending, so they do not spend. A tax cut provides a way round this; someone who finds he is denied a loan for £1000 and would otherwise cut his spending by this amount would presumably spend a tax cut of the same amount if this is offered. Temporary fiscal policy can also boost spending by reducing current prices relative to future prices; this is effectively how the VAT cut and the car scrappage scheme worked.

In the longer run, the fiscal deficits will generate much greater government debt. In the UK, the deficit for the 2009–10 financial year was about £165bn (or 11.7% of GDP), with government debt of 55% or so of GDP at the end of the year. The deficit in 2010–11 is estimated at £142.1bn, with the public sector net debt – GDP ratio of 61.9% in June 2011. In March 2011 the OBR forecast a deficit of £122bn for 2011–12.

Consider the following. The current 'structural' deficit (excluding the effects of the recession and the costs of the temporary measures taken to combat the recession) may be about 8% of GDP. Suppose we want to stabilise the debt at 80% of GDP in a few years time. Then this would imply a 'steady-state' deficit of about 4% of GDP, assuming nominal GDP growth of 5% or so. Reducing the deficit by 4% of GDP may not be painless, but it is certainly feasible. A reduction in the share of government spending to GDP of 2% could be achieved (given normal GDP growth) by freezing *real* government spending for two to three years. And a rise of 2% in the tax/GDP ratio could similarly be achieved over a course of several years. So although eliminating the growth in the ratio of government debt to GDP may be painful, it should be feasible.

It seems that a temporary increase in the fiscal deficit may be an entirely appropriate way of combating a short-run fall in aggregate demand. A more controversial question is when is it appropriate to reverse the direction of fiscal policy and move from expansion to contraction. This is something on which informed opinion seems to differ. However, we would point out that, as discussed in our chapter on fiscal policy, a fiscal tightening can be expansionary if it reduces long-term interest rates.

20.3.3 Regulatory Reform

Many would argue that regulatory reform is necessary to prevent such a crisis from ever happening again. But it is also important to get the reform right. We need a well-functioning financial system. In fact it may be impossible to ensure that a financial crisis never happens again; as has been argued earlier, there are some intrinsic features of the financial system that makes it liable to crises. Inasmuch as financial institutions perform liquidity transformation, then this exposes them to the possibility of bank runs and financial panic. Also, the 'too big to fail' syndrome plus the fact that bankers and shareholders are not exposed to the full negative downside implications of many of their actions means that they will have an incentive to make excessively risky loans – they gain if the project on which they are making the loan succeeds, but may not lose much if the project is unsuccessful. Perhaps it would be possible to prevent a crisis from ever happening again, by, for example, requiring that banks hold 100% reserves against deposits, but the costs of such a reform might be so great that the costs exceed the benefits. So we need 'optimal' regulation; such regulation would seek to ensure a maximum of benefits over costs; it might be a good idea to run the risk of an occasional crisis, if there are more than offsetting benefits from a financial system that usually functions well.

The regulatory system in the UK is currently being overhauled. A Financial Policy Committee (FPC) is being set up in the Bank of England; it is chaired by the Governor and a number of members of the MPC are also members of the FPC. It had its first meeting in June 2011. Responsibility for prudential regulation of financial firms is being transferred from the FSA to a newly established Prudential Regulatory Authority which will be a subsidiary of the Bank of England. It is envisaged that it will start operation in late 2012; transitional arrangements are currently in place. Its sole objective is promoting the safety and soundness of regulated firms. The consumer protection function of the FSA will be taken over by what will be called the Financial Conduct Authority. It remains to be seen how these arrangements will work in practice.

We do not offer any suggestions for institutional reform of the regulatory system in this book. However, we would offer the following suggestions for additional measures that may enhance financial stability as well as having other benefits:

1. A maximum loan to value ratio for mortgages for house purchase – e.g. 80%. So the maximum anyone buying a £100 000 property would be able to borrow would be £80 000. This would have a number of advantages:
   i. It would reduce the risk to banks from any given fall in house prices.
   ii. It would (almost certainly) reduce fluctuations in house prices, as well as leading to somewhat lower house prices on average.
   iii. Somewhat more speculatively, it would encourage more of a culture of thrift. Many people who otherwise would save a minimal amount would be forced to save in order to acquire the down payment on a house. This may give them more of a habit of saving, so they might save up to buy other items they would otherwise buy on credit. This might tend to reduce the general level of borrowing as well.
   iv. It could be varied to combat excessive increases or decreases in property prices, and for countercyclical reasons.

It might not be desirable to introduce such a measure until it is clear that the economy has recovered from the recession. However, once in place, it will give policy makers another tool to regulate demand in the economy. It probably would not be a good idea to change it too frequently, otherwise effects from agents anticipating that the ratio may be changed could make things worse: for example, suppose potential home buyers anticipate that the ratio will soon be increased, they may well postpone their purchases. One important question is who should make the decision about the ratio. The MPC might not be the appropriate body, as such a decision would have a large number of ramifications unrelated to inflation that the MPC might not have the knowledge or competence to deal with. Perhaps it might be preferable if the MPC could make recommendations to the government on what the ratio should be, but the decision should be the government's.

2. Another vexed question is that of bankers' bonuses. One possible reform is that most of bankers' bonuses be put into a special fund, from which the bankers could only withdraw certain amounts over time: for example, they might be allowed 25% of their bonus when it is paid, but the remainder would be paid into the fund, from which they could withdraw (say) 15% every year for the next five years. However, if their bank failed or needed to be rescued, the bankers in question would forfeit the remaining money in the fund, which instead could contribute towards the bailout and compensating those who had lost from the bank failure. This should deter bankers from taking risky decisions for which they are rewarded before the outcome of the decisions are realised.

However, we do not fully understand why bankers are paid such huge bonuses. Are they a reward for some special skill, or are they largely rents? In order to design appropriate ways of dealing with bankers' bonuses, we really need to understand what economic role, if any, they fulfil. A well functioning financial system is also vital for the health of the economy, and it is important that reform in this area does not damage the workings of the financial system unduly.

Two further issues that need careful consideration are whether there should be a split between retail and investment banks (along the lines of the Glass Steagall Act in the US, which was passed in 1933) and whether there should be more competition in banking. These are very complicated issues; the former question is being considered by the Independent Commission on Banking, which is due to report in September 2011. The second question is also complicated; although competition is generally regarded as desirable in an industry, in the case of financial services, it is possible that increased competition could create greater incentives for (undesirable) risk taking, make financial institutions less secure and create greater instability in the financial sector. Banking is quite concentrated in the UK; for example, the top six banks account for 88% of deposits (Independent Commission on Banking, 2010, p. 9).

20.4 The Future of Economics

Does the crisis mean that economics needs fundamental reappraisal? The crisis has clearly revealed much that is unsatisfactory about the state of economics. We have reacted much better to the crisis than we did in the past – consider the Great Depression, where a whole series of policy mistakes meant that (in the US) unemployment rose to 25% of the workforce, output fell for four years and it took eight years to return to the pre-Depression level of output. However, there are several areas in which economic analysis is currently inadequate and in which further work would be highly desirable.

1. Bubbles and Crashes. We have no satisfactory theories of bubbles and crashes. Such models would help explain how and why bubbles start, and how and why they end and turn into crashes. As suggested in Chapter 13, such models might well involve the

interaction of rational and irrational agents. Allen and Gale (2007) is a useful starting point for those wishing to develop such models.

2. Banking in General Equilibrium Models. There is a dearth of general equilibrium models that incorporate a financial or banking sector in a satisfactory way. Developing such models is an urgent priority for further research. One relevant reference is Goodfriend and McCallum (2007).

3. Uncertainty. Macroeconomic models have, by and large, not incorporated uncertainty in a satisfactory way. Agents can generally insure themselves to some extent against risk, but not completely. In discussing the Dornbusch model, we remarked that it involved an unanticipated change in a model with perfect foresight! Unfortunately we do not seem to have a much better way of analysing such changes now. We need a model where unanticipated changes can happen, but agents take into account the possibility that such shocks can occur and change their behaviour appropriately.

4. Bonuses. We need to understand the functioning of the banking system better – it is not clear why banks pay such large bonuses.

5. Economic History. Another lesson is that we need to study much more economic history. Bubbles and crises have happened periodically throughout history; if policy makers and economists had studied these episodes more, perhaps alarm bells would have started to ring much earlier than they actually did.

20.5 Conclusions

First of all, it might be said that although there are reforms that need to be made in the sphere of regulation, it does not appear that there is any case for a fundamental change in the way monetary policy is conducted. We have argued that there is no need to change the inflation target in either direction. Monetary policy makers will almost certainly pay more attention to asset price changes in fulfilling their remit; there is no need to change the remit. There are some things to consider in a longer term context, for example the possibility of moving to either a price level target or a GDP target.

As far as the crisis is concerned, it is of course not over yet, by any means. But it is important to recognise how far we have come. In late September 2008 there was a real danger of a collapse in the world financial system, with truly catastrophic consequences. That was averted. In March 2009, the FTSE 100 had fallen by 40%, manufacturing output was contracting at an annualised rate of almost 20%, unemployment was rising extremely rapidly, and corporate bond spreads and interbank spreads were extremely high (interbank spreads were around 15 times their pre-crisis levels).[4] By mid 2011, the situation had changed enormously. Spreads have declined, the economy is no longer in recession, un-employment is no longer rising and share prices have recovered. Nevertheless, we cannot

---

[4]See Dale (2010).

relax. The fact that short-term interest rates are still extremely low and that the government is intent on improving its fiscal position with some quite painful measures, entails that there is little that can be done if the economy stagnates except to introduce another round of quantitative easing. As far as monetary policy and economic policy more generally are concerned, we live in very interesting times.

DISCUSSION QUESTIONS

1. What difference would it have made to the financial crisis if Lehmann Brothers had been rescued?
2. Are bankers' bonuses a problem? If so, why? What should be done about them?
3. What was the role of asset price movements in causing the global financial crisis? Should policy makers seek to reduce asset price movements, and, if so, how?

CHAPTER 21

Recent Innovations in Monetary Policy: Quantitative Easing

T he credit crunch saw a number of innovations in monetary policy, the most notable of which was quantitative easing, whereby the central banks of a number of countries purchased assets, mainly longer-term government bonds, from the private sector. In this chapter, we will describe what happened in Section 21.1, discuss relevant theory in Section 21.2 and empirical evidence in Section 21.3. The future of such policies and implications for monetary policy is considered in Section 21.4, before some concluding thoughts are offered in Section 21.5.

21.1 Quantitative Easing in Practice

In the aftermath of the credit crunch that climaxed in September 2008, central banks around the world cut interest rates aggressively – in the UK, for example, the Bank of England cut its policy rate a number of times, reaching 0.5% in March 2009. They also embarked on an extensive programme of providing liquidity to the financial markets. When the first signs of tensions emerged in the financial markets in August 2007, money market spreads jumped upwards. These are the spreads between interbank interest rates, which may reflect default and liquidity risks and 'safe' interest rates such as 'swap' rates. The former may be measured by the London Interbank Offered Rate (or LIBOR), the latter by the overnight interest swap

Table 21.1   The Bank of England's Asset Purchase Operations ('Quantitative Easing').

Bank of England's Asset Purchase Facility Results, 7/7/11		
Purchases financed by:	Issue of Treasury Bills and the Debt Management Office's Cash Management Operations	Creation of Central Bank Reserves
Gilts	n/a	£198,275 m.
Corporate Bonds	£253 m.	£857 m.
Secured Commercial Paper	£30 m.	£0 m.
Total	£283 m.	£199,132 m.
(Total Asset Purchases however financed: £199,415 m.)		

(*Source:* Bank of England website, accessed 13/7/11)

(OIS) rate. After the failure of Lehmann Brothers in September 2008, these rates shot up dramatically. (See Lenza, Pill and Reichlin, 2010, for an account of what happened and of the measures central banks took to restore liquidity to the markets.) Since then the spreads have declined considerably, although not to pre-crisis levels.

We will not discuss these measures in any detail in this chapter, in spite of their importance; interested readers are invited to consult Lenza *et al.* (2010). Instead we will consider the policy of quantitative easing, initiated by the Bank of England in March 2009 whereby the Bank purchased large quantities of longer term assets, financed mainly, but not entirely by an increase in reserves at the Bank of England. More specifically, the Bank of England Asset Purchase Facility Fund was set up; in March 2009 it was authorised to purchase up to £150bn of assets; this limit was raised twice, to £175bn in August 2009 and to £200bn in November 2009. Figure 21.1 shows how the Bank of England's balance sheet changed over the relevant time period.[1]

Table 21.1 shows the composition (as of July 2011) of the Bank's assets which were acquired as a consequence of this programme. It can be seen that almost all the assets purchased are gilt-edged securities financed by an increase in reserves, although there have been some purchases of corporate bonds financed in the same way, and some asset purchases have been financed in other ways (mainly through an increase in Treasury bills). Other central banks also carried out such purchases.

The Federal Reserve has behaved similarly. In November 2008, it announced plans to purchase up to $100 billion in government-sponsored enterprise (GSE) debt and up to $500 billion in mortgage-backed securities. In March 2009, it announced plans to purchase up to $300 billion of longer-term Treasury securities in addition to increasing its total purchases of GSE debt up to $200 billion and of mortgage-backed securities up to $1.25 trillion. These purchases are equivalent to roughly 10% of GDP. The ECB has not purchased assets in the

---

[1]Dale (2010) is one account of the Bank's quantitative easing programme.

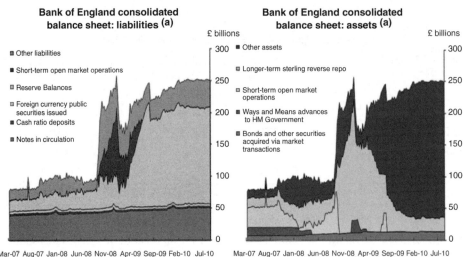

Bank of England consolidated balance sheet: liabilities (a)

Bank of England consolidated balance sheet: assets (a)

(a) Excludes loans and associated deposits in course of settlement

Figure 21.1   Changes in the Bank of England Balance Sheet between March 2007 and July 2010 (Reproduced with the kind permission of the Bank of England)

same way, but it has undertaken a large quantity of long-term repo operations, whereby central banks purchase assets with an agreed re-sale value. The reason for this may be that such operations do not expose the ECB to potential capital losses. This may be a problem as the ECB, unlike the Bank of England or the Fed, does not have a single fiscal authority behind it. (See Miles, 2010). The increase in the size of the ECB balance sheet (measured as a fraction of GDP) was comparable with the increase in that of the other two central banks.

21.2 Quantitative Easing: Theory

Quantitative easing measures have usually been undertaken when policy interest rates are low and the authorities seem unwilling to reduce them anymore.[2] It might be asked how they work, given that policy rates cannot go any lower; presumably the answer is that these measures affect other interest rates that are relevant for economic behaviour. One possibility is that they may affect other short-term interest rates such as inter-bank rates which may incorporate risk and liquidity premia. The purchases may reduce default risk and enhance liquidity. Another possibility is that they may reduce longer-term interest rates, which, as

---

[2]It might be asked why, in the UK, 0.5% and not zero is regarded as the 'floor' to interest rates. The explanation may be that many lending rates are tied to this interest rate, and a reduction of Official Bank Rate to zero would reduce these lending rates even further; as interest rates on many deposits are already at zero and cannot be reduced any further, this would squeeze banks' margins and the Bank may not wish to do this.

argued frequently in this book, are a crucial part of the mechanism whereby monetary policy impacts the economy. Here our discussion of the term structure of interest rates in Chapter 12 is relevant. Presumably quantitative easing can reduce longe-term interest rates either by lowering expectations of future short rates or by reducing the term premium on longer term bonds. It is not clear how they might do the former. It seems reasonable, then to suppose that it is by affecting the term premium that such operations work.

Some theoretical work has also appeared. For example, Cúrdia and Woodford (2010), discuss conditions under which quantitative easing can be effective. They present an irrelevance result under which central bank purchases of assets have no effect – these are (i) the assets in question are valued only for their pecuniary return and (ii) all investors can purchase arbitrary quantities of the same assets at the same (market) prices (Cúrdia and Woodford, 2010, p. 5). These may be standard assumptions in much of the literature, but in order to analyse quantitative easing rigorously, we need to build models that relax at least one of these assumptions. Cúrdia and Woodford indeed relax the second assumption and show that there may be circumstances under which a policy of quantitative easing may raise welfare, but these are usually when there is severe malfunctioning of financial markets.

Almost all theoretical macroeconomic models based on intertemporal optimisation do not allow for the possibility that short- and long-term bonds may be imperfect substitutes. It is not easy to modify these models so as to introduce this possibility, although this is clearly a high priority for research. One relevant paper is Harrison (2010).

21.3 Quantitative Easing: Empirical Evidence

Some studies have appeared which attempt to measure the effects of the quantitative easing programmes that were initiated in 2009. One such study is Gagnon *et al.* (2010), which found that the Federal Reserve's Large-Scale Asset Purchases programme (the US term for quantitative easing) had reduced the term premium on 10-year government bonds by between 30 and 100 basis points (i.e. between 0.3% and 1%). They stress that the policy seemed to have worked by affecting the term premium and not by altering expectations of future short rates. For the UK, one study is Joyce *et al.* (2010), which suggests that the quantitative easing programme may have depressed gilt yields by about 100 basis points, a non-negligible effect.

Unfortunately, we know of no estimates of the effects of such a decline in long-term nominal interest rates on economic activity (the effect on real interest rates will have been almost exactly the same, since it is unlikely that the policy had any major effect on inflationary expectations). Presumably the change will have many of the effects discussed in our chapter on the transmission mechanism of monetary policy in Chapter 18, but the change is a reduction in long-term interest rates holding constant expectations of short rates, not a reduction in both short and long rates.

21.4 Asset Purchases and Sales as an Instrument of Monetary Policy

One of the major issues facing monetary policy in the next few years is the question of how quantitative easing will be unwound – that is, how and when the £200bn of assets that the Bank of England bought starting in March 2009 will be sold; more generally there is the question of how such operations should be used in general. The Governor of the Bank of England has discussed this issue; in a press conference after the publication of the May 2011 *Inflation Report* he indicated that Official Bank Rate would be the first instrument to be used in a contractionary direction when the time came to raise interest rates.

Quantitative easing only really makes sense if the expectations hypothesis is false and something like Hicks's hypothesis holds, with the term premium dependent on the stock of bonds. If this is the case, then the monetary authorities have two instruments of monetary policy; as well as controlling the short-run interest rate, they can also influence the term premium, and hence longer-term interest rates, through purchases or sales of longer-term assets. The need for quantitative easing arose since, in the aftermath of the grave financial crisis of 2007–8, monetary policy was still not sufficiently expansionary even though short-term interest rates were as low as they could go, and hence it was necessary to use another instrument.

The question now arises as to which combination of policies the authorities should use when they are not constrained by the zero lower bound. This is an important issue which has scarcely been discussed so far, but should arise before long when central banks contemplate selling some of the large stocks of assets they accumulated during their quantitative easing programmes, something we will describe as quantitative contraction (QC), and we will describe actions which are either QE or QC as quantitative actions (QA). The following points may be relevant:

1. Changes in the policy interest rate will, provided they are expected to be reasonably persistent, change both short-term and longer-term interest rates whereas QAs will just affect the term premium and hence long-term rates. Longer-term rates may be more important for expenditure decisions than shorter-term rates, but the latter may not be completely irrelevant, so changes in the policy interest rate may be preferable from this perspective. Also, a number of interest rates in the economy (including many mortgage interest rates and rates on savings accounts) are linked to the central bank's policy rate, and this may be another, possibly powerful, way in which changes in this rate may have an impact on the economy.

2. It is not clear whether to choose a quantity or price target for QAs; for example, the central bank might decide either on a sale of government bonds worth £20bn, or on a target range for longer-term interest rates (it might decide on a range of 3.5–4% for longer term interest rates, for example). In the former case, it is not clear what effect these actions will have on interest rates and hence spending; in the latter case, it is not clear how large sales or purchases of bonds need to be to meet the target range; indeed, in some circumstances

meeting the target range may not be feasible. In general, it might be thought that QAs are less predictable in their effects than decisions to change the short-term interest rate.

3. Frequent purchases and sales of long-term bonds by the central bank may make the holding of such bonds riskier and hence make them more difficult to sell, or at least reduce the price at which they can be sold. This may be of importance if the government has a large budget deficit that it needs to finance largely through issuing such bonds. Also, a large-scale sale of long-term bonds by the central bank may, through depressing their price, cause balance-sheet problems for both financial and non-financial firms.

4. If it seems that lending growth by banks and other financial institutions is excessive, in the sense that it may lead to a breach of the inflation target, then QC, which may curtail such lending by mopping up these institutions' reserves, may be the appropriate remedy.

5. If there are asset price bubbles which the authorities wish to curtail, then QC may be the appropriate action if longer-term bonds are closer substitutes for shares and property than shorter-term bonds.[3]

6. If shorter-term interest rates are much higher than longer-term interest rates, but the authorities still wish to raise interest rates, they may prefer to raise longer-term rates by QC, rather than both shorter- and longer-term rates by raising their policy rate.

We would also point out that as well as conventional monetary policy being constrained by a zero-lower bound constraint, QC also has a lower bound – once the central bank has sold its entire stock of government bonds, it presumably cannot carry out any further quantitative contraction.

21.5 Conclusion

As far as QAs are concerned, it seems the monetary authorities now have two policy instruments. Nevertheless, it seems sensible that they employ changes in their policy rate as their main instrument, for the reasons discussed above. QAs should be employed sparingly, perhaps to mop up excess monetary or credit growth, to stabilise asset prices or to shift the term structure of interest rates in a favourable direction. Of course, their main role has been, and perhaps should continue to be, as a supplementary tool of monetary policy in circumstances when it is not possible to reduce the main instrument, the policy rate, when it is already as low as it can go.

DISCUSSION QUESTIONS

1. Are there any ways in which QE measures might work apart from changing the term premium?
2. How might QE work in an open economy?

---

[3]However, since many mortgage rates are tied to the Bank's policy rate, it is possible that conventional monetary policy measures may be more effective in curtailing house price bubbles than quantitative contraction.

CHAPTER 22

Current and Future Monetary Policy

F riedman and Schwartz conclude their classic history of money in the United States thus: 'One thing of which we are confident is that the history of money will continue to have surprises in store . . . – surprises that the student of money and the statesman will ignore at their peril' (Friedman and Schwartz, 1963, p. 700). These wise words are as true today as they were then.

Before the financial crisis emerged in 2007, a certain amount of smugness had crept into economists' discussion of monetary policy. There seemed to be a consensus that a policy regime of inflation targeting, implemented by operationally independent central banks, had produced a vast improvement in economic performance, sometimes described as 'The Great Moderation'. Inflation was low in most countries, and economic growth was proceeding at a reasonable pace. Some economists did draw attention to the large rises in both asset prices and indebtedness in many advanced Western economies, but it was not generally believed that they presaged anything dire. Perhaps it was believed that regulatory mechanisms would prevent a crisis; most economists were probably not aware of the sophisticated developments in corporate finance that may have played a crucial role in hiding the imminence of a disaster, and in any case it was believed that if a crash came, it could easily be offset by a sufficiently expansionary monetary policy, as happened with the collapse of the dot-com boom in the early years of the new millennium.

Whether monetary policy had an important role in causing the crisis is debatable, but the monetary policy response was much better than it was in the previous major worldwide financial crisis in the 1930s, for example, where GDP in the USA fell by 25% in the four years following the crisis and it took eight years for the pre-crisis level of economic activity to be restored. Central banks rapidly brought down short-term interest rates and pumped huge amounts of liquidity into the system; there were a number of policy innovations, the most important of which was quantitative easing. So it does seem that the inflation targeting regime produced a reasonably good policy response to the crisis.

In the remainder of this concluding chapter, we shall consider a number of important current issues relating to monetary policy.

22.1 Current Monetary Policy

The contention that monetary policy has been worked successfully may not command universal assent; at the time of writing (July 2011) inflation in the UK is considerably above its target; indeed, it has been above its target of 2% (as measured by the CPI) by at least one percentage point since January 2010. Nevertheless, the MPC has continued to keep their policy rate at its record low level ($\frac{1}{2}$%), generally regarded as the 'floor' to interest rates. There has been a certain amount of debate and discussion amongst economists both outside and inside the MPC about whether interest rates should be raised because of the rise in inflation. The majority opinion seems to be that a rise in interest rates is not required; the basic argument is that the current rise in inflation is temporary and will fall back in due course. The Bank of England can do nothing now to change inflation in the next few months. As emphasised repeatedly in this book, monetary policy decisions affect inflation with a long and variable lag, of at least one year and possibly two. What is relevant for monetary policy decisions is not the current rate of inflation but what it might be expected to be in (say) eighteen months, and there are reasons to believe that this should be low and not above target. One factor contributing to the current high rate of inflation is the rise in VAT to 20% in January 2011. This may have produced an increase in the price level of about 1%; this effect will raise inflation by about the same amount in this calendar year, but as from January 2012 this effect should drop out of the year by year comparison and hence not raise inflation further. Putting the point in another way, the rise in VAT may cause a permanent increase in the price level, but this translates into a rise in the inflation rate only for twelve months after it is implemented. The other main factors causing the current rise in inflation are the rise in world commodity prices and the depreciation in the value of sterling. One element behind the commodity price increase is the turmoil in the Middle East. A sudden decline in oil output, for example, means a decline in world oil supply and hence, given that demand for oil is pretty price inelastic in the short run, produces a large increase in world oil prices. As far as the effect of this on inflation is concerned, three points are worth making:

1. Even if the rise in world oil prices is permanent, it will only have a temporary effect on inflation for exactly the same reason as the VAT increase will only raise inflation temporarily.

2. Even if the decline in oil output is permanent, this will most likely not produce a permanent increase in world oil prices; over time, the higher world oil price will induce other producers to produce more and consumers to consume less, hence tending to attenuate the rise. This effect will be greater if it is anticipated that the price hike is temporary.

3. The decline in oil output will almost certainly not be permanent.

So our assessment would be that the MPC is right not to change policy in reaction to changes in the rate of inflation of this kind. What it should do is look at the underlying trend rate of inflation, and also the overall level of economic activity and how this is likely to develop over the next two years. Significant rises in the underlying trend rate of inflation and/or an impending boom in economic activity would be reasons for raising interest rates now, but neither of these is happening at all at the moment.

Sometimes it has been argued that the MPC needs to raise interest rates now to preserve its credibility. However, there is no evidence that its credibility is at all threatened. If it were to raise interest rates then, given the lags involved, it will have virtually no effect on inflation in the next few months, when it is likely to remain above target; its main effect will be on inflation in 2012 and 2013 when it may well be below target in any case and when it will hence make it miss the target by even more. It is difficult to see how a policy action which makes the Bank of England miss its inflation target for a longer period of time can plausibly be thought to enhance its credibility! A further point is that presumably the government can change the Bank of England's independence, or pass legislation that affects its behaviour in some way. If the Bank were to pursue policies that seemed contrary both to what the government wanted and to public opinion, then the government might conceivably do something on these lines. Presumably this is something the MPC needs to bear in mind when making its decisions.

Taking a somewhat broader perspective, we might ask whether the current policy of the Bank of England is right for the economy. It can be argued that a temporary rise in inflation might indeed be appropriate for a heavily indebted economy emerging from a credit crunch as it reduces the real value of both public and private debt. Also the rise in inflation may raise spending by reducing real interest rates. An increase in interest rates now would probably be quite damaging to the economy given that the recovery is fairly fragile as it is. However, it is important that the MPC does raise interest rates as and when it becomes necessary to do so.

22.2 Monetary Policy and Asset Price Bubbles and Collapses

The last two decades have seen large asset price bubbles and collapses, in both share and house prices. Such large asset price movements are almost certainly not desirable, but we know little about how they are caused and what their consequences are. Although there is a great deal of literature on bubbles, the questions why they start, and why and how they end have hardly been tackled at all. It is probably the case that monetary policy has an important relationship with the creation, persistence and ending of asset price bubbles, but beyond that we know very little. Should, for example, the Federal Reserve have done more to burst the internet price bubble in the later years of the 1990s? At the moment, we do not have any appropriate analytic framework for examining such a phenomenon. Developing a better understanding of asset price bubbles and collapses is an important area for further research. However, it does seem reasonable to argue that, on the basis of what we know now, it would be desirable if policy, including monetary policy, could, as one of its goals, seek greater stability in asset prices.

22.3 Monetary Policy and Crises

Many economies are subject to periodic financial and banking crises of various types; moreover, when these crises occur, they often come as complete surprises to most of the participants. Having lived through the turmoil of the past few years we do not need reminding of this fact. The Asian financial crisis of 1998 is another example of how crises can effectively come out of the blue. There is a great deal about crises that we do not understand. There are important issues relating to monetary policy. What should the central bank do if the economy is in a recession as a consequence of such a crisis but interest rates are at their lower bound? Should the central bank always act as lenders of last resort? What about the moral hazard problem of intervention? What is the role of regulation?

It is almost certainly inevitable that crises of some sort will continue to occur periodically. Improved regulation is the main way in which we should seek to prevent crises from happening again, but such regulation cannot completely prevent crises from occurring; indeed, it can be argued that optimal regulation will leave a positive probability of a crisis. Monetary policy can make a contribution in preventing a crisis from having too large an effect on output and employment, and in facilitating recovery from any such effects it might have. Fiscal policy can also contribute to combating a crisis; one reason for reducing the debt-GDP ratio is to give the Treasury enough 'spare capacity' to raise government spending and cut taxes temporarily in a time of crisis. Quantitative easing can also contribute; so recovery is by no means dependent on the central bank being able to cut its policy rate, although this probably should continue to be the main instrument of monetary policy. There is no need to raise the inflation target so as to give greater scope for interest rate reductions in a time of crisis. This would impose the costs of a permanently higher rate of inflation; the likelihood and severity of crises can be mitigated through better regulation and there are two other policy tools – fiscal policy and quantitative easing – that can also be used to combat a downturn in demand. However, it would not be a good idea to reduce the inflation target below its current 2%.

22.4 Conclusion

There is no case at the moment for any significant change in the monetary policy framework in the United Kingdom. It is working well. Nevertheless, the next few years will not be easy ones for monetary policy, with the current sluggish recovery from the recession and the unwinding of quantitative easing to manage. They should be interesting years for students of monetary policy.

DISCUSSION QUESTIONS

1. What are the main lessons of the financial crisis for monetary policy?
2. Are there any circumstances under which the government should change the inflation target?
3. Should monetary policy decisions ever be coordinated between central banks?

Glossary

Bubble   Where an asset price is above its 'efficient' price (i.e. that determined by fundamentals), but continues to rise since agents believe its price will continue to rise in the future.

Disintermediation   Where borrowing and lending activities, which formerly went through financial intermediaries, now are carried out directly between final borrowers and final lenders.

Dynamic inefficiency   An intertemporal economy where a central planner can make every generation better off by redistributing goods between agents. A common condition for dynamic inefficiency is that it occurs when the real interest rate is less than the population growth rate.

Efficient markets hypothesis   The hypothesis that the price of shares equals the discounted present value of the stream of dividend payments that the owner of the shares expects to receive.

Fiat currency   An intrinsically useless object that becomes a medium of exchange because of a government decree (or *fiat*) that it be so.

Fisher effect   The hypothesis that the nominal interest rate rises one-to-one with the rate of expected inflation, so that the real interest rate is invariant with respect to fully anticipated inflation.

Law of One Price   States that the price of a good in one country equals the price in another country when converted at the exchange rate between the countries.

Natural rate of unemployment   Rate of unemployment consistent with constant inflation.

Non accelerating inflation rate of unemployment (NAIRU)   Another term sometimes used for the natural rate of unemployment.

Pareto efficiency   A state of affairs where it is impossible to make any agent better off without making some other agent worse off.

Purchasing Power Parity (PPP)   States that price levels in different countries, converted at the relevant exchange rate, are identical.

Quantitative easing   The purchase by the central bank of longer term government bonds and certain other assets, financed by an increase in banks' deposits at the central bank.

Real interest rate   The interest rate adjusted for inflation; usually defined as $i - \pi^*$, where i is the nominal interest rate and π^* is expected inflation.

Uncovered interest parity condition (UIP)   States that interest rate differentials between countries equal the expected rate of change of the exchange rate between their two currencies, so that expected returns are the same irrespective of the currency denomination of one's assets.

References

Acemoglu, D., Johnson, S., Querubín, P. and Robinson, J. (2008) 'When does Policy Reform Work? The Case of Central Bank Independence', *Brookings Papers on Economic Activity*, Spring, pp. 351–417.

Akerlof, G. (1979) 'Irving Fisher on his Head: The Consequences of Constant-Threshold-Target Monitoring of Money Holdings', *Quarterly Journal of Economics*, 93(2), pp. 169–87.

Akerlof, G., Dickens, W. and Perry, G. (1996) 'The Macroeconomics of Low Inflation', *Brookings Papers on Economic Activity*, pp. 1–59.

Akerlof, G., Dickens, W. and Perry, G. (2000) 'Near Rational Wage and Price Setting and the Long-Run Phillips Curve', *Brookings Papers on Economic Activity*, pp. 1–44.

Alesina, A. and Summers, L.H. (1993) 'Central Bank Independence and Macroeconomic Performance: Some Comparative Evidence', *Journal of Money, Credit and Banking*, 25(2), pp. 151–62.

Allen, F. and Gale, D. (2007) *Understanding Financial Crises*, Oxford: Oxford University Press.

Amato, J., Morris, S. and Shin, H. (2008) 'Communication and Monetary Policy', *Oxford Review of Economic Policy*, 18(4), pp. 495–503.

Aron, J., Duca, J. V., Muellbauer, J., Murata, K. and Murphy, A. (2010) 'Credit, Housing Collateral and Consumption: Evidence from the UK, Japan and US', *Discussion Paper* No. 487, Department of Economics, University of Oxford.

Ascari, G. and Rankin, N. (2002) 'Staggered Wages and Output Dynamics under Disinflation', *Journal of Economic Dynamics and Control*, 26, pp. 653–80.

Azariadis, C. (1993) *Intertemporal Macroeconomics*, Oxford: Blackwell.

Bakshi, H., Haldane, A. and Hatch, N. (1997) 'Quantifying some Benefits of Price Stability', *Bank of England Quarterly Bulletin*, August, pp. 274–84.

Ball, L. (1994a) 'Credible Disinflation with Staggered Price Setting', *American Economic Review*, 84, pp. 282–9.

Ball, L. (1994b) 'What Determines the Sacrifice Ratio?', in Mankiw, N.G. (ed.), *Monetary Policy*, Chicago: University of Chicago Press.

Ball, L. (2001) 'Another Look at Long-run Money Demand', *Journal of Monetary Economics*, 47(1), pp. 31–44.

Banerjee, A. and Maskin, E. (1996) 'A Walrasian Theory of Money and Barter', *Quarterly Journal of Economics*, 111(4), pp. 955–1005.

Banerjee, A. and Russell, B. (2004) 'A Reinvestigation of the Markup and the Business Cycle', *Economic Modeling*, 21, pp. 267–84.

Bank of England (2011) *Inflation Report*, May.

Barker, K. (2008) 'Planning Policy, Planning Practice and Housing Supply', *Oxford Review of Economic Policy*, 24(1), pp. 34–49.

Barrell, R. and Weale, M. (2009) 'The Economics of a Reduction in VAT', *Fiscal Studies*, 30(1), pp. 17–30.

Barro, R.J. (1974) 'Are Government Bonds New Wealth?', *Journal of Political Economy*, 82, pp. 1095–117.

Barro, R.J. (1979) 'On the Determination of the Public Debt', *Journal of Political Economy*, 87, pp. 940–71.

Barro, R.J. (1989) 'The Ricardian Approach to Budget Deficits', *Journal of Economic Perspectives*, 3(2), pp. 37–54.

Barro, R.J. (1995) 'Inflation and Economic Growth', *Bank of England Quarterly Bulletin*, May, pp. 166–76.

Barro, R.J. and Gordon, D. (1983a) 'A Positive Theory of Monetary Policy in a Natural Rate Model', *Journal of Political Economics*, 91, pp. 589–610.

Barro, R.J. and Gordon, D. (1983b) 'Rules, Discretion and Reputation in a Model of Monetary Policy', *Journal of Monetary Economics*, 12, pp. 101–22.

Baumol, W. (1952) 'The Transactions Demand for Cash', *Quarterly Journal of Economics*, 67, pp. 545–56.

Bean, C. (2010) '*Joseph Schumpeter Lecture:* The Great Moderation, the Great Panic and the Great Contraction', *Journal of the European Economic Association*, 8(2-3), pp. 289–325.

Benati, L. (2008) 'Investigating Inflation Persistence across Monetary Regimes', *Quarterly Journal of Economics*, 123(3), pp. 1005–60.

Bernanke, B. and Gertler, M. (1995) 'Inside the Black Box: The Credit Channel of Monetary Policy Transmission', *Journal of Economic Perspectives*, 9(4), pp. 27–48.

Bernanke, B., Boivin, J. and Elaisz, P. (2005) 'Measuring the Effects of Monetary Policy: a Factor-Augmented Vector Autoregressive Approach', *Quarterly Journal of Economics*, 120(1), pp. 387–422.

Bernheim, B.D. (1987) 'Ricardian Equivalence: An Evaluation of Theory and Evidence', *NBER Macroeconomics Annual* 2, pp. 263–304.

Bernheim, B.D. and Bagwell, K. (1988) 'Is Everything Neutral?' *Journal of Political Economy*, 96, pp. 308–38.

Bils, M. and Klenow, P. (2004) 'Some Evidence on the Importance of Sticky Prices', *Journal of Political Economy*, 112(5), pp. 947–85.

Blanchard, O.J. (1985) 'Debt, Deficits and Finite Horizons', *Journal of Political Economy*, 93, pp. 223–47.

Blanchard, O.J. (1990) 'Why does Money affect Output?', Chapter 15 in Friedman, B. and Hahn, F.H. (eds.), *Handbook of Monetary Economics*, Vol. 2, Amsterdam: North-Holland.

Blanchard, O.J. and Fischer, S. (1989) *Lectures on Macroeconomics*, Cambridge: MIT Press.

Blanchard, O.J. and Kiyotaki, N. (1987) 'Monopolistic Competition and the Effects of Aggregate Demand', *American Economic Review*, 77, pp. 647–66.

Blanchard, O.J. and Summers, L. (1986) 'Hysteresis and the European Unemployment Problem' in *NBER Macroeconomics Annual*, 1, pp. 15–78.

Blinder, A.S., Ehrmann, M., Fratzscher, M., De Haan, J, and Jensen, D-J. (2008) 'Central Bank Communication and Monetary Policy: A Survey of Theory and Evidence', *Journal of Economic Literature*, 46(4), pp. 910–45.

Blundell, R. (2009) 'Assessing the Temporary VAT Cut Policy in the UK', *Fiscal Studies*, 30(1), pp. 31–38.

Boivin, J., Giannoni, M. and Mihov, I. (2009) 'Sticky Prices and Monetary Policy: Evidence from Disaggregated US Data', *American Economic Review*, 99(1), pp. 350–84.

Buiter, W.H. (2010) 'Housing Wealth Isn't Wealth', *Economics: The Open-Access, Open Assessment E-Journal*, Vol. 3(22).

Burstein, A., Eichenbaum, M. and Rebelo, S. (2005) 'Large Devaluations and the Real Exchange Rate', *Journal of Political Economy*, 113(4), pp. 742–84.

Caballero, R. (1999) 'Aggregate Investment', in Taylor, J.B.and Woodford, M. (eds.) *Handbook of Macroeconomics* 1B, Amsterdam: Elsevier.

Calvo, G. (1983) 'Staggered Prices in a Utility Maximizing Framework', *Journal of Monetary Economics*, 12, pp. 383–98.

Campbell, J.Y. (1995) 'Some Lessons from the Yield Curve', *Journal of Economic Perspectives*, 9(3), pp. 129–52.

Campbell, J. Y. and Cocco, J. (2007) 'How do House Prices Affect Consumption? Evidence from Micro Data', *Journal of Monetary Economics*, 54, pp. 591–621.

Carroll, C.D. (2001) 'A Theory of the Consumption Function With and Without Liquidity Constraints', *Journal of Economic Perspectives*, 15(3), pp. 23–45.

Carruth, A., Dickerson, A. and Henley, A. (2000) 'Econometric Modelling of UK Aggregate Investment: The Role of Profits and Uncertainty', *Manchester School*, 68(3), pp. 276–300.

Case, K., Quigley, J.M. and Shiller, R.J. (2005) 'Comparing Wealth Effects: The Stock Market versus the Housing Market', *Advances in Macroeconomics*, 5(1), article 1.

Chadha, J., Haldane, A. and Janssen, N. (1998) 'Shoe-leather Costs Reconsidered', *Economic Journal*, 108(447), pp. 363–82.

Chadha, J., MacMillan, P. and Nolan, C. (2007) 'Independence Day for the "Old Lady": A Natural Experiment on the Implications of Central Bank Independence', *Manchester School*, 75(3), pp. 311–327.

Chan, L.K.C. (1983) 'Uncertainty and the Neutrality of Government Financing Policy', *Journal of Monetary Economics*, 11, pp. 351–72.

Chirinko, R.S. (1993) 'Business Fixed Investment Spending: a Critical Survey of Modelling Strategies, Empirical Results and Policy Implications', *Journal of Economic Literature*, 31, pp. 1875–911.

Christiano, L., Eichenbaum, M. and Evans, C. (1999) 'Monetary Policy Shocks: What have we Learned and to what End?' Chapter 2 in Taylor, J.B. and Woodford, M. (eds.), *Handbook of Macroeconomics*, Volume 1C, Amsterdam: Elsevier.

Christiano, L., Eichenbaum, M. and Evans, C. (2005) 'Nominal Rigidities and the Dynamic Effects of a Shock to Monetary Policy', *Journal of Political Economy*, 113(1), pp. 1–45.

Christiano, L., Eichenbaum, M. and Rebelo, S. (2011) 'When is the Government Spending Multiplier Large?' *Journal of Political Economy*, 119(1), pp. 78–121.

Clarida, R., Galí, J. and Gertler, M. (1999) 'The Science of Monetary Policy: A New Keynesian Perspective', *Journal of Economic Literature*, 37, pp. 1661–707.

Clarida, R., Galí, J. and Gertler, M. (2000) 'Monetary Policy Rules and Macroeconomic Stability: Evidence and Some Theory', *Quarterly Journal of Economics*, 115(1), pp. 147–80.

Clower, R. (1967) 'A Reconsideration of the Microfoundations of Monetary Theory', *Western Economic Journal*, 6, pp. 1–9.

Cogley, T. and Sbordone, A. (2008) 'Trend Inflation, Indexation, and Inflation Persistence in the New Keynesian Phillips Curve', *American Economic Review*, 98(5), pp. 2101–26.

Crossley, T., Leicester, A. and Levell, P. (2010) 'Fiscal Stimulus and the Consumer', Chapter 3 in Chote, R., Emmerson, C. and Shaw, J., *The IFS Green Budget: February 2009*, London: Institute for Fiscal Studies.

Crossley, T., Low, H. and Wakefield, M. (2009) 'The Economics of a Temporary VAT Cut', *Fiscal Studies*, 30(1), pp. 3–16.

Crowe, C. and Meade, E. (2007) 'The Evolution of Central Bank Governance around the World', *Journal of Economic Perspectives*, 21(4), pp. 69–90.

Cúrdia, V. and Woodford, M. (2010) 'The Central Bank Balance Sheet as an Instrument of Monetary Policy', Federal Reserve Bank of New York Staff Report no. 463.

Cuthbertson, K. and Gasparro, D. (1993) 'The Determinants of Manufacturing Inventories in the UK', *Economic Journal*, 103, pp. 1479–92.

Cuthbertson, K. and Gasparro, D. (1995) 'Fixed Investment Decisions in UK Manufacturing – The Importance of Tobin's q, Output and Debt', *European Economic Review*, 39(5), pp. 919–41.

Cuthbertson, K. and Nitzsche, D. (2004) *Quantitative Financial Economics*, Second Edition, Chichester: John Wiley.

Dale, S. (2010) 'QE – One Year On', Paper presented at CIMF and MMF conference, Cambridge on 'New Instruments of Monetary Policy: The Challenges', March.

De Grauwe, P. (2009) *Economics of Monetary Union*, Eighth Edition, Oxford: Oxford University Press.

Dhyne, E., Álvarez, L., Le Biham, H., Veronese, G., Dias, D., Hoffman, J., Jonker, N., Lünnemann, P., Rumler, F. and Vilmunun, J. (2006) 'Price Changes in the Euro Area and the United States: Some Facts from Individual Consumer Price Data', *Journal of Economic Perspectives*, 20(2), pp. 171–92.

Diamond, D.W. (1984) 'Financial Intermediation and Delegated Monitoring', *Review of Economic Studies*, 51(3), pp. 393–414.

Diamond, D.W. and Dybvig, P. (1983) 'Bank Runs, Deposit Insurance and Liquidity', *Journal of Political Economy*, 91, pp. 401–19.

Diamond, P. (1993) 'Search, Sticky Prices, and Inflation', *Review of Economic Studies*, 60, pp. 53–68.

Dickens, W., Goette, L., Groshen, E., Holden, S., Messina, J., Schweitzer, M., Turunen, J. and Ward, M. (2007) 'How Wages Change: Micro Evidence from the International Wage Flexibility Project', *Journal of Economic Perspectives*, 21(2), pp. 195–214.

Dixit, A.K. and Pindyck, R.S. (1994) *Investment Under Uncertainty*, Princeton, New Jersey: Princeton University Press.

Dornbusch, R. (1976) 'Expectations and Exchange Rate Dynamics', *Journal of Political Economy*, 84(6), pp. 1161–76.

Dow, S. (1996) 'Why the Banking System Should be Regulated', *Economic Journal*, 106(436), pp. 698–707.

Duffy, J. and Ochs, J. (1999) 'Emergence of Money as a Medium of Exchange: An Experimental Study', *American Economic Review*, 89(4), pp. 847–77.

Eggertsson, G. and Woodford, M. (2003) 'The Zero Bound on Interest Rates and Optimal Monetary Policy', *Brookings Papers on Economic Activity* 2003, pp. 139–211.

Eichenbaum, M. and Evans, C. (1995) 'Some Empirical Evidence on the Effects of Shocks to Monetary Policy on Exchange Rates', *Quarterly Journal of Economics*, pp. 975–1009.

Ellis, C. and Price, S. (2004) 'UK Business Investment and the User Cost of Capital', *Manchester School*, 72(Supplement), pp. 72–93.

Elmendorf, D. and Mankiw, N.G. (1999) 'Government Debt', Chapter 25 in Taylor, J.B. and Woodford, M. (eds.), *Handbook of Macroeconomics*, Volume 1C, Amsterdam: Elsevier.

Evans, P. (1985) 'Do Large Deficits Produce High Interest Rates?', *Journal of Political Economy*, 75(1), pp. 68–87.

Faust, J. and Rogers, J. (2003) 'Monetary Policy's Role in Exchange Rate Behavior', *Journal of Monetary Economics*, 50(7), pp. 1403–24.

Feldstein, M.S. (1969) 'Mean-Variance Analysis in the Theory of Liquidity Preference and Portfolio Selection', *Review of Economic Studies*, 35(1), pp. 5–12.

Fender, J. (1981) *Understanding Keynes: an Analysis of 'the General Theory'*, Brighton: Harvester Wheatsheaf.

Fender, J. (1990) *Inflation – a Contemporary Perspective*, Brighton: Harvester Wheatsheaf.

Fender, J. (2002) 'Nominal Rigidity' in Snowden, B. and Vane, H. (eds.) *An Encyclopedia of Macroeconomics*, Cheltenham, UK: Edward Elgar.

Fischer, S. (1990) 'Rules versus Discretion in Monetary Policy', Chapter 21 in Friedman, B.M. and Hahn, F.H. (eds.) *Handbook of Monetary Economics*, Volume II, Amsterdam: North-Holland, pp. 1155–84.

Fischer, S. and Summers, L. (1989) 'Should Governments Learn to Live with Inflation?' *American Economic Review*, papers and proceedings, pp. 382–7.

French, K. and Poterba, J. (1991) 'International Diversification and International Equity Markets', *American Economic Review*, papers and proceedings, pp. 222–6.

Friedman, B. and Woodford, M. (2011) *Handbook of Monetary Economics*, Volumes 3A and 3B, Amsterdam: North-Holland.

Friedman, M. (1953) *Essays in Positive Economics*, Chicago: University of Chicago Press.

Friedman, M. (1957) *A Theory of Consumption Function*, Princeton: Princeton University Press.

Friedman, M. (1968) 'The Role of Monetary Policy', *American Economic Review*, 58(1), pp. 1–17.

Friedman, M. (1969) 'The Optimal Quantity of Money' in Friedman, M. (ed.), *The Optimal Quantity of Money and Other Essays*, pp. 1–50, Chicago: Aldine Publishing Company.

Friedman, M. and Schwartz, A. (1963) *A Monetary History of the United States, 1867–1960*, Princeton, New Jersey: Princeton University Press.

FSA (Financial Services Authority, 2010) *The Turner Review: a Regulatory Response to the Global Banking Crisis*, March.

Fuertes, A-M and Heffernan, S.A. (2009) 'Interest Rate Transmission in the UK: A Comparative Analysis across Financial Firms and Products', *International Journal of Finance and Economics*, 14, pp. 45–63.

Fuhrer, J. and Moore, G. (1995) 'Inflation Persistence', *Quarterly Journal of Economics*, 110(1), pp. 127–59.

Gagnon, E. (2009) 'Price Setting during Low and High Inflation: Evidence from Mexico', *Quarterly Journal of Economics*, 124(3), pp. 1221–64.

Gagnon, J., Raskin, M., Remache, J. and Sack, B. (2010) 'Large-scale Asset Purchases by the Federal Reserve: Did They Work?', Federal Reserve Bank of New York Staff Report no. 441.

Galbraith, J.K. (1961) *The Great Crash*, Boston: Houghton Mifflin.

Geraats, P.M. (2002) 'Central Bank Transparency', *Economic Journal*, 112, pp. F532–65.

Gertler, M. and Gilchrist, S. (1994) 'Monetary Policy, Business Cycles and the Behavior of Small Manufacturing Firms', *Quarterly Journal of Economics*, 109(2), pp. 309–40.

Giavazzi, F. and Pagano, M. (1988) 'The Advantage of Tying One's Hands: EMS Discipline and Central Bank Credibility', *European Economic Review*, 32, pp. 1055–82.

Goodfriend, M. and McCallum, B. (2007) 'Banking and Interest Rates in Monetary Policy Analysis: A Quantitative Exploration', *Journal of Monetary Economics*, 54(5), pp. 1480–507.

Goodhart, C.A.E. (1989) *Money, Information and Uncertainty*, 2nd Edition, Cambridge, MA: MIT Press.

Goodhart, C.A.E. and Hoffman, B. (2008) 'House Prices, Money, Credit, and the Macroeconomy', *Oxford Review of Economic Policy*, 24(1), pp. 180–205.

Gowland, D. and Goodhart, C.A.E. (1978) 'The Relationship between Long-dated Gilt Yields and Other Variables', *Bulletin of Economic Research*, 30(2), pp. 59–70.

Grossman, S.J. and Stiglitz, J.E. (1980) 'On the Impossibility of Informationally Efficient Markets', *American Economic Review*, 70, pp. 393–408.

Guimaraes, B. and Sheedy, K. (2011) 'Sales and Monetary Policy', *American Economic Review*, 101(2), pp. 844–76.

Hahn, F. (1982) *Money and Inflation*, Oxford: Basil Blackwell.

Handa, J. (2000) *Monetary Economics*, London: Routledge.

Hansen, S. and McMahon, M. (2010) 'What Do Outside Experts Bring to a Committee? Evidence from the Bank of England', unpublished paper, University of Warwick.

Harris, M.N., Levine, P. and Spencer, C. (2011) 'A Decade of Dissent: Explaining the Dissent Voting Behavior of Bank of England MPC Members', *Public Choice*, 146, pp. 413–42.

Harrison, R. (2010) 'Asset Purchase Policy at the Effective Lower Bound for Interest Rates', Paper presented at CIMF and MMF conference, Cambridge on 'New Instruments of Monetary Policy: the Challenges', March.

Hart, O.D. and Kreps, D. (1986) 'Price Destabilizing Speculation', *Journal of Political Economy*, 94(5), pp. 927–52.

He, P., Huang, L. and Wright, R. (2008) 'Money, Banking and Monetary Policy', *Journal of Monetary Economics*, 55, pp. 1013–24.

Heffernan, S. (2005) *Modern Banking*, Chichester: John Wiley & Sons.

Hicks, J.R. (1937) 'Mr. Keynes and the Classics; a Suggested Interpretation', *Econometrica*, 5(2), pp. 147–59.

Hicks, J.R. (1946) *Value and Capital*, Second Edition, Oxford: Clarendon Press.

Hicks, J.R. (1973) 'Recollections and Documents', *Economica*, 40(157), pp. 2–11.

Hobijn, B., Ravenna, F. and Tambalotti, A. (2006) 'Menu Costs at Work: Restaurant Prices and the Introduction of the Euro', *Quarterly Journal of Economics*, 121(3), pp. 1103–31.

Hoffman, D. and Rasche, R. (1991) 'Long Run Income and Interest Elasticities of Money Demand in the United States,' *Review of Economics and Statistics*, 73, pp. 665–74.

ICB (Independent Commission on Banking, 2010), *Issues Paper: Call for Evidence*, September.

Ireland, P. (2009) 'On the Welfare Cost of Inflation and the Recent Behavior of Money Demand', *American Economic Review*, 99(3), pp. 1040–52.

Jones, C. and Lamont, O. (2002) 'Short-sale Constraints and Stock Returns', *Journal of Financial Economics*, 66(2-3), pp. 207–39.

Joyce, M., Lasaosa, A., Stevens, I. and Tong, M. (2010) 'The Financial Market Impact of Quantitative Easing', Bank of England Working Paper No. 393.

Kashyap, A. and Stein, J. (1994) 'Monetary Policy and Bank Lending', Chapter 7 in Mankiw, N.G. (ed.) *Monetary Policy*, Chicago: University of Chicago Press.

Keynes, J.M. (1936) *The General Theory of Employment, Interest and Money*, London: Macmillan.

Kiyotaki, N. and Moore, J. (1997) 'Credit Cycles', *Journal of Political Economy*, 105(2), pp. 211–48.

Kiyotaki, N. and Wright, R. (1989) 'On Money as a Medium of Exchange', *Journal of Political Economy*, 97(4), pp. 927–54.

Klenow, P. and Malin, B. (2011) 'Microeconomic Evidence on Price-Setting', Chapter 6 in Friedman and Woodford (2011), pp. 231–84.

Klomp, J. and de Haan, J. (2010) 'Central Bank Independence and Inflation Revisited', *Public Choice*, 144, pp. 445–457.

Kuhn, T. (1970) *The Structure of Scientific Revolutions*, Chicago: University of Chicago Press.

Kydland, F.E. and Prescott, E.C. (1982) 'Time to Build and Aggregate Fluctuations', *Econometrica* (50), pp. 1345–70.

Laubach, T. (2009) 'New Evidence on the Interest Rate Effects of Budget Deficits and Debt', *Journal of the European Economic Association*, 7(4), pp. 858–65.

Lenza, M., Pill, H. and Reichlin, L. (2010) 'Monetary Policy in Exceptional Times', *Economic Policy*, 62, pp. 295–339.

Levy, D., Bergen, M., Dutta, S. and Venable, R. (1997) 'The Magnitude of Menu Costs', *Quarterly Journal of Economics*, 112(3), pp. 791–825.

Lewis, M. and Mizen, P. (2000) *Monetary Economics*, Oxford: Oxford University Press.

Long, J.B. Jr. and Plosser, C.I. (1983) 'Real Business Cycles', *Journal of Political Economy* (91), pp. 39–69.

Lucas, R.E. Jr. (1976) 'Econometric Policy Evaluation: A Critique', *Carnegie-Rochester Conference Series on Public Policy*, 1, pp. 19–46.

Lucas, R.E. Jr. (2000) 'Inflation and Welfare', *Econometrica*, 68(2), pp. 247–74.

Maćkowiak, B. and Wiederholt, M. (2009) 'Optimal Sticky Prices under Rational Inattention', *American Economic Review*, 99(3), pp. 769–803.

Mankiw, N.G. (1985) 'Small Menu Costs and Large Business Cycles: A Macroeconomic Model of Monopoly', *Quarterly Journal of Economics*, 100(2), pp. 529–37.

Mankiw, N.G. and Reis, R. (2002) 'Sticky Information versus Sticky Prices: A Proposal to Replace the New Keynesian Phillips Curve', *Quarterly Journal of Economics*, 117(4), pp. 1295–328.

Mayer, C., Pence, K. and Sherlund, S. (2009) 'The Rise in Mortgage Defaults', *Journal of Economic Perspectives*, 23(1), pp. 27–50.

McCallum, B. (2000) 'Theoretical Analysis Regarding a Zero Lower Bound on Nominal Interest Rates', *Journal of Money, Credit and Banking*, 32(4), pp. 870–904.

Mertens, K. and Ravn, M. (2011) 'Understanding the Aggregate Effects of Anticipated and Unanticipated Tax Policy Shocks', *Review of Economic Dynamics*, 14(1), pp. 27–54.

Miles, D. (2010) 'Interpreting Monetary Policy', speech given at Imperial College London, 25 February.

Miller, M.H. and Orr, D. (1966) 'A Model of the Demand for Money by Firms', *Quarterly Journal of Economics*, 80(3), pp. 413–35.

Mishkin, F.S. (2007) *Monetary Policy Strategy*, Cambridge, MA: MIT Press.

Morris, S. and Shin, H. (2000) 'Rethinking Multiple Equilibria in Macroeconomic Modelling', *NBER Macroeconomics Annual*, 15, pp. 139–61.

Muellbauer, J. and Murphy, A. (1997) 'Booms and Busts in the UK Housing Market', *The Economic Journal*, 107(445), pp. 1701–27.

Muellbauer J. and Murphy, A. (2010) 'Housing Markets and the Economy: the Assessment', *Oxford Review of Economic Policy*, 24(1), pp. 1–33.

Mulligan, C. and Sala-i-Martin, X. (2000) 'Extensive Margins and the Demand for Money at Low Interest Rates', *Journal of Political Economy*, 108(5), pp. 961–91.

Mussa, M. (1977) 'The Welfare Cost of Inflation and the Role of Money as a Unit of Account', *Journal of Money, Credit and Banking*, 9, pp. 276–86.

Nakamura, E. and Steinsson, J. (2008) 'Five Facts about Prices: A Reevaluation of Menu Cost Models', *Quarterly Journal of Economics*, 123(4), pp. 1415–64.

Nicolini, J. (1998) 'Tax Evasion and the Optimal Inflation Tax', *Journal of Development Economics*, 55, pp. 215–232.

Niehans, J. (1984) *International Monetary Economics*, Baltimore, Maryland: The Johns Hopkins University Press.

Obstfeld, M. and Rogoff, K. (1986) 'Ruling out Divergent Speculative Bubbles', *Journal of Monetary Economics*, 17(3), pp. 349–62.

Obstfeld, M. and Rogoff, K. (1995a) 'The Mirage of Fixed Exchange Rates', *Journal of Economic Perspectives*, 9(4), pp. 73–96.

Obstfeld, M. and Rogoff, K. (1995b) 'Exchange Rate Dynamics Redux', *Journal of Political Economy*, 103(3), pp. 624–60.

Obstfeld, M. and Rogoff, K. (1996) *Foundations of International Macroeconomics*, Cambridge, MA: MIT Press.

Ofek, E. and Richardson, M. (2002) 'The Valuation and Market Rationality of Internet Stock Prices', *Oxford Review of Economic Policy*, 18(3), pp. 265–87.

Ortalo-Magné, F. and Rady, S. (2006) 'Housing Market Dynamics: On the Contribution of Income Shocks and Credit Constraints', *Review of Economic Studies*, 73, pp. 459–85.

Perotti, R. (1999) 'Fiscal Policy in Good Times and Bad', *Quarterly Journal of Economics*, 114(4), pp. 1399–436.

Phelps, E. (1970) *Microeconomic Foundations of Employment and Inflation Theory*, New York: W. W. Norton.

Phelps, E. (1973) 'Inflation in the Theory of Public Finance', *Swedish Journal of Economics*, 75, pp. 67–82.

Phillips, A.W. (1958) 'The Relation between Unemployment and the Rate of Change of Money Wage Rates in the United Kingdom, 1861–1957', *Economica* 25(100), pp. 283–99.

Poole, W. (1970) 'Optimal Choice of Monetary Policy Instruments in a Simple Stochastic Macro Model', *Quarterly Journal of Economics*, 84(2), pp. 197–216.

Poterba, J. (2000) 'Stock Market Wealth and Consumption', *Journal of Economic Perspectives*, 14(2), pp. 99–118.

Ramey, V. and West, K. (1999) 'Inventories', Chapter 13 in Taylor, J. and Woodford, M. (eds.) *Handbook of Macroeconomics*, Volume 1B, Amsterdam: Elsevier Science.

Reinhart, C. and Rogoff, K. (2009) *This Time is Different: Eight Centuries of Financial Folly*, Princeton, New Jersey: Princeton University Press.

Rogoff, K. (1985) 'The Optimal Degree of Commitment to an Intermediate Monetary Target', *Quarterly Journal of Economics*, 100, pp. 1169–90.

Romer, C. and Romer, D. (1989) 'Does Monetary Policy Matter? A New Test in the Spirit of Friedman and Schwartz', *NBER Macroeconomics Annual*, pp. 121–70.

Romer, C. and Romer, D. (1990) 'New Evidence on the Monetary Transmission Mechanism', *Brookings Papers on Economic Activity* (1), pp. 149–98.

Romer, C. and Romer, D. (2004) 'A New Measure of Monetary Shocks: Derivation and Implications', *American Economic Review*, 94(4), pp. 1055–84.

Romer, C. and Romer, D. (2010) 'The Macroeconomic Effects of Tax Changes: Estimates Based on a New Measure of Fiscal Shocks', *American Economic Review*, 100, pp. 763–801.

Romer, D. (1986) 'A Simple General Equilibrium Baumol-Tobin Model', *Quarterly Journal of Economics*, 101(4), pp. 663–85.

Romer, D. (1993) 'Openness and Inflation: Theory and Evidence', *Quarterly Journal of Economics*, 108, pp. 869–904.

Romer, D. (2000) 'Keynesian Economics without the LM Curve', *Journal of Economic Perspectives*, 14(2), pp. 149–69.

Rudd, J. and Whelan, K. (2005) 'New Tests of the New-Keynesian Phillips Curve', *Journal of Monetary Economics*, 52, pp. 1167–81.

Rudd, J. and Whelan, K. (2006) 'Can Rational Expectations Sticky-Price Models Explain Inflation Dynamics?' *American Economic Review*, 96(1), pp. 303–20.

Saborowski, C. (2010) 'Inflation Targeting as a Means of Achieving Disinflation', *Journal of Economic Dynamics and Control*, 34(12), pp. 2510–32.

Samuelson, P.A. (1958) 'An Exact Consumption Loan Model of Interest with or without the Social Contrivance of Money', *Journal of Political Economy*, 66, pp. 1002–11.

Santos, M.S. and Woodford, M. (1997) 'Rational Asset Pricing Bubbles', *Econometrica*, 65(1), pp. 19–57.

Sargent, T. and Wallace, N. (1981) 'Some Unpleasant Monetarist Arithmetic', *Federal Reserve Bank of Minneapolis Quarterly Review*, 5, pp. 1–17.

Sbordone, A.M. (2007) 'Inflation Persistence: Alternative Interpretations and Policy Implications', *Journal of Monetary Economics*, 54, pp. 1311–39.

Schmitt-Grohé, S. and Uribe, M. (2011) 'The Optimal Rate of Inflation', Chapter 13 in Friedman and Woodford (2011).

Shapiro, C. and Stiglitz, J.E. (1984) 'Equilibrium Unemployment as a Worker-Discipline Device', *American Economic Review*, 74, pp. 434–44.

Sheedy, K. (2010) 'Intrinsic Inflation Persistence', *Journal of Monetary Economics*, 57(8), pp. 1049–61.

Shi, S. (1997) 'A Divisible Theory of Fiat Money', *Econometrica*, 65(1), pp. 75–102.

Shiller, R.J. (1981) 'Do Stock Prices Move too Much to Be Justified by Subsequent Movements in Dividends?' *American Economic Review*, 71(3), pp. 421–36.

Shiller, R.J. (1990) 'The Term Structure of Interest Rates', Chapter 13 in Friedman, B.M. and Hahn, F.H. (eds.), *Handbook of Monetary Economics, Volume 1*, Amsterdam: North-Holland.

Shin, H. (2009) 'Reflections on Northern Rock: The Bank Run that Heralded the Global Financial Crisis', *Journal of Economic Perspectives*, 23(1), pp. 101–19.

Shleifer, A. (1986) 'Do Demand Curves for Stocks Slope Down?' *Journal of Finance*, 41, pp. 579–90.

Siegel, J. (2002) *Stocks for the Long Run: The Definitive Guide to Financial Market Returns and Long-Term Investment Strategies*, New York: McGraw-Hill.

Sims, C. (1980) 'Macroeconomics and Reality', *Econometrica*, 48, pp. 1–47.

Sinai, T. and Souleles, N. (2005) 'Owner-occupied Housing as a Hedge against Rent Risk', *Quarterly Journal of Economics*, 120(2), pp. 763–89.

Sinclair, P.J.N. (2003) 'The Optimal Rate of Inflation: An Academic Perspective', *Bank of England Quarterly Bulletin*, Autumn, pp. 343–51.

Sinclair, P.J.N. (2005) 'The Transmission of Monetary Policy through Interest Rates: Policy Rate Effects on other Interest Rates, Asset Prices, Consumption and Investment', pp. 5–49 in Mahadeva, L. and Sinclair, P.J.N. (eds.) *How Monetary Policy Works*, London: Routledge.

Sorkin, A.R. (2009) *Too Big to Fail*, London: Penguin.

Stein, J. (1995) 'Prices and Trading Volume in the Housing Market: A Model with Down-Payment Effects', *Quarterly Journal of Economics*, 110(2), pp. 379–406.

Stiglitz, J.E. and Weiss, A. (1981) 'Credit Rationing in Markets with Imperfect Information', *American Economic Review*, 71, pp. 393–410.

Stock, J and Watson, M. (1999) 'Business Cycle Fluctuations in US Macroeconomic Time Series', Chapter 1 in Taylor, J. and Woodford, M. (eds.) *Handbook of Macroeconomics*, Volume 1A, Amsterdam: Elsevier Science.

Svensson, L. (1997a) 'Optimal Inflation Targets, "Conservative" Central Banks, and Linear Inflation Contracts', *American Economic Review*, 87, pp. 98–114.

Svensson, L. (1997b) 'Inflation Forecast Targeting: Implementing and Monitoring Inflation Targets', *European Economic Review*, 41, pp. 1111–46.

Svensson, L. (2011) 'Inflation Targeting', Chapter 22 in Friedman and Woodford (2011) pp. 1237–302.

Sweezy, P.M. (1939) 'Demand under Conditions of Oligopoly', *Journal of Political Economy*, 47(4), pp. 568–73.

Taylor, J. (1980) 'Aggregate Dynamics and Staggered Contracts', *Journal of Political Economy* 88, pp. 1–24.

Taylor, J. (1993) 'Discretion versus Policy Rules in Practice', *Carnegie-Rochester Conference Series on Public Policy*, 39, pp. 195–214.

Temin, P. and Voth, H-J. (2004) 'Riding the South Sea Bubble', *American Economic Review*, 94(5), pp. 1654–68.

Tobin, J. (1956) 'The Interest Elasticity of the Transactions Demand for Cash', *Review of Economics and Statistics*, 38, pp. 241–7.

Tobin, J. (1958) 'Liquidity Preference as Behavior towards Risk', *Review of Economic Studies*, 25, pp. 65–86.

Tobin, J. (1970) 'Money and Income: Post Hoc Ergo Propter Hoc?' *Quarterly Journal of Economics*, 84(2), pp. 301–17.

Trejos, A. and Wright, R. (1995) 'Search, Bargaining, Money and Prices', *Journal of Political Economy*, 103(1), pp. 118–41.

Tsoukalas, J. (2011) 'Input and Output Inventories in the UK', *Economica*, 78, pp. 460–79.

Twigger, R. (1999) 'Inflation: The Value of the Pound 1750–1998', House of Commons Library Research Paper 99/20.

Walsh, C. (1995) 'Optimal Contracts for Central Bankers', *American Economic Review*, 85(1), pp. 150–67.

Walsh, C. (2010) *Monetary Theory and Policy*, 3rd Edition, Cambridge, MA: MIT Press.

Woodford, M. (1990) 'The Optimum Quantity of Money', Chapter 20 in Friedman, B. and Hahn, F. (eds.) *The Handbook of Monetary Economics*, Amsterdam: North-Holland, pp. 1067–152.

Woodford, M. (2003a) *Interest & Prices – Foundations of a Theory of Monetary Policy*, Princeton, New Jersey: Princeton University Press.

Woodford, M. (2003b) 'Optimal Interest-Rate Smoothing', *Review of Economic Studies*, 70, pp. 861–86.

Wren-Lewis, S. (2010) 'Macroeconomic Policy in the Light of the Credit Crunch; the Return of Counter-Cyclical Fiscal Policy?' *Oxford Review of Economic Policy*, 26(1), pp. 71–86.

Yotsuzuka, T. (1987) 'Ricardian Equivalence in the Presence of Credit Market Imperfections', *Journal of Monetary Economics*, 20, pp. 411–36.

Zbaracki, M., Ritson, M., Levy, D., Dutta, S. and Bergen, M. (2004) 'The Managerial and Customer Costs of Price Adjustment: Direct Evidence from Industrial Markets', *Review of Economics and Statistics*, 86(2), pp. 514–33.

Index

Note: Italic page numbers refer to figures and tables.